AUSTRALIAN
Signpost
MATHS

Alan McSeveny Rachel McSeveny Diane McSeveny-Foster

Pearson Australia
(a division of Pearson Australia Group Pty Ltd)
459–471 Church St, Level 1, Building B, Richmond, Victoria, 3121
PO Box 23360, Melbourne, Victoria 8012
www.pearson.com.au

Copyright © Pearson Australia 2024
(a division of Pearson Australia Group Pty Ltd)
First published 2024 by Pearson Australia
2028 2027 2026 2025
10 9 8 7 6 5 4 3 2 1

Reproduction and communication for educational purposes
The Australian *Copyright Act 1968* (the Act) allows a maximum of one chapter or 10% of the pages of this work, whichever is the greater, to be reproduced and/or communicated by any educational institution for its educational purposes provided that that educational institution (or the body that administers it) has given a remuneration notice to the Copyright Agency under the Act. For details of the copyright licence for educational institutions contact the Copyright Agency (www.copyright.com.au).

Reproduction and communication for other purposes
Except as permitted under the Act (for example any fair dealing for the purposes of study, research, criticism or review), no part of this book may be reproduced, stored in a retrieval system, communicated or transmitted in any form or by any means without prior written permission. All enquiries should be made to the publisher at the address above.

This book is not to be treated as a blackline master; that is, any photocopying beyond fair dealing requires prior written permission.

PHOTOCOPYING OF BOOKS IS RESTRICTED UNDER LAW

Publishers: Sophie Matta and Rachel Elliott
Project Manager: Michelle Thomas
Production Editor: Laura Rentsch
Editor: Katie Millar
Designers: Anne Donald and Jennifer Johnston
Typesetter: Integra
Proofreader: Laura Rentsch
Rights & Permissions Editor: Alice McBroom
Cover art: Michael Barter
Illustrator: Michael Barter
Production Services: Jit-Pin Chong
Printed in Malaysia by Vivar

ISBN 978 0 6557 0874 2
Pearson Australia Group Pty Ltd ABN 40 004 245 943

Attributions
We would like to thank the following for permission to reproduce copyright material.

© Australian Curriculum, Assessment and Reporting Authority (ACARA) 2010 to present, unless otherwise indicated. This material was downloaded from the Australian Curriculum website (www.australiancurriculum.edu.au) **(Website)** (accessed 2022-23) and was modified. The material is licensed under CC BY 4.0 (https://creativecommons.org/licenses/by/4.0). Version updates are tracked in the 'Curriculum version history' section on the 'About the Australian Curriculum' page (http://australiancurriculum.edu.au/about-the-australian-curriculum/) of the Australian Curriculum website.

ACARA does not endorse any product that uses the Australian Curriculum or make any representations as to the quality of such products. Any product that uses material published on this website should not be taken to be affiliated with ACARA or have the sponsorship or approval of ACARA. It is up to each person to make their own assessment of the product, taking into account matters including, but not limited to, the version number and the degree to which the materials align with the content descriptions and achievement standards (where relevant). Where there is a claim of alignment, it is important to check that the materials align with the content descriptions and achievement standards (endorsed by all education Ministers), not the elaborations (examples provided by ACARA).

Acknowledgement of Country
Pearson respects and honours Aboriginal and Torres Strait Islander Elders past, present and future. We acknowledge the stories, traditions and living cultures of the Traditional Custodians of the lands on which our company is located and where we conduct our business. Pearson is committed to honouring Australian Aboriginal and Torres Strait Islander peoples' unique cultural and spiritual relationships to the land, waters and seas and their rich contribution to society.

Aboriginal and Torres Strait Islander peoples are advised that this text may contain images, voices and names of deceased persons.

What is Australian Signpost Maths?

Australian Signpost Maths is a mathematics program providing direction and support for teaching and learning. The series covers the content and skills presented in the Australian Curriculum (v9) Mathematics F–10.

A Student Book and an online Teacher Resource are provided for Foundation.

For Years 1 to 6, a Student Book, an online Teacher Resource and a Mentals Book are provided for each year level. The online Teacher Resources provide a wealth of support for teachers.

The content has been carefully sequenced within each year level and across the F–6 series to take into account students' expected mathematical development. However, from the rich and varied material provided, teachers can develop individual learning programs to meet the needs of each student.

The Student Books are designed to support explicit teaching methods. Many group activities are provided in Activity, Investigation and Fun spots within the Student Books and the online Teacher Resource.

To maximise the benefits of the program, the Student Book, the online Teacher Resource and the Mentals Book should be used together.

Student Books

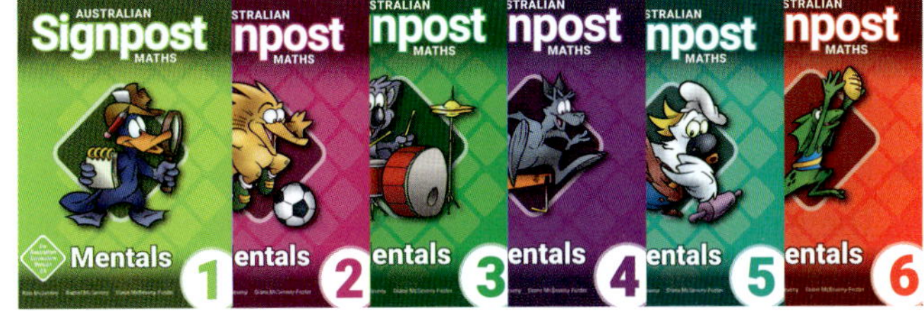

Mentals Books

Teacher Resource

Structure of Australian Signpost Maths

In the F–2 books, the worksheet pages covering all of the strands are presented in a recommended order. Each unit of 4 pages usually begins with Number or Algebra. The Contents cross-reference allows teachers to quickly find the pages where each concept has been covered.

Within the program, explicit teaching, critical and creative thinking, language development and identification and treatment of weaknesses are given high priority.

Identifying and addressing areas of need

Five progress tests are designed to identify each student's areas of need, and the follow-up program after each of the tests is designed to address these needs. For each test question, a reference to the relevant worksheet page is given. A remediation record page is used to track the student's progress.

These testing resources can be found in the online Teacher Resource.

Parallel progress retests are provided for further testing after remediation has taken place. See pages 128 and 129 of this book for more information.

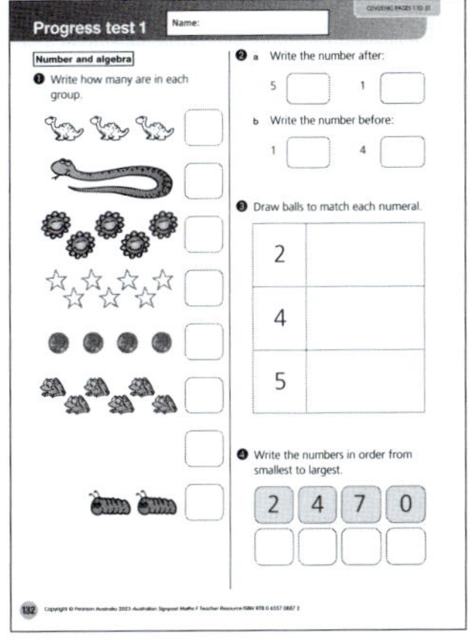
Progress test 1 Name:

Number and algebra

1 Write how many are in each group.

2 a Write the number after:

5 1

b Write the number before:

1 4

3 Draw balls to match each numeral.

2	
4	
5	

4 Write the numbers in order from smallest to largest.

2 4 7 0

132

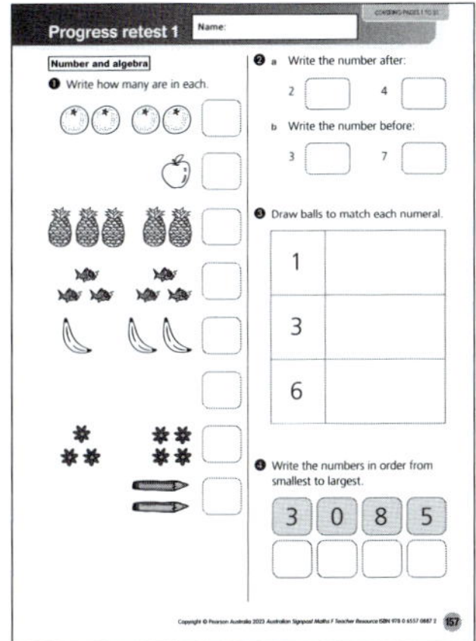
Progress retest 1 Name:

Number and algebra

1 Write how many are in each.

2 a Write the number after:

2 4

b Write the number before:

3 7

3 Draw balls to match each numeral.

1	
3	
6	

4 Write the numbers in order from smallest to largest.

3 0 8 5

157

Special features of Australian Signpost Maths

- **The traffic light icons**
  These are found on the top right of each worksheet page in the Student Books. They allow students to assess their own progress and give feedback to the teacher.
  - ☐ **Green:** I found this work easy.
  - ☐ **Orange:** I found some work on the page difficult.
  - ☐ **Red:** I don't understand the work on this page.

- **Dictionary**
  Terms used in the Student Book and terms that should be understood at this level are recorded here to provide a reference for students and teachers. This is found on pages xii–xiv of this book.

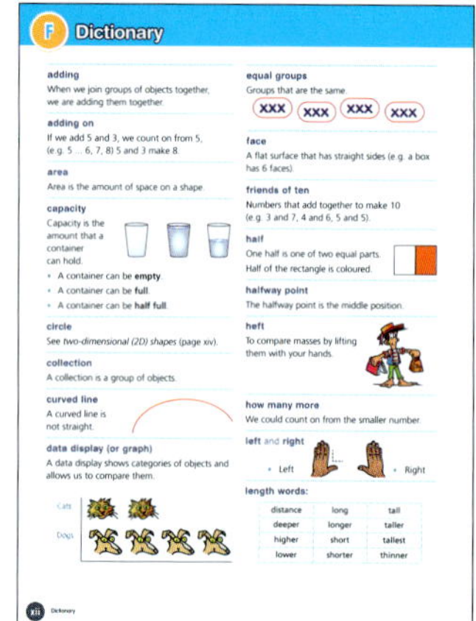

F Dictionary

adding
When we join groups of objects together, we are adding them together.

adding on
If we add 5 and 3, we count on from 5, (e.g. 5 ... 6, 7, 8) 5 and 3 make 8.

area
Area is the amount of space on a shape.

capacity
Capacity is the amount that a container can hold.
- A container can be **empty**.
- A container can be **full**.
- A container can be **half full**.

circle
See *two-dimensional (2D) shapes* (page xiv).

collection
A collection is a group of objects.

curved line
A curved line is not straight.

data display (or graph)
A data display shows categories of objects and allows us to compare them.

Cats
Dogs

equal groups
Groups that are the same.
XXX XXX XXX XXX

face
A flat surface that has straight sides (e.g. a box has 6 faces).

friends of ten
Numbers that add together to make 10 (e.g. 3 and 7, 4 and 6, 5 and 5).

half
One half is one of two equal parts.
Half of the rectangle is coloured.

halfway point
The halfway point is the middle position.

heft
To compare masses by lifting them with your hands.

how many more
We could count on from the smaller number.

left and right
- Left
- Right

length words:

distance	long	tall
deeper	longer	taller
higher	short	tallest
lower	shorter	thinner

xii Dictionary

- **ID cards (Years 1 to 6)**
  These cards review the language of Mathematics by asking students to identify common terms, shapes and symbols. They are designed to be reused and are found in the online Teacher Resource and in the front of the Mentals Books.

- **Progress tests**
  These allow the teacher to identify each student's strengths and needs. The cross-references for each question direct teachers and students to the pages where that work is introduced. Tables are provided to record the follow-up that takes place and parallel tests are provided for retesting. These tests can be found in the online Teacher Resource.

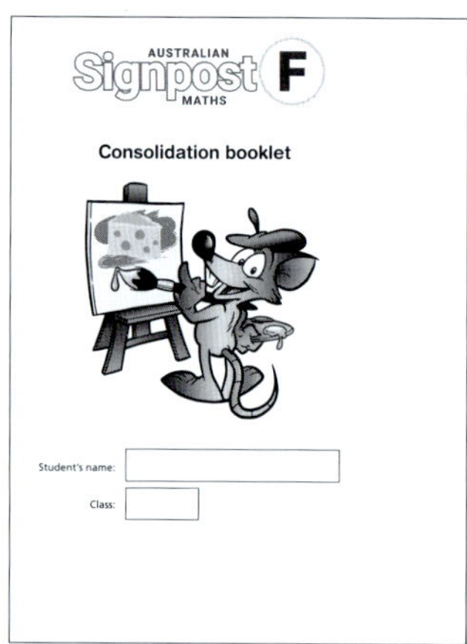

- **Year F Consolidation booklet**
  This 30-page booklet is found in the online Teacher Resource. It is designed to reinforce work completed in class and provides practice of important skills and addition and subtraction facts. The booklet can be used when there is limited supervision or when a student finishes classwork early.

- **Answers**
  These are supplied in the online Teacher Resource.

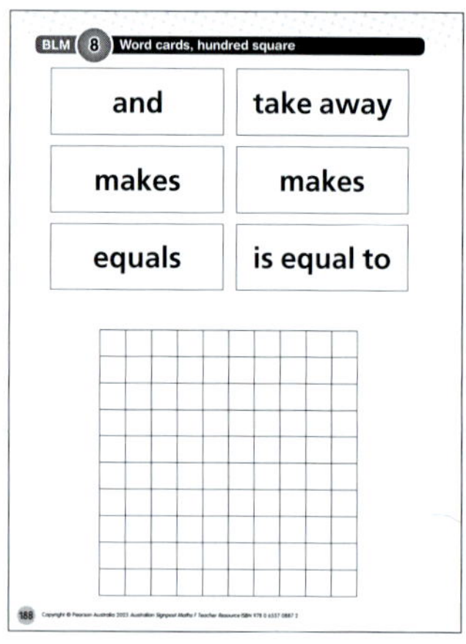

- **Blackline masters (BLM)**
  References are made to the blackline masters in the teaching suggestions provided for each student work page.

- **Differentiation**
  Each student work page has a Teacher Resource page to support it. Cross-references direct the teacher to pages where the concept is introduced and developed. These references may be from the Student Book for the previous year, current year or the next year.

  The Teacher Resource support pages provide additional learning activities for students who need remediation or extension activities. The blackline masters provide activities to support students of various learning abilities.

- **Cartoons**
  Cartoons are used to motivate and instruct.

Australian Signpost Maths icons

Signpost icons are used throughout the book as cues to the essential nature of exercises and activities, and as a guide to ways of engaging with them. These icons often indicate alternative or more concrete approaches to dealing with concepts.

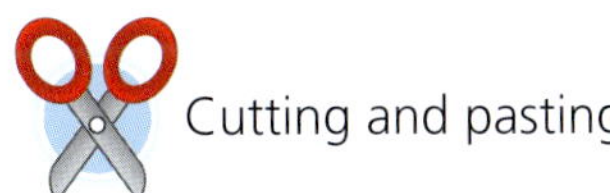
Cutting and pasting.

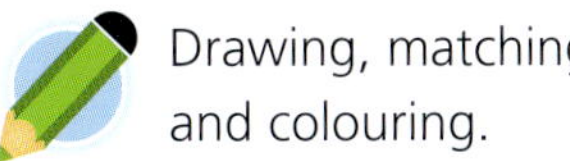
Drawing, matching and colouring.

Circle Circling the best or correct answer.

This icon highlights **important rules and concepts** occurring throughout the book. It often appears with worked examples.

Investigations allow students to **explore and discover** maths concepts.

Activities provide **applications and enrichment**. These activities usually involve the use of concrete materials and partner or group work.

These enjoyable activities are used to **motivate and involve** students in mathematical pursuits. They usually involve games and puzzles.

Structure of the Australian Curriculum, F–6 (v9)

Numeracy elements

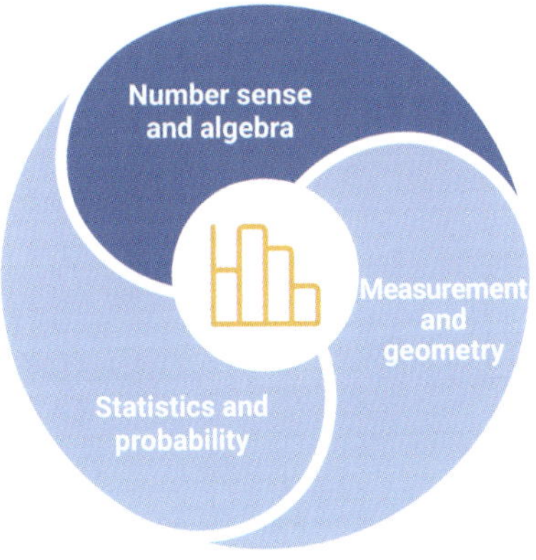

Curriculum content is organised under 6 interrelated strands: Number, Algebra, Measurement, Space, Statistics and Probability.

Sub-elements for Number sense and algebra

- Number and place value
- Counting processes
- Additive strategies
- Multiplicative strategies
- Interpreting fractions
- Number patterns and algebraic thinking
- Understanding money

Sub-elements for Measurement and geometry

- Understanding units of measurement
- Understanding geometric properties
- Positioning and locating
- Measuring time

Sub-elements for Statistics and probability

- Understanding chance
- Interpreting and representing data

The Curriculum strives to develop in students proficiency in Mathematics, highlighting Understanding, Fluency, Reasoning and Problem solving.

Mathematics content of the Australian Curriculum

- Both the content description in the Curriculum F–6 (e.g. AC9MFSP02 of the Space strand) and the sub-element in the Numeracy progression levels (e.g. Positioning and locating) define the content and skill expectations (e.g. for the element Measurement and Geometry) of the Year (e.g. Foundation) for the learning area Mathematics.
- The General capabilities that relate to teaching Mathematics are Numeracy, Critical and creative thinking, Literacy, Digital literacy and Ethical understanding.

F Contents and syllabus overview

Contents cross-reference x
Dictionary xii
Identifying and addressing areas of need 128
Extra support pages 130

KEY

Colour	Strand
Dark blue	Number / algebra
Green	Measurement / space
Orange	Statistics / probability

Page	Unit	Title	Strand			Content area									
			Number / algebra	Measurement / space	Statistics / probability	Numbers / money	Addition / subtraction	Sharing / grouping	Patterns	2D shapes / 3D objects	Position / directions	Length / area / mass	Capacity / volume	Time / duration	Data displays
1	Thinking Skills		Critical and creative thinking is covered throughout.												
2	1A	Zero	■			●									
3	1B	The number one	■			●									
4	1C	The number two	■			●									
5	1D	Long, short and tall		■								●			
6	2A	The number three	■			●									
7	2B	The number four	■			●									
8	2C	The number five	■			●									
9	2D	Data			■										●
10	3A	Numbers to five	■			●									
11	3B	Counting to five	■			●									
12	3C	The number six	■			●									
13	3D	Curved and straight		■						●					
14	4A	The number seven	■			●									
15	4B	Dot patterns	■			●									
16	4C	Circles		■						●					
17	4D	Comparing objects		■								●			
18	5A	Same and different	■			●									
19	5B	Same and different	■			●									
20	5C	Squares		■						●					
21	5D	Full, empty and half full		■									●		
		Progress test 1: Administer test then address weaknesses.													
22	6A	The number eight	■			●									
23	6B	Comparing groups	■			●									
24	6C	Ordering collections	■			●									
25	6D	Comparison of mass		■								●			
26	7A	The number nine	■			●									
27	7B	The number ten	■			●									
28	7C	Rectangles		■						●					
29	7D	Daytime and night-time		■										●	

KEY

Colour	Strand
■ (blue)	Number / algebra
■ (green)	Measurement / space
■ (orange)	Statistics / probability

Page	Unit	Title	Strand	Number / algebra	Measurement / space	Statistics / probability	Content area	Numbers / money	Addition / subtraction	Sharing / grouping	Patterns	2D shapes / 3D objects	Position / directions	Length / area / mass	Capacity / volume	Time / duration	Data displays
30	8A	Numbers to ten		■				●									
31	8B	Numbers to ten		■				●									
32	8C	Position			■								●				
33	8D	Language of location			■								●				
34	9A	Numbers to 10		■				●									
35	9B	Numbers 11 and 12		■				●									
36	9C	Longer and shorter			■									●			
37	9D	Triangles			■							●					
38	10A	Adding two groups		■					●								
39	10B	Adding two groups		■					●								
40	10C	Cutting shapes			■							●					
41	10D	Numbers to 12		■				●									
42	11A	Numbers 13 to 20		■				●									
43	11B	Numbers 11 to 20		■				●									
44	11C	Shape pictures			■							●					
45	11D	3D objects			■							●					
46	12A	Adding dots		■					●								
47	12B	Using five to form numbers		■				●	●								

Progress test 2: Administer test then address weaknesses.

Page	Unit	Title	Strand	Number / algebra	Measurement / space	Statistics / probability	Content area	Numbers / money	Addition / subtraction	Sharing / grouping	Patterns	2D shapes / 3D objects	Position / directions	Length / area / mass	Capacity / volume	Time / duration	Data displays
48	12C	Rolling, sliding and stacking			■							●					
49	12D	Stacking and packing			■							●					
50	13A	Adding two groups		■					●								
51	13B	Adding two groups		■					●								
52	13C	Ball-shaped objects			■							●					
53	13D	Box-shaped objects			■							●					
54	14A	Adding two groups		■					●								
55	14B	Addition		■					●								
56	14C	Sorting objects			■							●					
57	14D	Using data displays				■											●
58	15A	Dominoes and dice		■					●								
59	15B	Adding groups		■					●								
60	15C	Sequencing events in a day			■											●	
61	15D	Days of the week			■											●	
62	16A	Adding groups		■					●								
63	16B	Adding rows of dots		■							●						
64	16C	Cone-shaped objects			■							●					
65	16D	Using data displays				■											●

KEY

■	Number / algebra
■	Measurement / space
■	Statistics / probability

			Strand			Content area									
Page	Unit	Title	Number / algebra	Measurement / space	Statistics / probability	Numbers / money	Addition / subtraction	Sharing / grouping	Patterns	2D shapes / 3D objects	Position / directions	Length / area / mass	Capacity / volume	Time / duration	Data displays
66	17A	Adding groups	■				●								
67	17B	Ordinal numbers	■			●									
68	17C	Can-shaped objects		■						●					
69	17D	Duration of events		■										●	
70	18A	Looking for patterns	■						●						
71	18B	Patterns	■						●						
72	18C	Shapes		■						●					
73	18D	Shapes		■						●					
74	19A	Adding groups	■				●								
75	19B	Counting to 20	■			●									
76	19C	Comparing objects		■						●					
77	19D	Gathering data			■										●
78	20A	Comparing collections	■			●									
79	20B	Counting to 30	■			●									
80	20C	Sequencing events		■										●	
81	20D	Days of the week		■										●	
82	21A	Taking objects away	■				●								
83	21B	Taking away	■				●								

Progress test 3: Administer test then address weaknesses.

Page	Unit	Title	Number / algebra	Measurement / space	Statistics / probability	Numbers / money	Addition / subtraction	Sharing / grouping	Patterns	2D shapes / 3D objects	Position / directions	Length / area / mass	Capacity / volume	Time / duration	Data displays
84	21C	Classifying 2D shapes		■						●					
85	21D	Describing objects in our world		■						●					
86	22A	Taking away	■				●								
87	22B	Taking away	■				●								
88	22C	Comparing two lengths		■								●			
89	22D	Position and length		■							●	●			
90	23A	Taking away	■				●								
91	23B	Taking away	■				●								
92	23C	Left and right		■							●				
93	23D	Giving and following directions		■							●				
94	24A	Separating a number into parts	■				●								
95	24B	Separating a number into parts	■				●								
96	24C	Adding on and counting back	■				●								
97	24D	2D shapes		■						●					
98	25A	Everyday patterns	■						●						
99	25B	Making patterns	■						●						
100	25C	Comparing quantities	■			●									
101	25D	Data displays			■										●

KEY

■ (blue)	Number / algebra
■ (teal)	Measurement / space
■ (orange)	Statistics / probability

Page	Unit	Title	Strand	Number / algebra	Measurement / space	Statistics / probability	Content area	Numbers / money	Addition / subtraction	Sharing / grouping	Patterns	2D shapes / 3D objects	Position / directions	Length / area / mass	Capacity / volume	Time / duration	Data displays
102	26A	Groups of equal size		■						●							
103	26B	Matching equal groups		■						●							
104	26C	Comparing lengths			■									●			
105	26D	Data displays				■											●
106	27A	Equal groups		■						●							
107	27B	Using grouping to share		■						●							
108	27C	Telling the time			■											●	
		Progress test 4: Administer test then address weaknesses.															
109	27D	Using o'clock			■											●	
110	28A	How many more?		■					●								
111	28B	Equal groups		■						●							
112	28C	Patterns using sounds and actions		■							●						
113	28D	Using data displays				■											●
114	29A	Sharing		■						●							
115	29B	Sharing		■						●							
116	29C	Comparing capacities			■										●		
117	29D	Comparing objects			■									●	●		
118	30A	Sharing in other ways		■						●							
119	30B	Sharing among 3 or more		■						●							
120	30C	Comparing capacity			■										●		
121	30D	Comparing capacity			■										●		
122	31A	Location			■								●				
		Progress test 5: Administer test then address weaknesses.															
123	31B	Recording the weather				■											●
124	31C	Comparing distances			■									●			
125	31D	Pattern blocks			■								●	●			
126	32A	Sorting and classifying coins		■				●									
127	32B	Australian money		■				●									

Page			
128	Identifying and addressing areas of need		
130	**1** Number charts	**2** Ten frames	**3** Adding two groups
133	**4** Before and after to 10	**5** Adding 1 or 2	**6** Subtracting 1 or 2
136	**7** Addition number facts to 10	**8** Number bond houses	**9** Number bonds (addition)

Contents cross-reference

Number and algebra

1	Whole numbers	Pages
	Counting	2, 3, 4, 6, 7, 8, 10, 11, 12, 14, 22, 23, 24, 26, 27, 30, 31, 34, 35, 42, 43, 49, 75, 78, 79, 100, 124, 126, 130
	Counting forwards from a given number	22, 31, 35, 43, 47, 75, 79, 96
	Counting backwards from a given number	22, 31, 35, 43, 75, 79, 96
	State the number after (one more) or before (one less)	6, 12, 34, 35, 75, 79, 133
	Subitising for small groups (instant recognition)	4, 6, 7, 8, 15, 18, 19, 23, 24, 26, 31, 34, 46, 47, 58, 98
	Recognising dice, domino and finger patterns	3, 4, 6, 7, 8, 10, 12, 15, 18, 19, 26, 31, 46, 47, 58, 96, 98
	Represent and recognising numbers using words, numerals and objects	2, 3, 4, 6, 7, 8, 10, 11, 12, 14, 22, 23, 26, 27, 30, 31, 34, 35, 41, 42, 43, 47, 75, 79, 100
	Distinguish between 'teen' numerals and multiples of 10	42, 43, 78
	Compare and order numbers and collections to 20	7, 8, 18, 19, 23, 24, 27, 43, 78, 100
2	**Addition and subtraction**	**Pages**
	Part–whole relationships up to 10	46, 51, 94, 95, 137
	Addition	38, 39, 46, 50, 51, 54, 55, 58, 59, 62, 63, 66, 74, 94, 95, 96, 110, 134, 136
	Subtraction	82, 83, 86, 87, 90, 91, 96, 110, 135, 137, 138
	Using concrete materials to add or subtract	51, 55, 58, 74, 82
	How many more?	23, 46, 102, 110
	Money	100, 126, 127
3	**Multiplication and division**	**Pages**
	Equal groups	6, 102, 103, 106, 107, 111, 118
	Combining equal groups	106, 107, 111
	Sharing	107, 114, 115, 118, 119
4	**Algebra**	**Pages**
	Patterns	70, 71, 72, 80, 98, 99, 112
	Same and different	18, 19

Measurement and space

1	Measurement	Pages
	Length	5, 36, 76, 88, 89, 104, 117, 124
	Capacity	21, 116, 117, 120, 121
	Mass	17, 25, 76, 117
	Duration	69
	Sequencing events / the language of time	29, 60, 61, 69, 80, 81
	Days of the week	61, 80, 81
	Telling time on the hour	29, 41, 108, 109
2	**Space**	**Pages**
	2D shapes	13, 16, 20, 28, 37, 40, 44, 72, 73, 84, 97, 125
	3D objects	45, 48, 49, 52, 53, 56, 64, 68, 85
	Describing position	32, 33, 67, 89, 92, 93, 122
	Left and right	92, 109, 122
	Giving and following directions	93
	Ordinal numbers	67, 80

Statistics and probability

1	Statistics	Pages
	Collecting information	57, 77, 101, 105, 113, 123
	Using data displays	9, 57, 65, 77, 101, 105, 113, 123

F Dictionary

adding
When we join groups of objects together, we are adding them together.

adding on
If we add 5 and 3, we count on from 5, (e.g. 5 ... 6, 7, 8) 5 and 3 make 8.

area
Area is the amount of space on a shape.

capacity
Capacity is the amount that a container can hold.

- A container can be **empty**.
- A container can be **full**.
- A container can be **half full**.

circle
See *two-dimensional (2D) shapes* (page xiv).

collection
A collection is a group of objects.

curved line
A curved line is not straight.

data display (or graph)
A data display shows categories of objects and allows us to compare them.

equal groups
Groups that are the same.

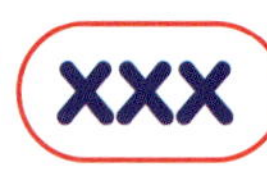

face
A flat surface that has straight sides (e.g. a box has 6 faces).

friends of ten
Numbers that add together to make 10 (e.g. 3 and 7, 4 and 6, 5 and 5).

half
One half is one of two equal parts.

Half of the rectangle is coloured.

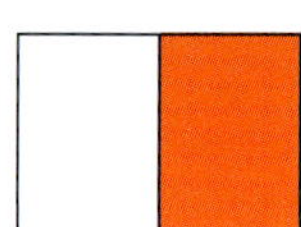

halfway point
The halfway point is the middle position.

heft
To compare masses by lifting them with your hands.

how many more
We could count on from the smaller number.

left and right
- Left

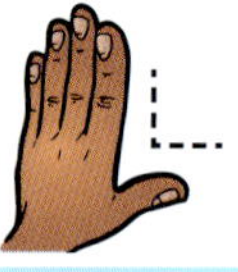
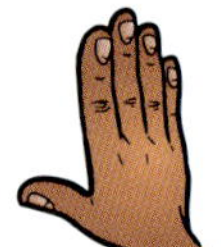

- Right

length words:

distance	long	tall
deeper	longer	taller
higher	short	tallest
lower	shorter	thinner

mass words:

heavy	light	weigh
heavier	lighter	weight

numbers

0 zero
1 one ●
2 two ●●
3 three ●●●
4 four ●●●●
5 five ●●●●●
6 six ●●●●●●
7 seven ●●●●●●●
8 eight ●●●●●●●●
9 nine ●●●●●●●●●
10 ten ●●●●●●●●●●

number bonds

Pairs of numbers that add to make a specific number (e.g. 0 and 4, 1 and 3, and 2 and 2 all make 4).

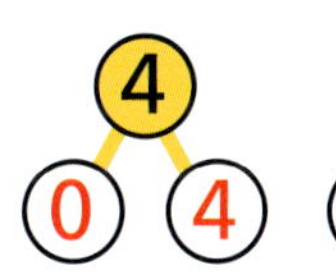
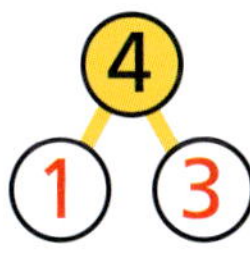

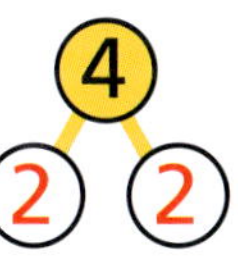

number sentence

Uses numerals and symbols (e.g. 4 and 6 makes 10. This can be written as 4 + 6 = 10).

numeral

A numeral is a written number symbol.

7, 18, 92, 120

ordering

We can order objects or numbers by placing them from smallest to largest or from largest to smallest.

We can use words like first, next, last, before, after, 1st, 2nd, 3rd.

ordinal numbers

Ordinal numbers describe the order or position of something.

1st, 2nd, 3rd, 4th, 5th

pattern

A pattern is a group of numbers, objects, shapes, colours, sounds or actions that are repeated over and over again.

rectangle

See *two-dimensional (2D) shapes* (page xiv).

row

A row is a line of objects going across. Here are 2 rows of 5.

sharing

When sharing, we make sure that each share is the same size.

If 2 people could share these 6 balls, each person would get 3 balls.

If two groups are not the same, we can make fair shares by moving items from the larger group to the smaller group.

sorting, classifying

When sorting or classifying, we put similar objects in each group.

square

See *two-dimensional (2D) shapes.*

straight line

A straight line has no bends or curves.

take away (subtraction)

When we remove objects from a group, we call this "take away".

three-dimensional (3D) objects

Solid objects are three-dimensional.
They have length, width and height.

Ball-shaped objects (spheres)

are curved and round.
They can roll.

Box-shaped objects (cubes)

have 6 square faces.
They can slide and stack.

Can-shaped objects (cylinders)

have 2 surfaces that are circles and 1 curved surface. They can roll, slide and stack.

Cone-shaped objects (cones)

have 1 surface that is a circle and 1 curved surface. They can roll and slide.

time words:

morning	daytime
afternoon	night time

Days			
Sunday	Monday	Tuesday	Wednesday
Thursday	Friday	Saturday	

Clocks

3 o'clock

o'clock:
When the long hand is pointing to 12, the time is an o'clock time.

triangle

See *two-dimensional (2D) shapes.*

two-dimensional (2D) shapes

Flat shapes are two-dimensional.
They have length and width.

Circle

1 curved side

Triangle

3 straight sides

Square

4 equal straight sides

Rectangle

2 equal long sides and 2 equal short sides, like a stretched square. All sides are straight.

volume

Volume is the amount of space an object takes up.

The mice and the parrot

1. What are the mice wearing?
2. How many hats are in this picture?
3. How many balloons are in this picture?
4. What else can you count in the picture?
5. What things are round? Colour the round things.
6. What is the parrot doing?
7. What could happen when the mouse sticks the needle into the balloon?
8. Why is the mouse with balloons worried?
9. How many legs can you see in this picture?
10. Which of these questions do you like best? Why do you like it?

1 **Circle** the containers that hold zero things.  Trace the numerals and the word "zero".

2 These stalls were at the show. Look at the picture and then answer the questions.

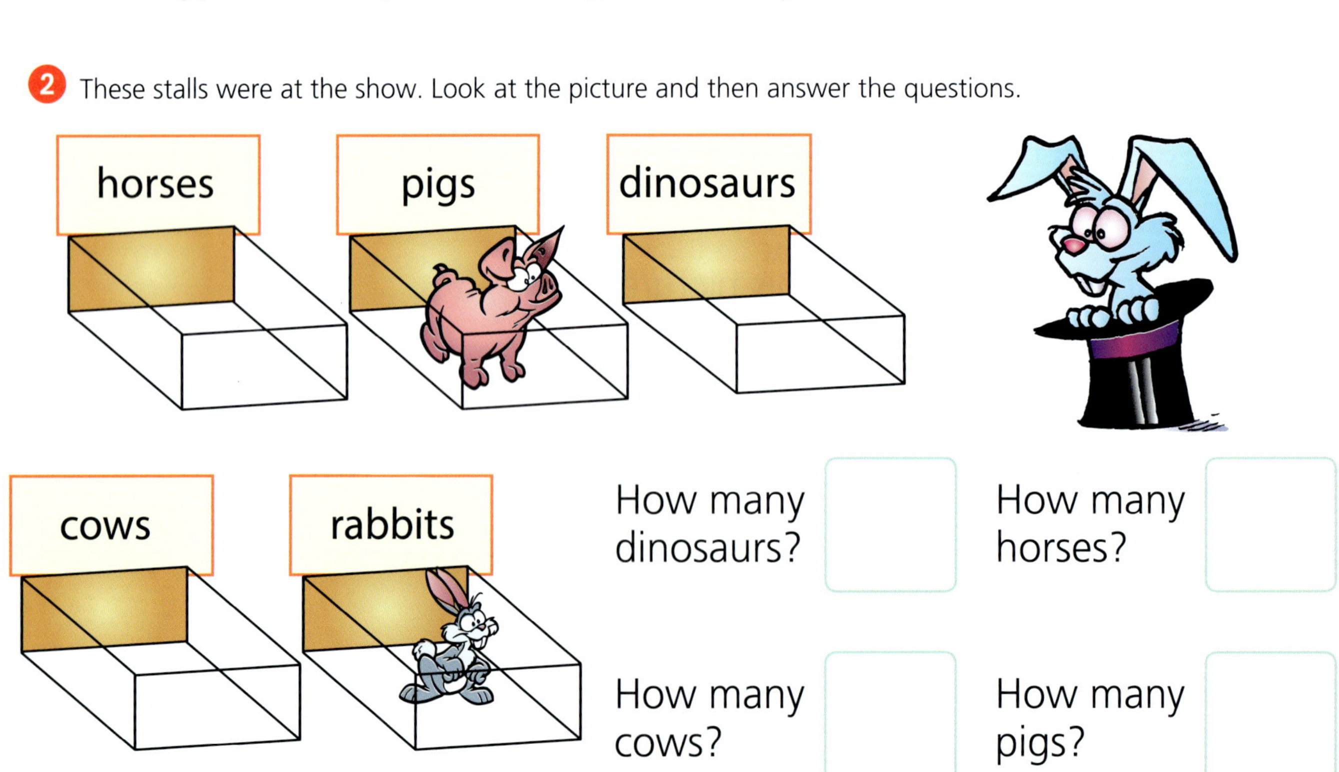

How many dinosaurs? ☐

How many horses? ☐

How many cows? ☐

How many pigs? ☐

© PEARSON AUSTRALIA 2024 • *AUSTRALIAN SIGNPOST MATHS F* • ISBN 9780655708742

1B The number one

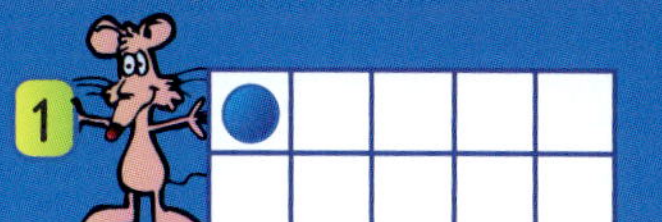

1 Circle the groups with one object. Trace the numerals and the word "one".

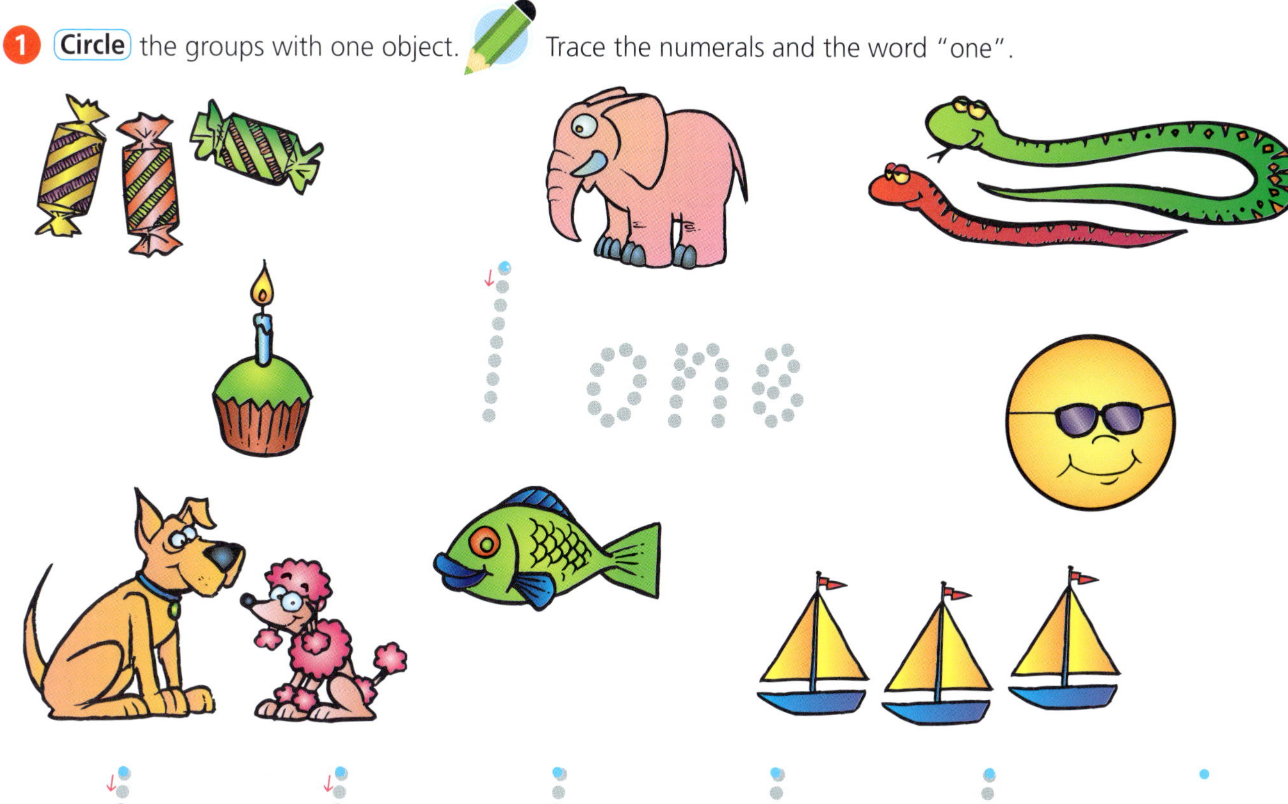

2 Draw one fish.

How many fish did you draw?

Colour the parts that are shown only once.

© PEARSON AUSTRALIA 2024 • *AUSTRALIAN SIGNPOST MATHS F* • ISBN 9780655708742

1C The number two

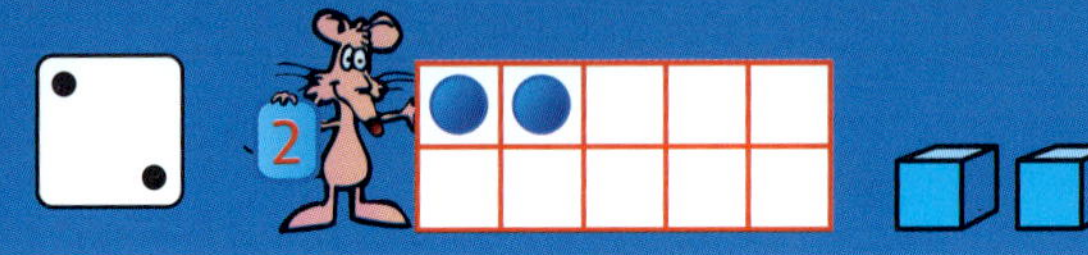

1 Circle the groups of two. Trace the numerals and the word "two".

2 two

2 2 2 2 2

Discuss which groups above have the same number.

2 Colour two in each row. Trace the numbers.

Draw two balloons.

Tell a story about the balloons.

© PEARSON AUSTRALIA 2024 • *AUSTRALIAN SIGNPOST MATHS F* • ISBN 9780655708742

1D Long, short and tall

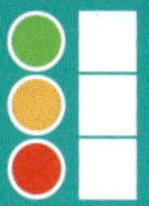

1 Draw lines to match each word to a picture.

short | long | tall

2 Draw a tall tree. | Draw one long arrow. | Draw a long scarf.

Draw two short trees. | Draw two short arrows. | Draw two short scarves.

3 Colour the long snakes. Draw two more short snakes.

© PEARSON AUSTRALIA 2024 • *AUSTRALIAN SIGNPOST MATHS F* • ISBN 9780655708742

2A The number three

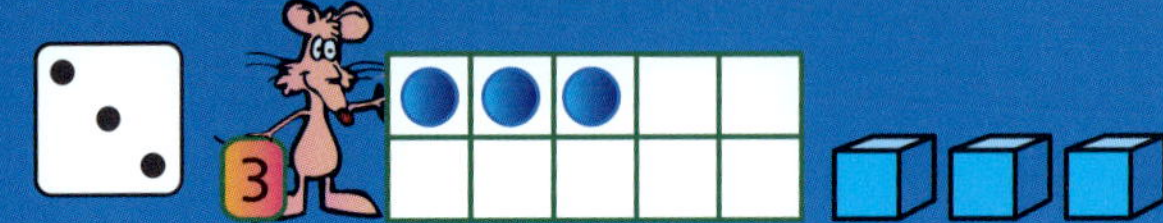

1 Colour groups that show three. Trace the numerals and the word "three".

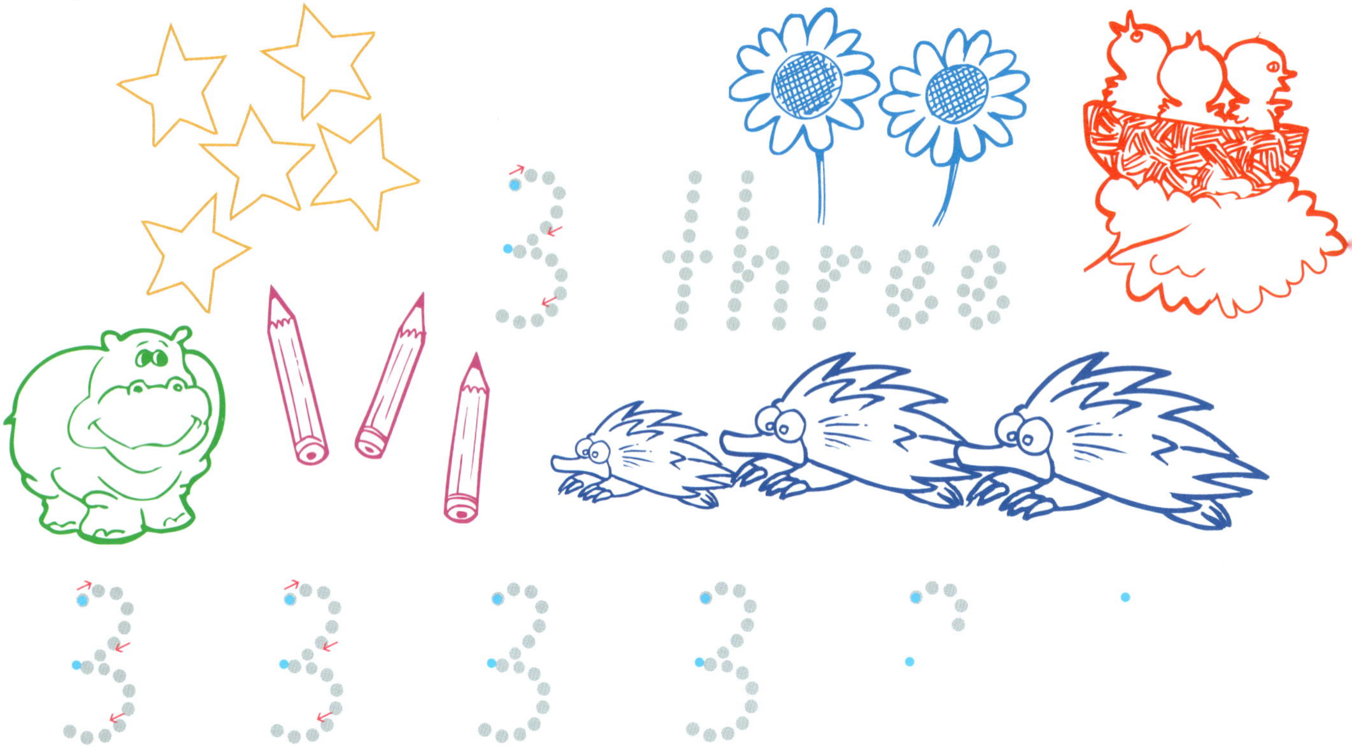

2 Draw three spots on each ladybird.

INVESTIGATION

Circle groups of two lollies.

How many groups did you circle?

→ Talk about your answer.

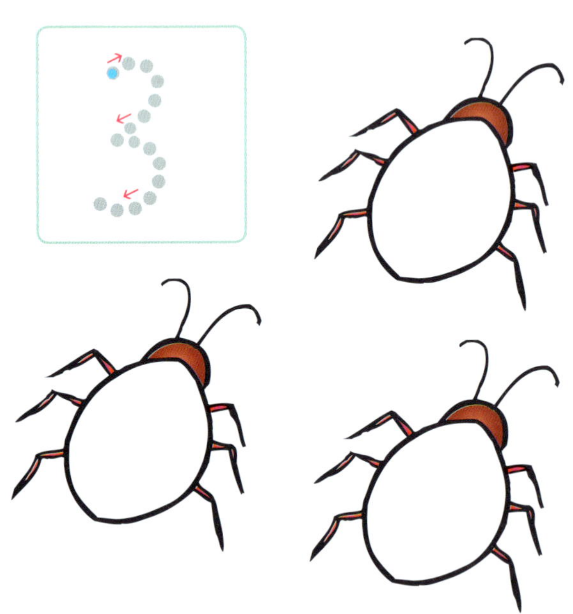

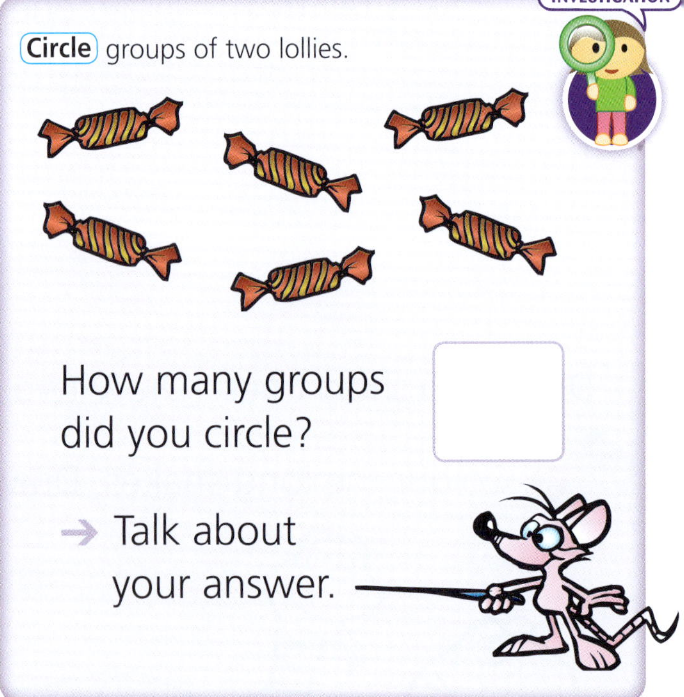

3 Write the numeral after or before.

	3	2			1	0	

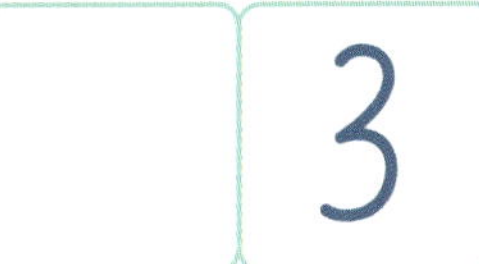

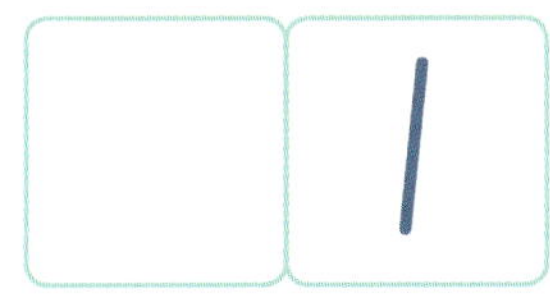

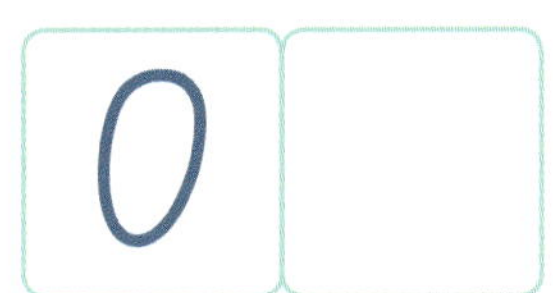

© PEARSON AUSTRALIA 2024 • *AUSTRALIAN SIGNPOST MATHS F* • ISBN 9780655708742

2B The number four

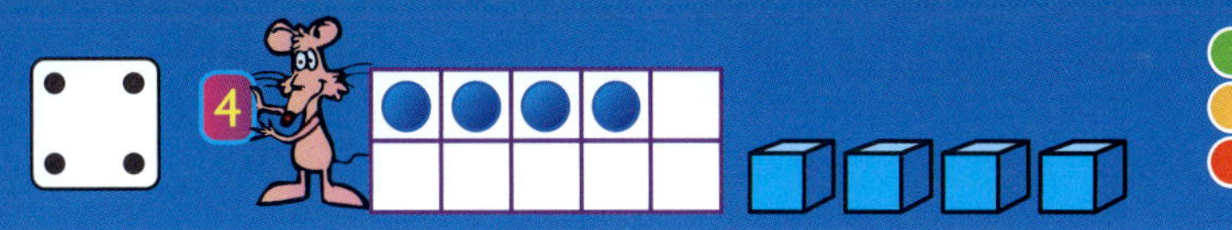

1 Circle groups that show four.

Trace the numerals and the word "four".

four

4 4 4 4

2 Draw objects to match each numeral.

4	
2	
3	

INVESTIGATION

Make different dot patterns for four.

→ Talk about your answer.

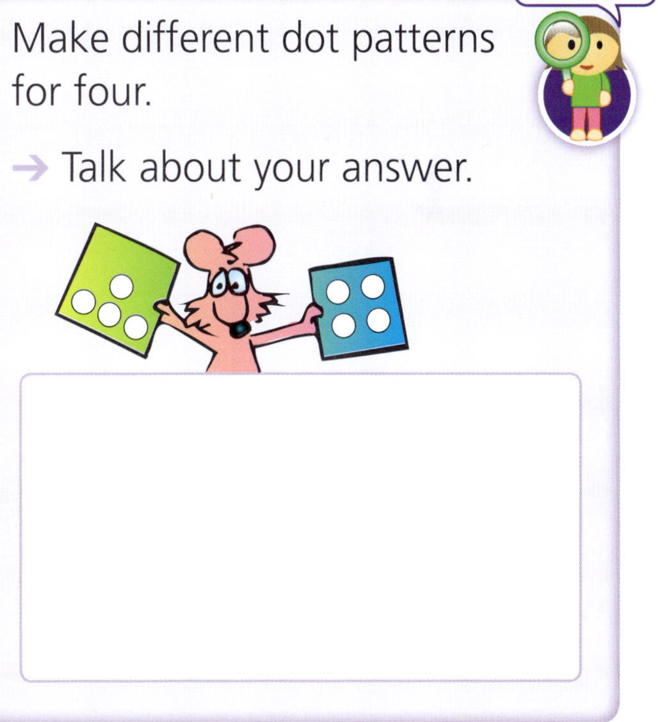

3 Write the numbers 0, 1, 2, 3 and 4 from smallest to largest.

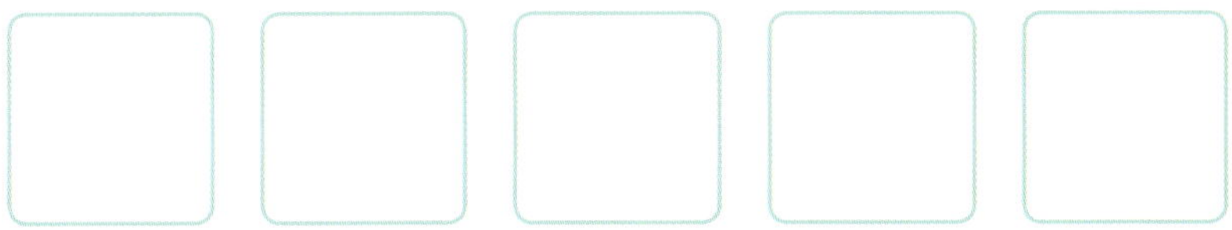

© PEARSON AUSTRALIA 2024 • *AUSTRALIAN SIGNPOST MATHS F* • ISBN 9780655708742

2C The number five

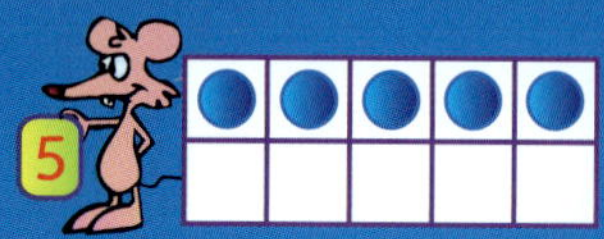

1 Colour the groups of five. Trace the numerals and the word "five".

2 Write the numbers in order.

a forwards

b backwards

3 Write 2, 0, 5 and 4 in order, smallest to largest.

4 Write 3, 5, 0 and 2 in order, smallest to largest.

ACTIVITY

Draw your hand on paper. Number the fingers 1 to 5.

© PEARSON AUSTRALIA 2024 • *AUSTRALIAN SIGNPOST MATHS F* • ISBN 9780655708742

1 Colour each group differently.

How have you sorted the objects?

Which group has the most?

ACTIVITY

Sort groups of objects in your classroom. Talk about how you sorted the objects.

© PEARSON AUSTRALIA 2024 • *AUSTRALIAN SIGNPOST MATHS F* • ISBN 9780655708742

Numbers to five

1 Trace the numerals.

1 2 3 4 5

2 How many?

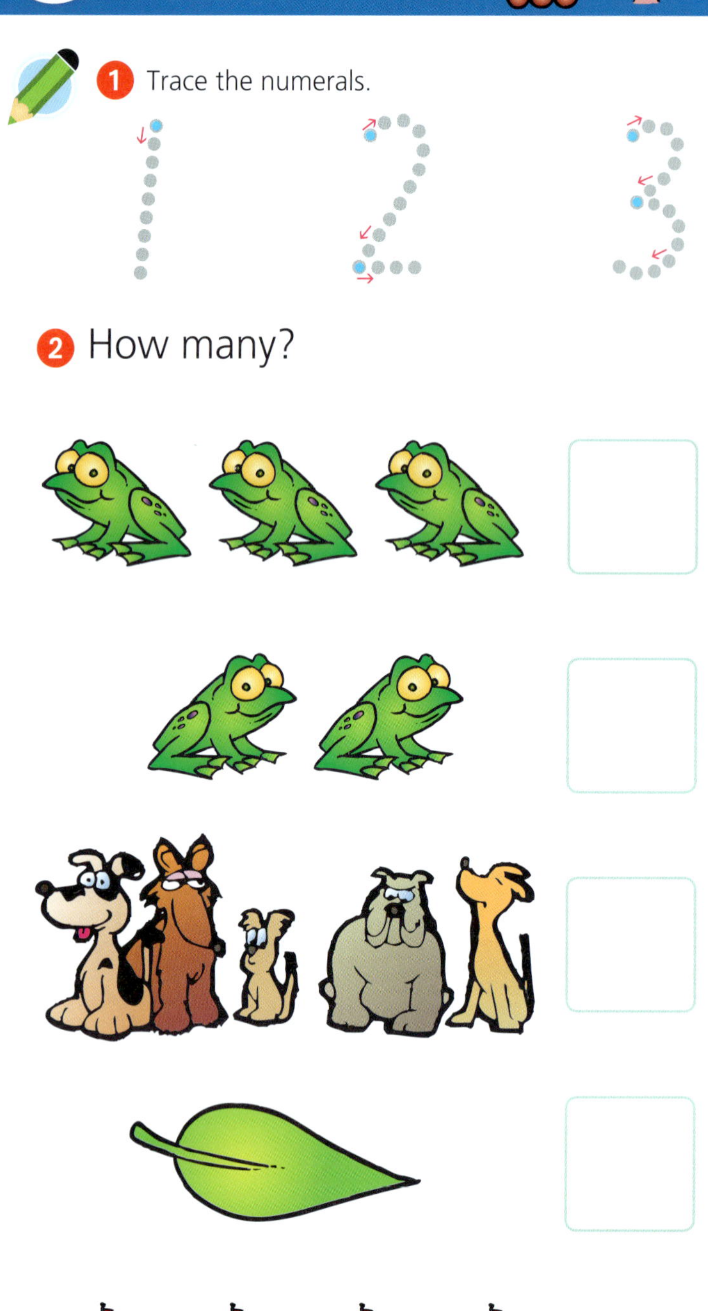

3 Join the numbers in order. Join the words in order.

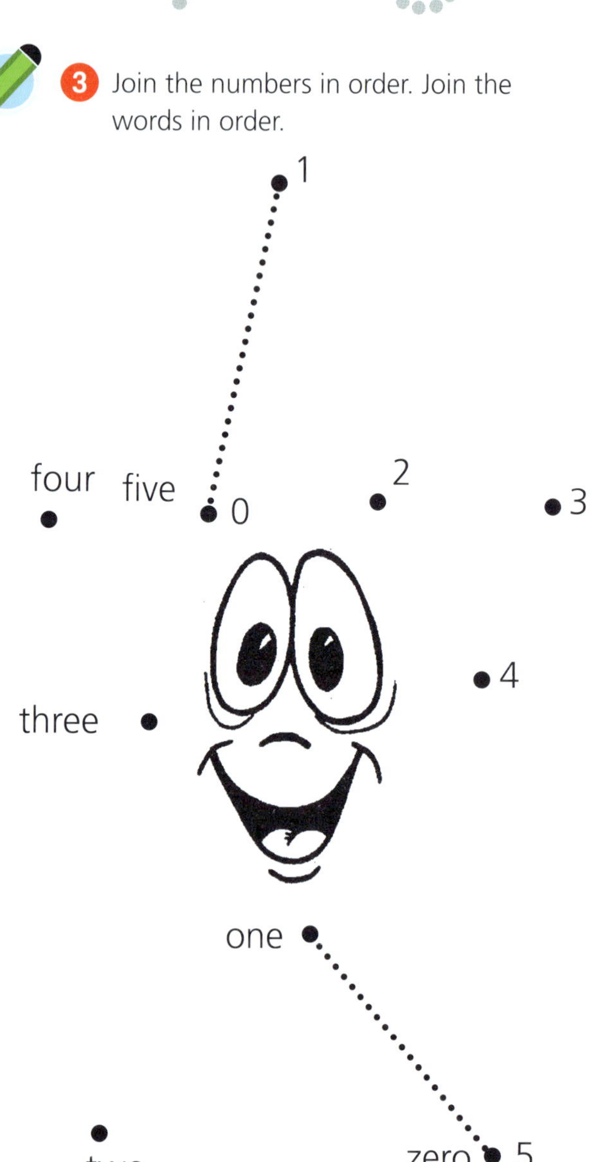

FUN SPOT

Give each person 2 legs. Give each animal 4 legs.

© PEARSON AUSTRALIA 2024 • *AUSTRALIAN SIGNPOST MATHS F* • ISBN 9780655708742

3B Counting to five

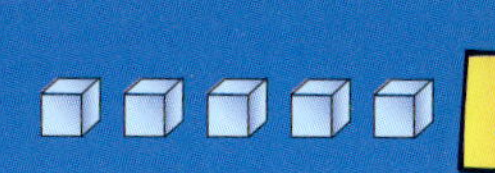
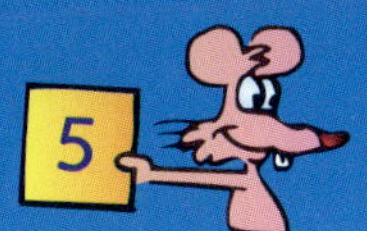

1 Trace the numerals.

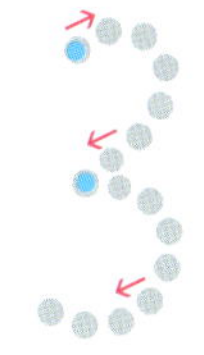
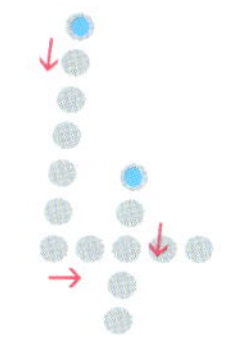
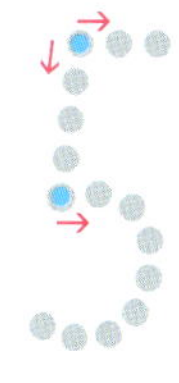

2 Talk about the picture and answer the questions.

How many ?

How many ?

How many ?

How many ?

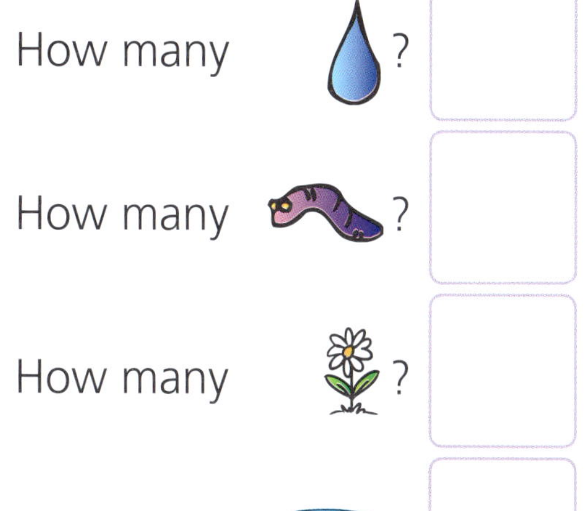

How many ?

How many ?

How many ?

How many ?

© PEARSON AUSTRALIA 2024 • *AUSTRALIAN SIGNPOST MATHS F* • ISBN 9780655708742

The number six

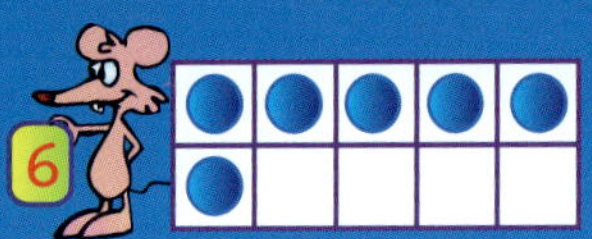

1 Colour the groups that show six. Trace the numerals and the word "six".

2 Write the number before (one less).

	1		2

3 Write the number after (one more).

5		3	

4 Draw six legs on each beetle.

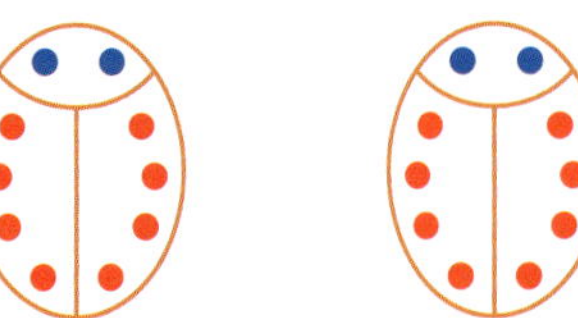

Challenge a friend

- What is one more than: 2, 4, 5, 3, 1?
- What is one less than: 3, 6, 4, 2, 5?

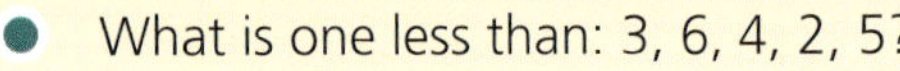

Egg carton game

Cut an egg carton into parts containing six cups. Place counters into each cup, one at a time, counting as you go. Repeat the process of placing the counters several times.

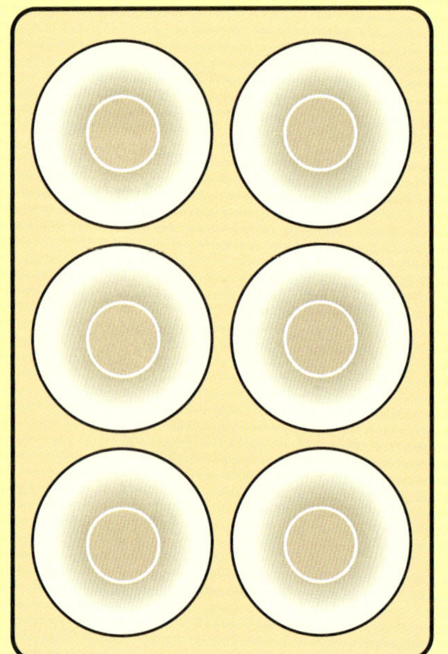

© PEARSON AUSTRALIA 2024 • *AUSTRALIAN SIGNPOST MATHS F* • ISBN 9780655708742

3D Curved and straight

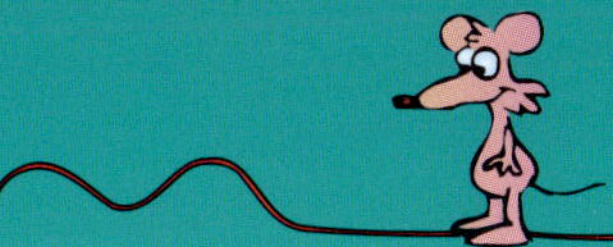

CONCEPT

- This line is curved. 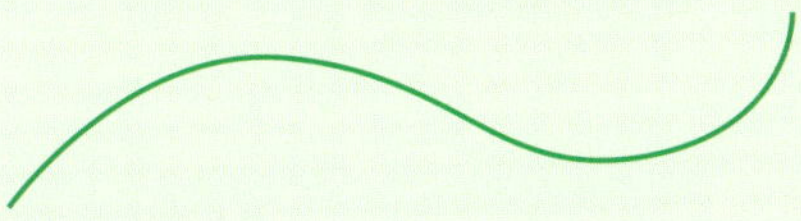
- This line is straight.

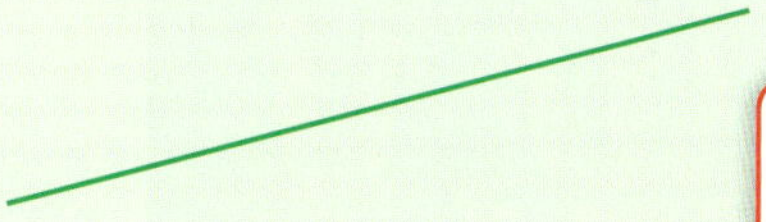

Shapes have curved or straight sides.

1 Trace the curved lines red and the straight lines blue.

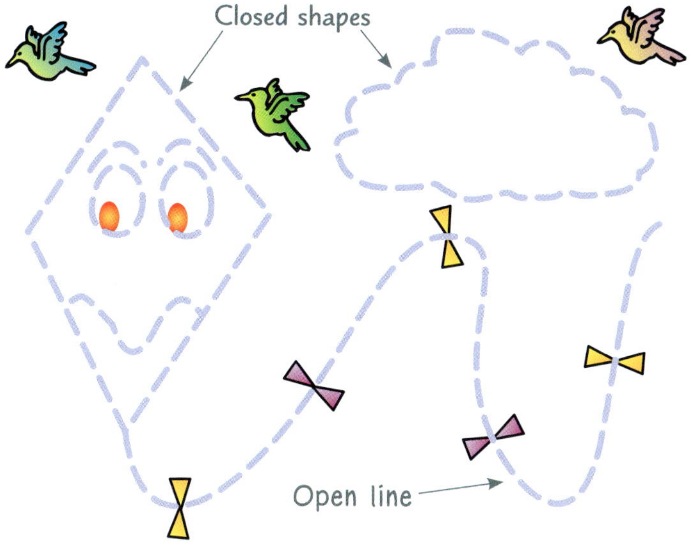

Closed shapes

Open line

2 Draw some straight and curved lines.

Straight

Curved

3 Trace these closed shapes and add some funny faces.

How many curved shapes?

How many straight shapes?

© PEARSON AUSTRALIA 2024 • *AUSTRALIAN SIGNPOST MATHS F* • ISBN 9780655708742

4A The number seven

1 Add dots to make seven. Trace the numerals and the word "seven".

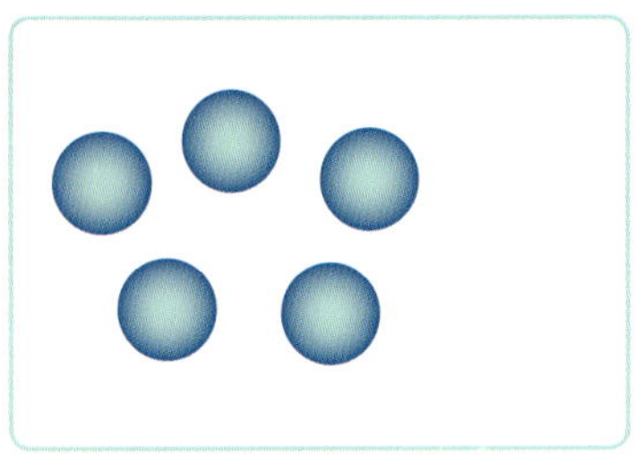

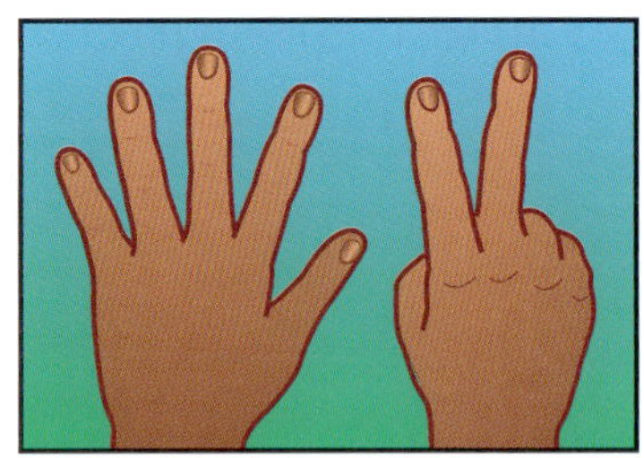

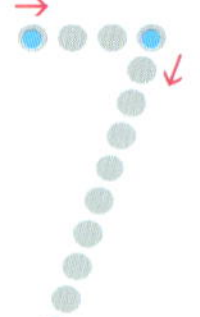

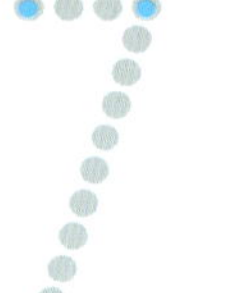

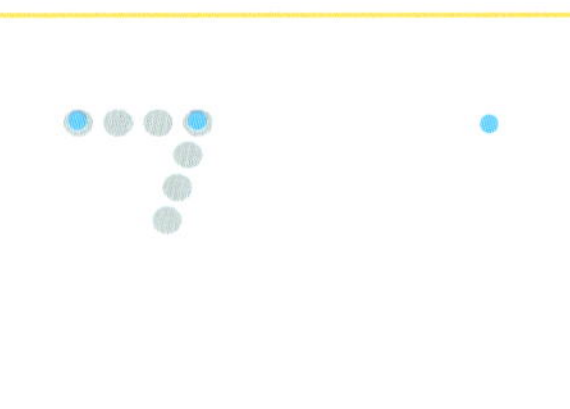

2 Write the numerals 1 to 7.

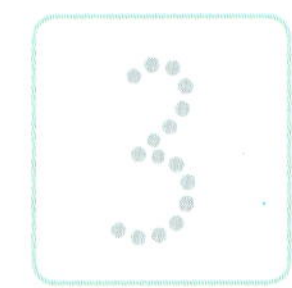

cakes

3 Draw more candles to make seven.
Draw more balloons to make seven.

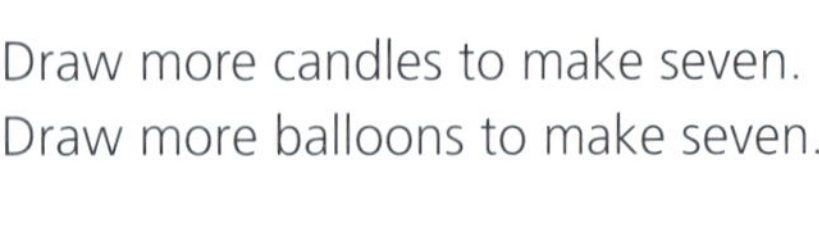

FUN SPOT

Play segur etug

How many stones?

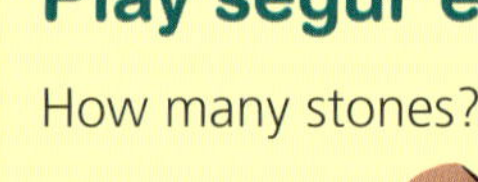

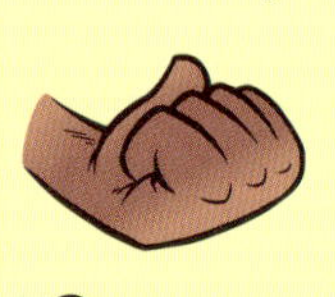

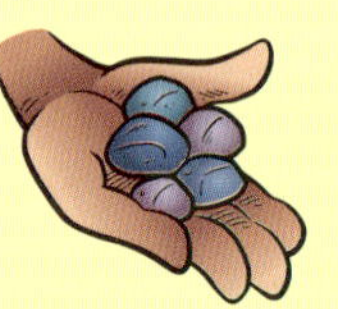

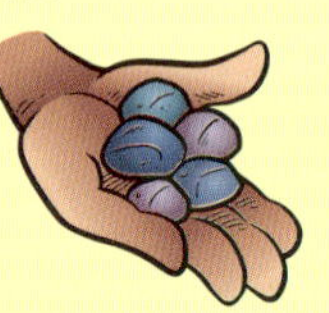

Join the numbers in order.

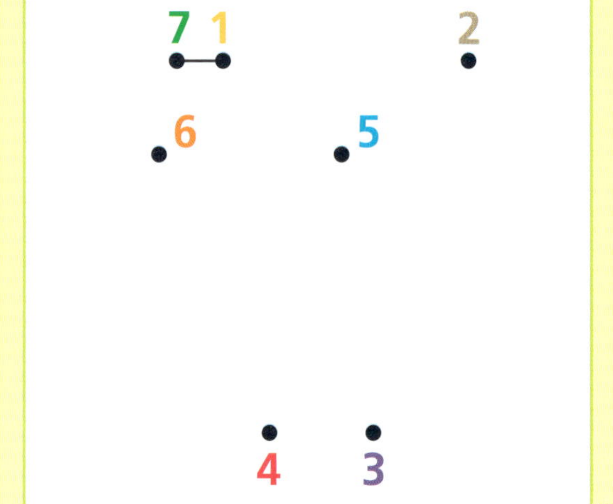

© PEARSON AUSTRALIA 2024 • *AUSTRALIAN SIGNPOST MATHS F* • ISBN 9780655708742

4B Dot patterns

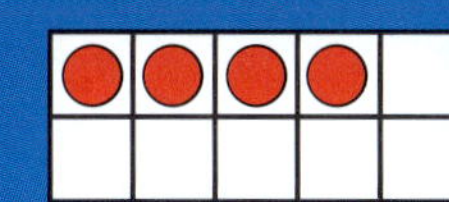
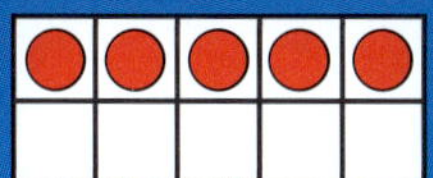
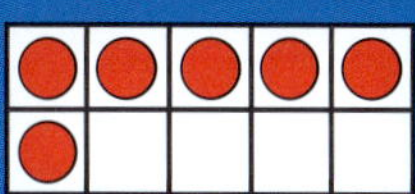

CONCEPT

Say the number of dots in each square without counting the dots.

1 In each answer square write the number of dots above it. Discuss the position of the dots in each pattern.

ACTIVITY

- Put a set of dominoes into a box. Take out one domino at a time. Say the two numbers without counting the dots.

- Keep throwing a dice.
✔ Tick the boxes below when you throw:

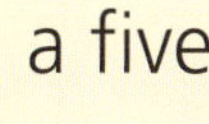
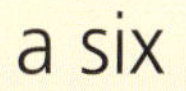

a three	a five	a six

© PEARSON AUSTRALIA 2024 • *AUSTRALIAN SIGNPOST MATHS F* • ISBN 9780655708742

4C Circles

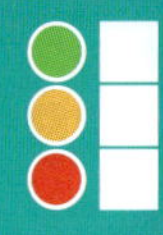

CONCEPT

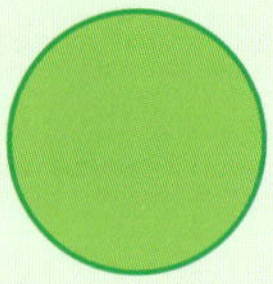

This is a circle.
It has a curved side.

1 Trace the circles in these pictures.

circle

2 Colour the circles. Discuss what makes a circle.

3 Trace the circles.

FUN SPOT

Draw a picture using circles.

This is my circle picture.

© PEARSON AUSTRALIA 2024 • *AUSTRALIAN SIGNPOST MATHS F* • ISBN 9780655708742

Comparing objects

1 Colour the light objects. **Circle** the heavy ones.

heavy

light

Hefting: holding an object in each hand to feel which is heavier.

2 In each case, **circle** the item that is heavier. (You could compare by hefting.)

5A Same and different

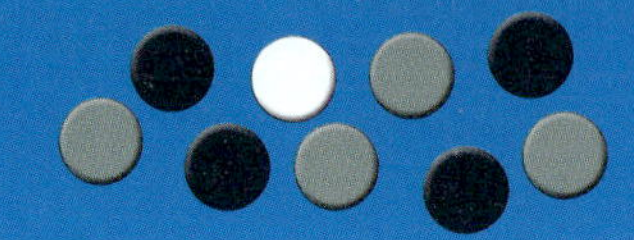

1 Draw lines to match one-to-one and then count each group.

a

the same / different

b

the same / different

c

the same / different

d

the same / different

e

the same / different

f

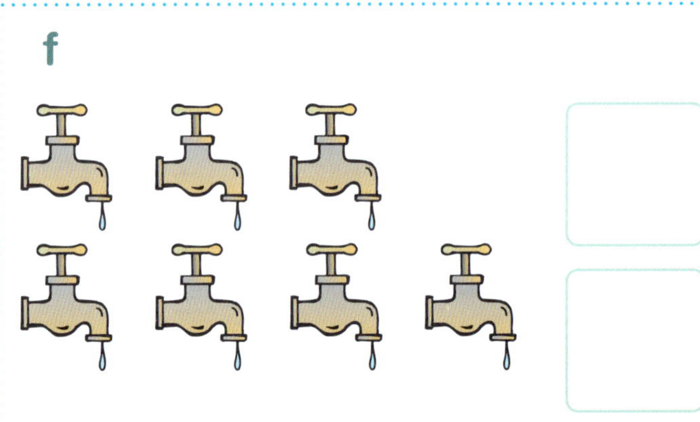

the same / different

2 **Circle** the parts in question 1 that show groups that are equal in size.

3 Colour the row that has more.

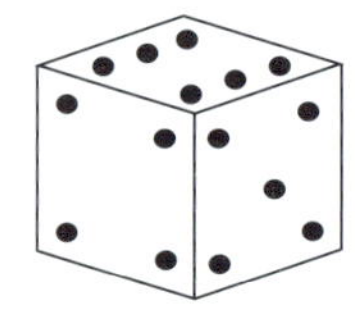
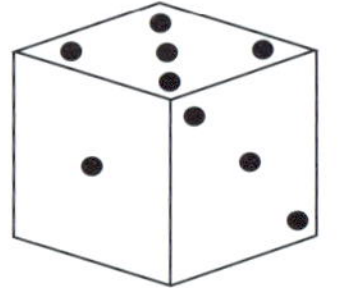
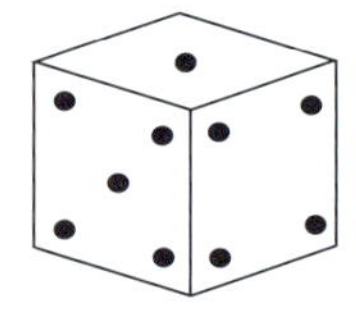

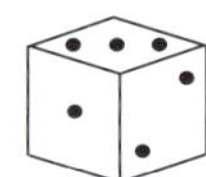
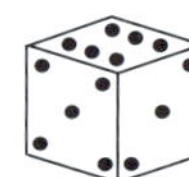
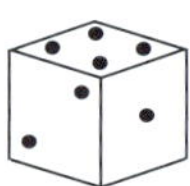
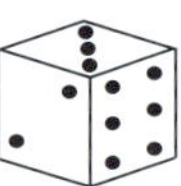

© PEARSON AUSTRALIA 2024 • *AUSTRALIAN SIGNPOST MATHS F* • ISBN 9780655708742

5B Same and different

Not the same

1 Compare each row and colour the correct label.

the same as

different

the same as

different

2 Draw seven jellybeans in each jar so they are the **same**.

3 Draw balls in each row so that the rows are **not the same**. Write the numbers.

INVESTIGATION

Colour the groups that **are the same** size. Cross out the group that **is not the same**.

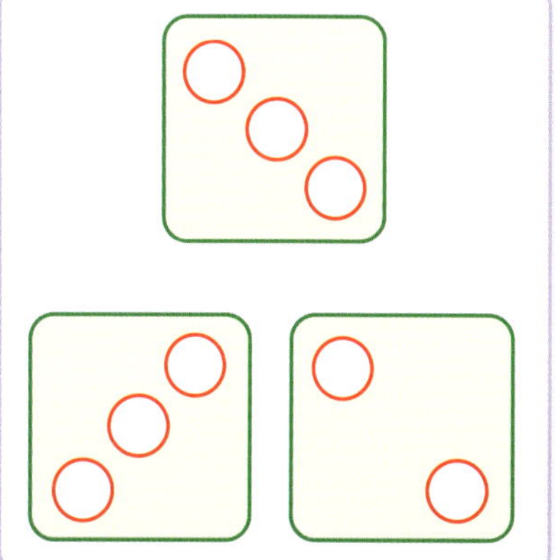

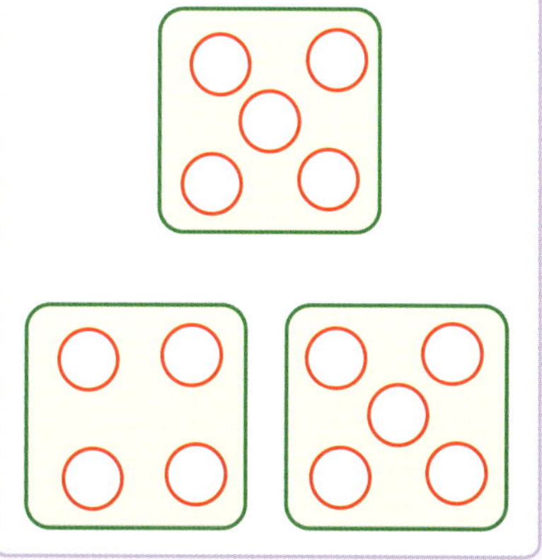

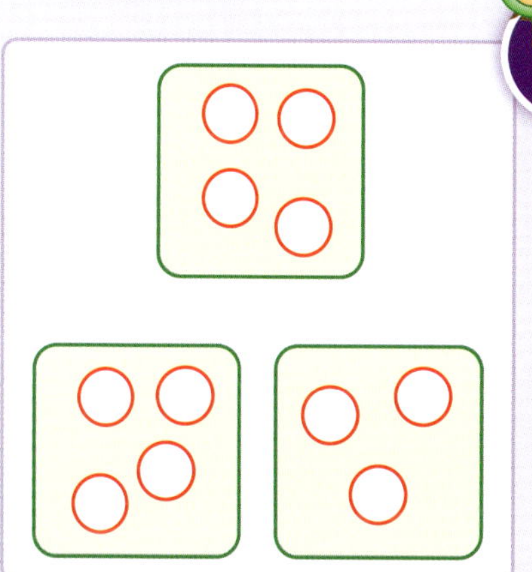

Make two groups of counters that are the same.

Make two groups of counters that are not the same.

Ask a partner if your two groups are the same or not the same. Take turns.

© PEARSON AUSTRALIA 2024 • *AUSTRALIAN SIGNPOST MATHS F* • ISBN 9780655708742

Squares

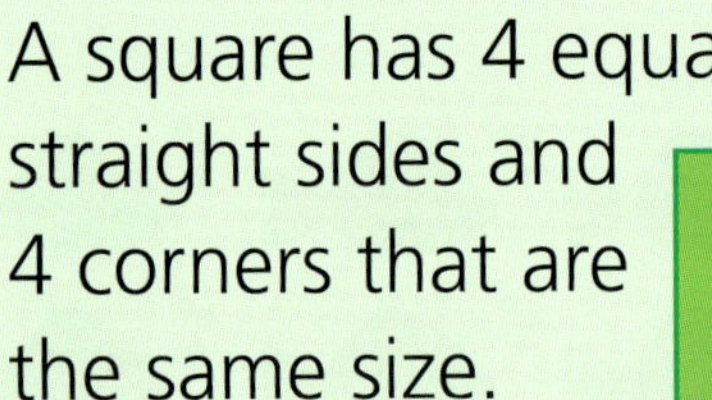

A square has 4 equal straight sides and 4 corners that are the same size.

2 ✔ Tick the squares. Discuss.

1 Trace the squares in these pictures.

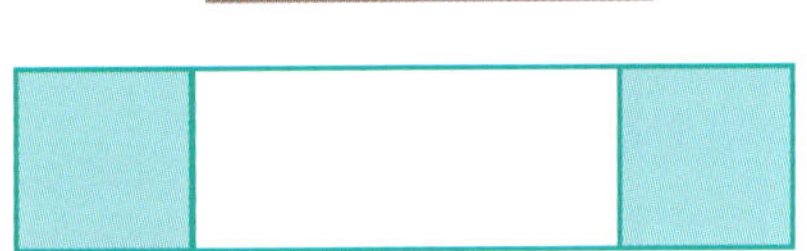

3 Trace the squares.

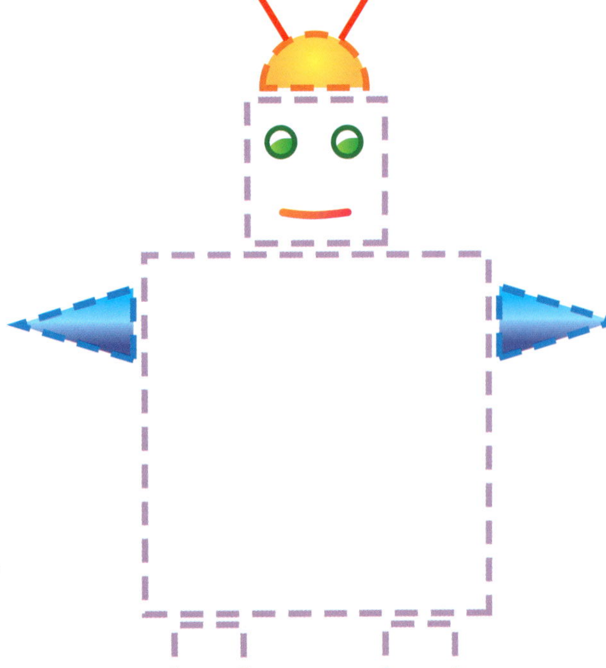

FUN SPOT

Draw a picture using squares.

This is my square picture.

© PEARSON AUSTRALIA 2024 • *AUSTRALIAN SIGNPOST MATHS F* • ISBN 9780655708742

5D Full, empty and half full

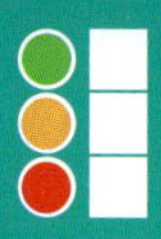

1 Circle the things that are full. ✔ Tick the things that are empty.

How many glasses are about half full? ☐ Talk about the picture.

© PEARSON AUSTRALIA 2024 • *AUSTRALIAN SIGNPOST MATHS F* • ISBN 9780655708742

The number eight

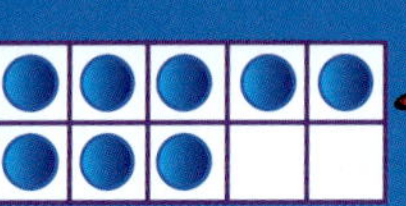

1 Trace the numerals and the word "eight".

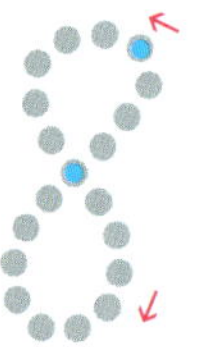
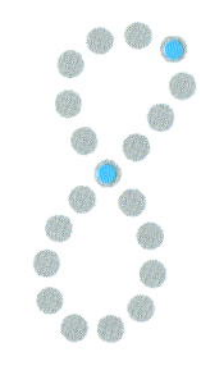
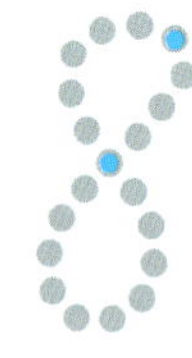

2 Circle boxes that show eight.

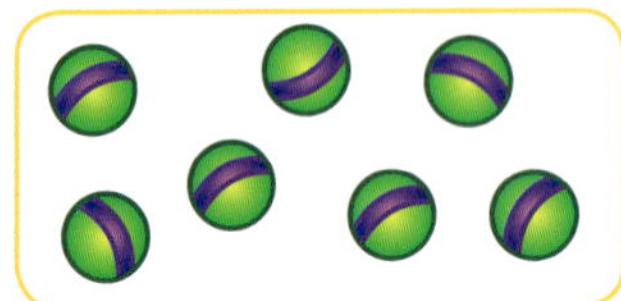

3 Count on.

6		
3		

4 Count back.

8		
4		

5 Draw a face in each window.

[ ] faces

INVESTIGATION

Craft stick patterns

Ask students to count out eight craft sticks and use them to make two squares. Count the craft sticks used for each shape.

Draw the shapes you have made.

© PEARSON AUSTRALIA 2024 • *AUSTRALIAN SIGNPOST MATHS F* • ISBN 9780655708742

6B Comparing groups

1 **a** Count the objects.

b Circle to show the largest group above.

c Circle to show the smallest group above.

d Colour: 3 5 6 7

INVESTIGATION

Balloons at the party

green	red	blue	yellow

- How many balloons of each colour?
- There are more ______ balloons than blue balloons.

© PEARSON AUSTRALIA 2024 • *AUSTRALIAN SIGNPOST MATHS F* • ISBN 9780655708742

6C Ordering collections

1 Write the number of fish in each group. Order the groups from smallest to largest.

A

B

C

☐ fish ☐ fish ☐ fish

Order: ☐ ☐ ☐

These are not the same.
Talk about how many more.

2 Write the number of teddy bears and order the groups, smallest to largest.

A ☐ teddy bears

B ☐ teddy bears

C ☐ teddy bears

Order: ☐ ☐ ☐

These are not the same.

Guess my number

FUN SPOT

Take turns selecting some cubes to put behind a barrier. Have your partner guess how many cubes. See how many guesses are needed to find the correct number.

I need more blocks.

My number is more than 3. Guess again.

© PEARSON AUSTRALIA 2024 • *AUSTRALIAN SIGNPOST MATHS F* • ISBN 9780655708742

6D Comparison of mass

CONCEPT

Holding an object in each hand helps you decide which one is heavier. This is called hefting.

1 Colour the light objects.

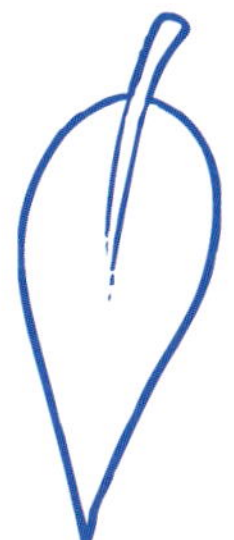

ACTIVITY

Predict which of two objects is heavier or lighter. Compare two objects by hefting.
Circle the lightest object. ✘ Cross the heaviest object.

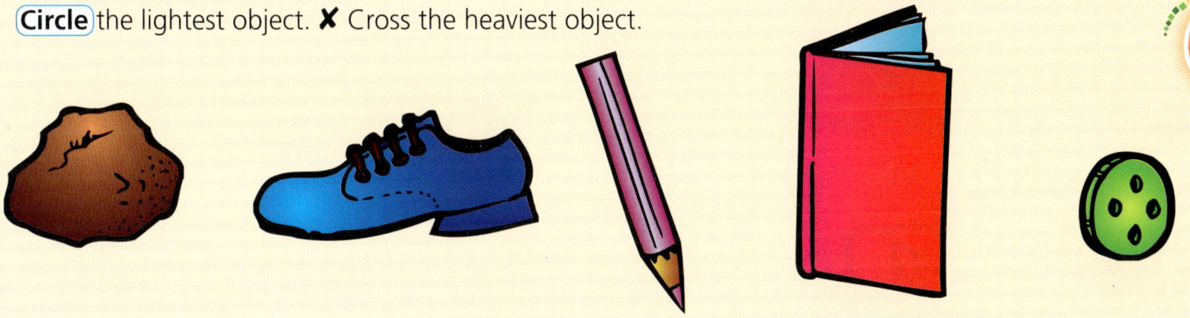

rock	shoe	pencil	book	button

______	is heavier than	______	.
______	is lighter than	______	.
______	is heavier than	______	.

The number nine

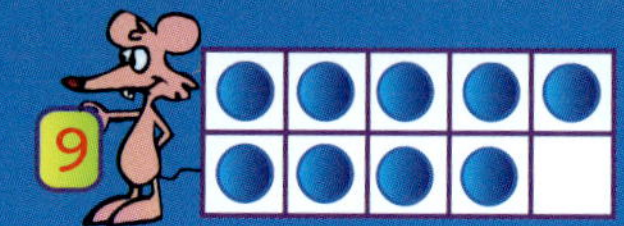

1 Draw a dot pattern for nine. Trace the numerals and the word "nine".

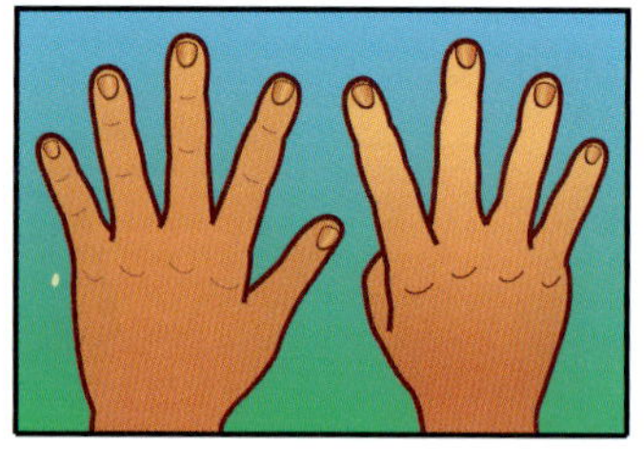
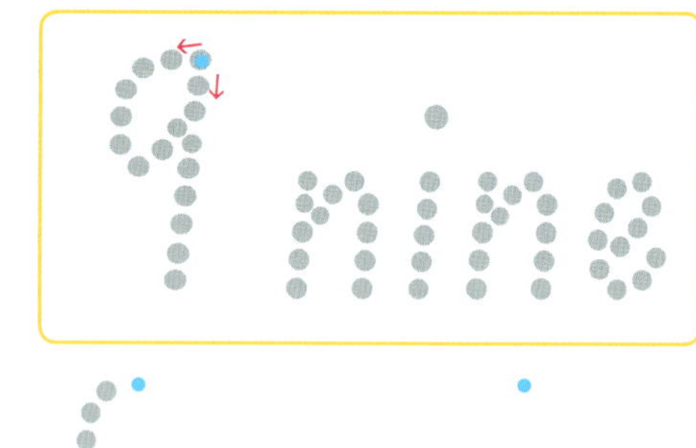

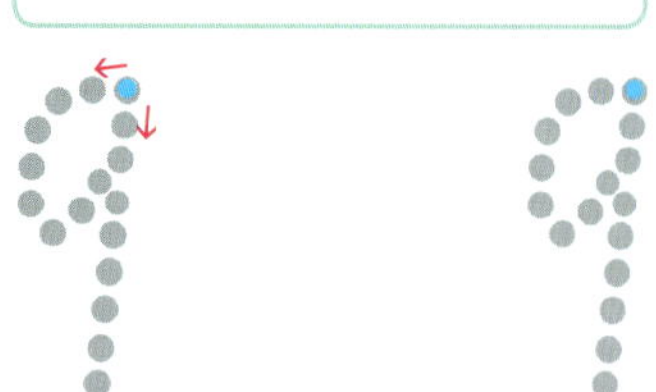

2 Write how many dots you can see in each domino altogether.

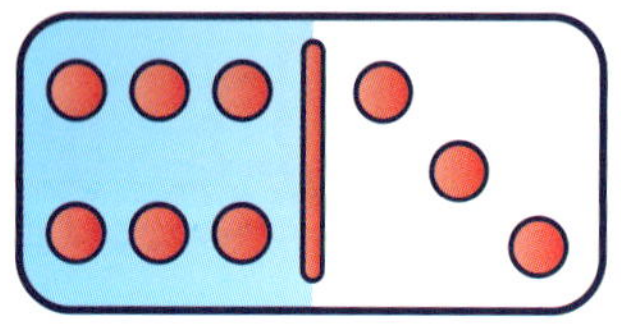
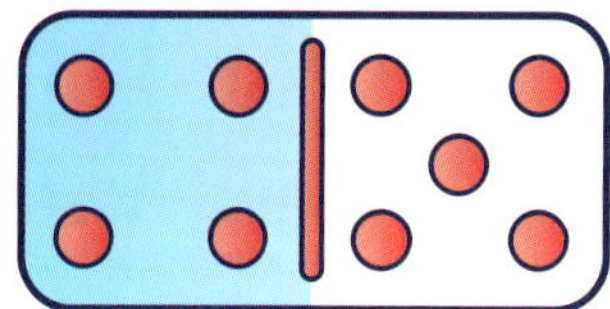
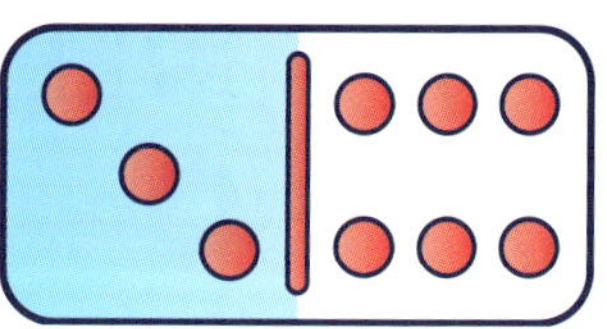

3 Join the dots in order. Start at 1.

How many ants?

Draw nine faces.

Go outside

Ask students to skip, bounce a ball or hop while the rest of the class counts.

© PEARSON AUSTRALIA 2024 • *AUSTRALIAN SIGNPOST MATHS F* • ISBN 9780655708742

7B The number ten

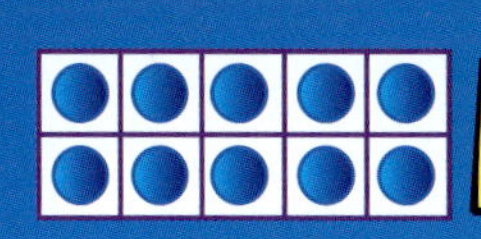

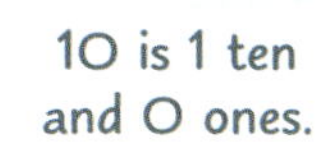

1 Draw a dot pattern for 10. Trace the numerals and the word "ten".

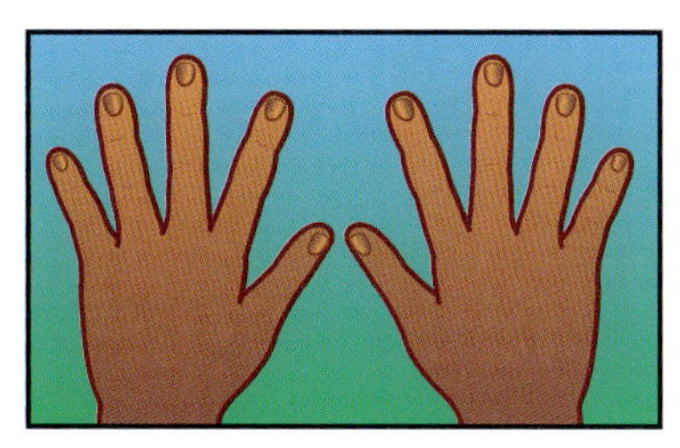

10 10 10

2 **Circle** the cards that have 10 pictures.

3 Order the cards from smallest to largest.

5	3	2	4
8	10	7	9

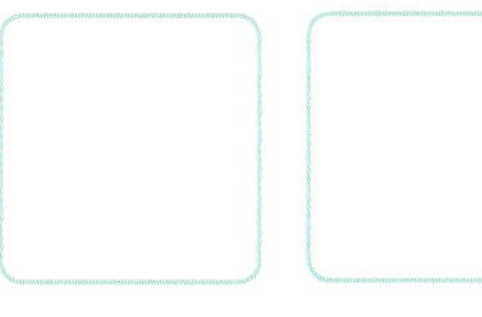

4 How many fingers on two hands?

FUN SPOT

Concentration

Make two sets of 6–10 number cards, as shown. Place both sets of cards face down on a table. Students take turns to turn over two cards. If the cards match, the student keeps them.

Match these cards.

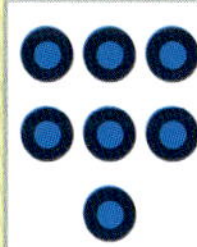
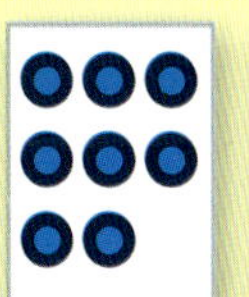
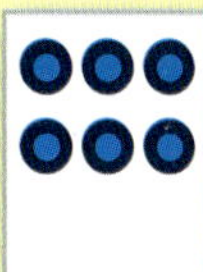

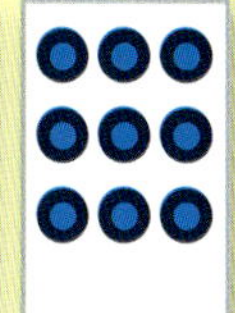

© PEARSON AUSTRALIA 2024 • *AUSTRALIAN SIGNPOST MATHS F* • ISBN 9780655708742

7C Rectangles

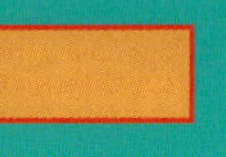
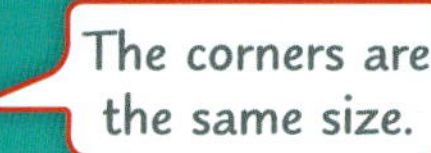

CONCEPT

A rectangle has two equal long sides and two equal short sides, like a stretched square.

1 Trace the rectangles in these pictures.

2 Draw patterns on the rectangles. Discuss.

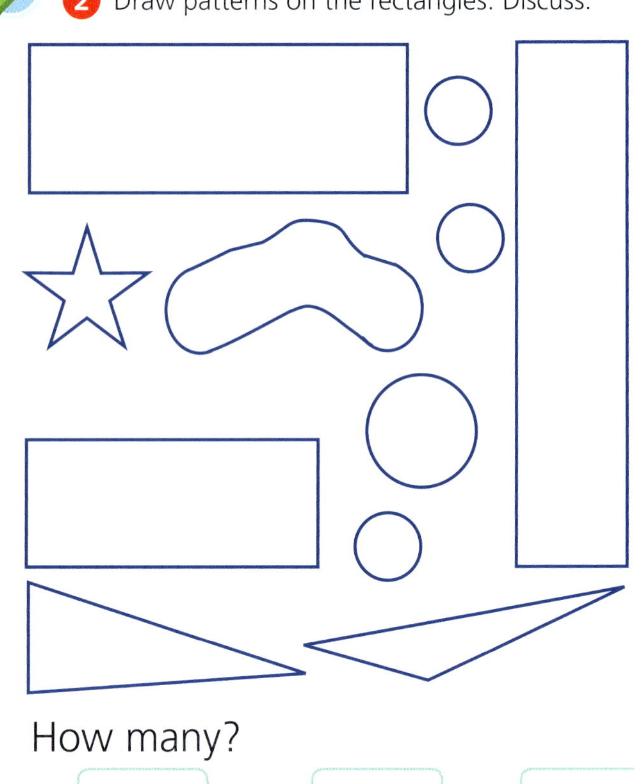

How many?

3 Trace the rectangles.

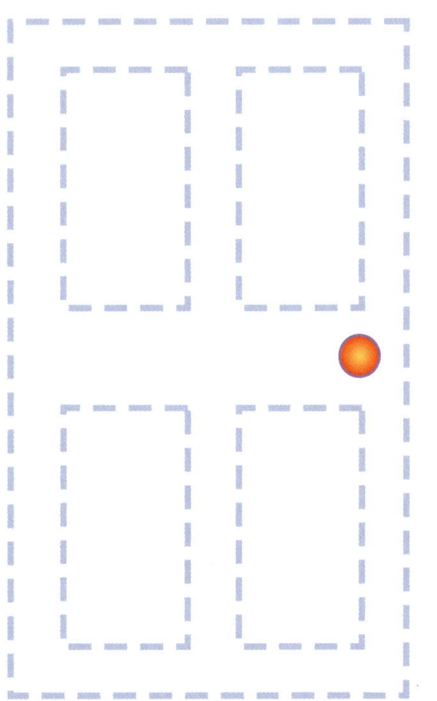

FUN SPOT

Draw a picture using rectangles.

This is my rectangle picture.

© PEARSON AUSTRALIA 2024 • *AUSTRALIAN SIGNPOST MATHS F* • ISBN 9780655708742

7D Daytime and night-time

1 Draw something you do when it's daytime.

8 o'clock.

2 Draw something you do when it's night-time.

3 Colour things that you do in the morning. ✔ Tick what you might do in the afternoon. Circle the event that takes the longest time. Discuss the order of these events.

© PEARSON AUSTRALIA 2024 • *AUSTRALIAN SIGNPOST MATHS F* • ISBN 9780655708742

8A Numbers to ten

10 is 1 ten
and 0 ones.

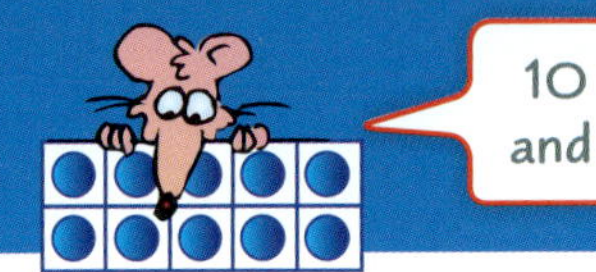

1 Write the numerals on the rocket. Match the words and numerals. Trace the numerals and words.

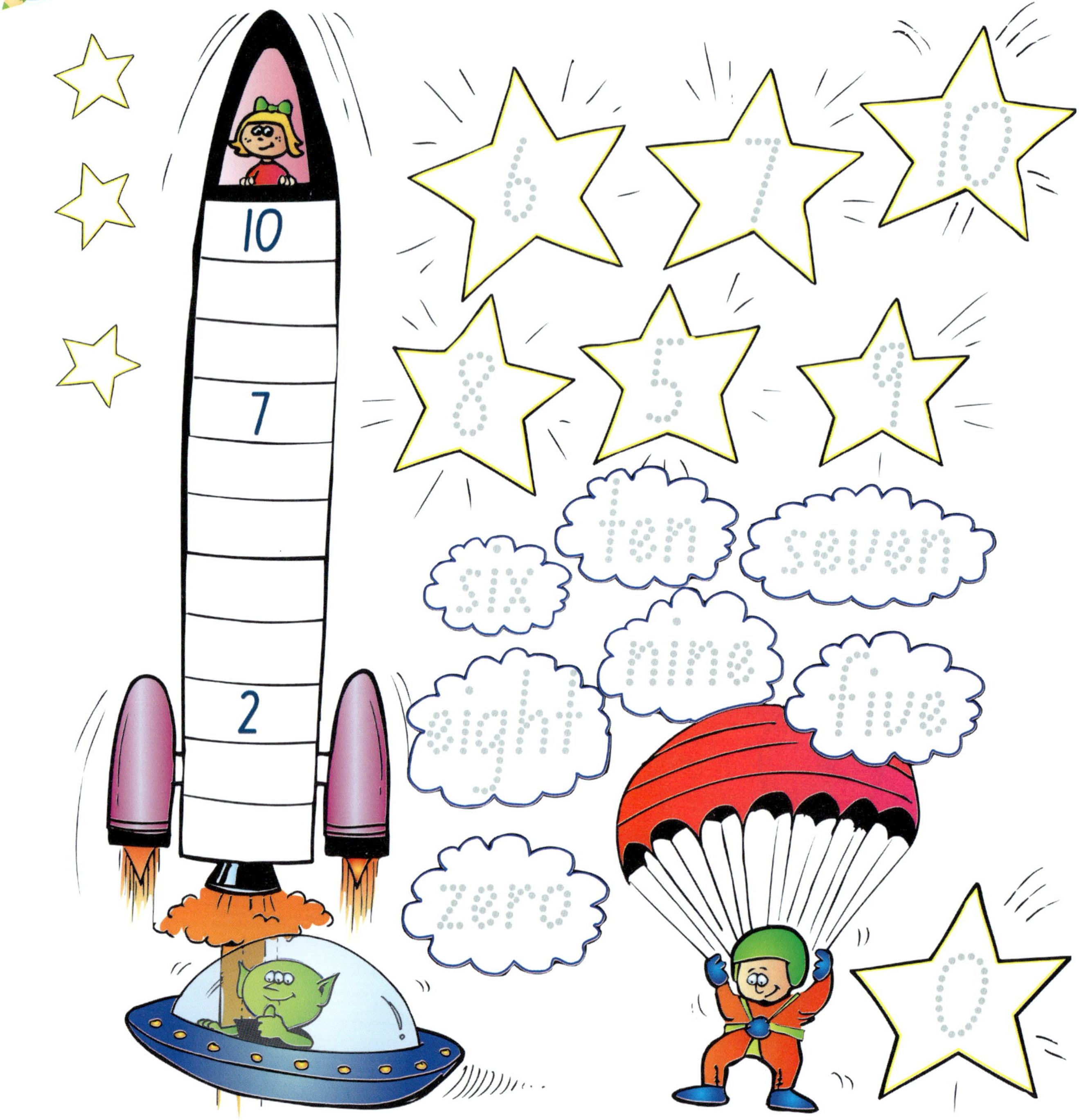
10
7
2
6
7
10
8
5
9
ten
seven
six
nine
eight
five
zero
0

2 Talk about the picture above and answer the questions.

How many?

 ☐ ☐ ☐ ☐

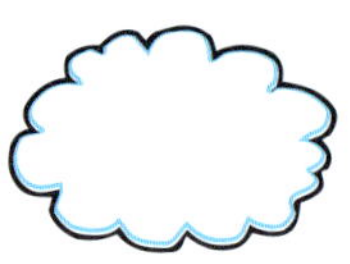

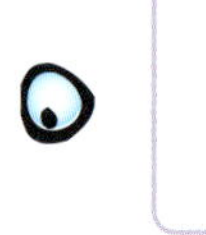

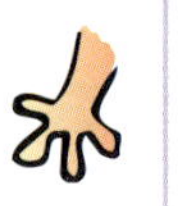

© PEARSON AUSTRALIA 2024 • *AUSTRALIAN SIGNPOST MATHS F* • ISBN 9780655708742

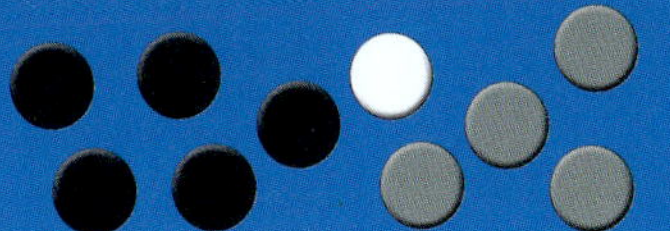

1 Talk about the picture and answer the questions. Compare two groups (more / less).

How many ?

How many ?

How many ?

How many  ?

How many  ?

How many  ?

2 Count forwards.

2

6

3 Count backwards.

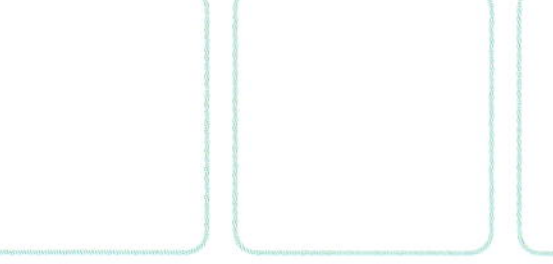

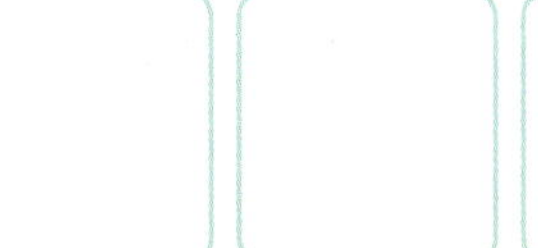

Draw dots to make 10 on each domino.

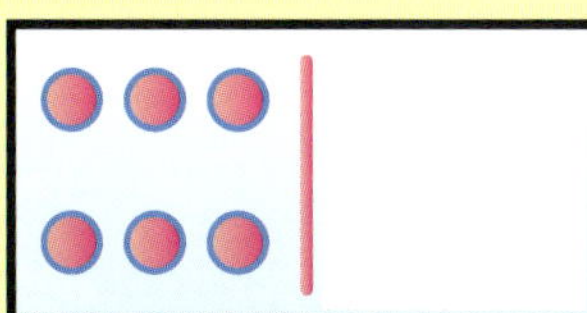
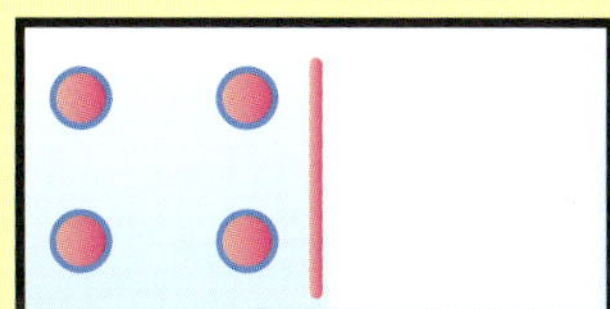
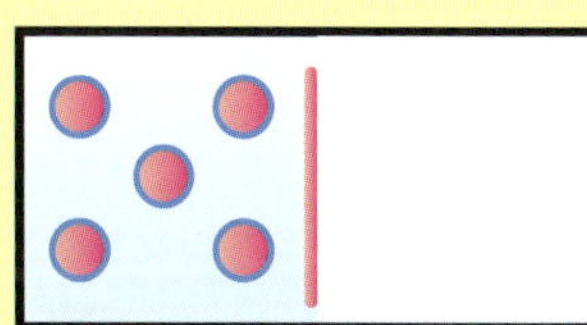

- Count all of the dots already drawn in pink.
- See if you can count to 20.
- How high can you count?

© PEARSON AUSTRALIA 2024 • *AUSTRALIAN SIGNPOST MATHS F* • ISBN 9780655708742

8C Position

FUN SPOT

Colour what is:

- on the log black
- in front of the tree pink
- inside the tent purple
- near the fire orange
- under the log red
- close to the log brown
- behind the tent green
- up on a tree branch orange
- beside the mouse yellow.

Talk about the positions of the other objects.

ZZZ

© PEARSON AUSTRALIA 2024 • *AUSTRALIAN SIGNPOST MATHS F* • ISBN 9780655708742

Language of location

1 Draw:

 on top of

 inside

 outside

 behind

 between

under

 in

 in front of

 next to

2 Draw a circle behind the student, a square next to him, and a triangle in front of him.

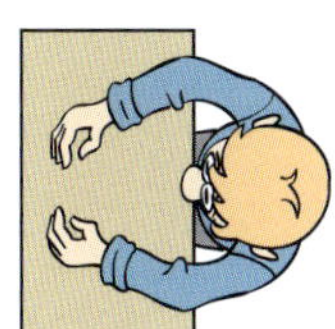

3 Write up or down.

© PEARSON AUSTRALIA 2024 • *AUSTRALIAN SIGNPOST MATHS F* • ISBN 9780655708742

9A Numbers to 10

1 Write the numbers up to 10 on the clothes. Draw ten flowers under the washing line.

2 How many dots?

Draw other patterns using 10 dots.

3 Write the number that comes:

before		after
	9	
	4	
	6	
	7	
	5	

4

How many legs?

5

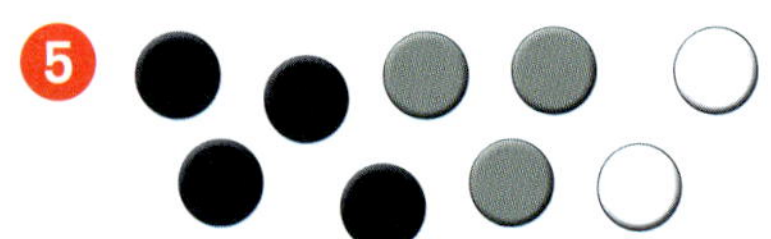

How many grey circles?

How many black circles?

6 See if you can count to 30.

© PEARSON AUSTRALIA 2024 • *AUSTRALIAN SIGNPOST MATHS F* • ISBN 9780655708742

9B Numbers 11 and 12

11 is 1 ten and 1 one.

12 is 1 ten and 2 ones.

1 Trace the numerals and words below.

2 Count and write the number of objects.

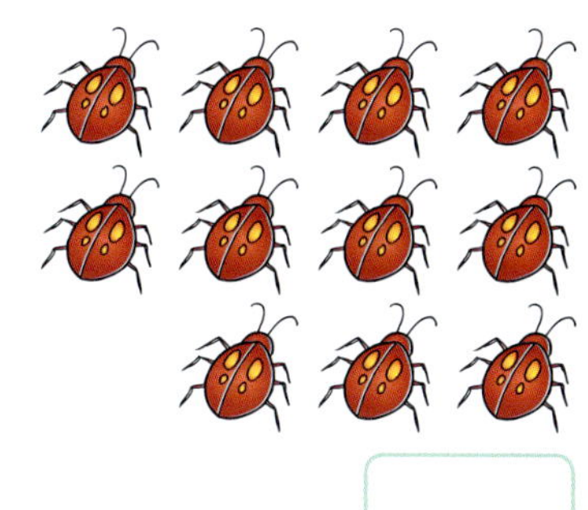

3 Draw 12 circles. (○) Draw 11 stars. (∗)

4 Count forwards and backwards from any number. Discuss numbers "before" and "after" a given number.

1	2	3	4	5	6	7	8	9	10
11	12	13	14	15	16	17	18	19	20

9C Longer and shorter

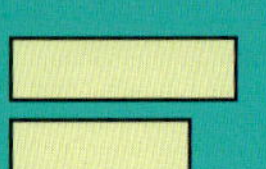

1 Length is the measure of an object from end to end. Colour the longer things. Circle the shorter things.

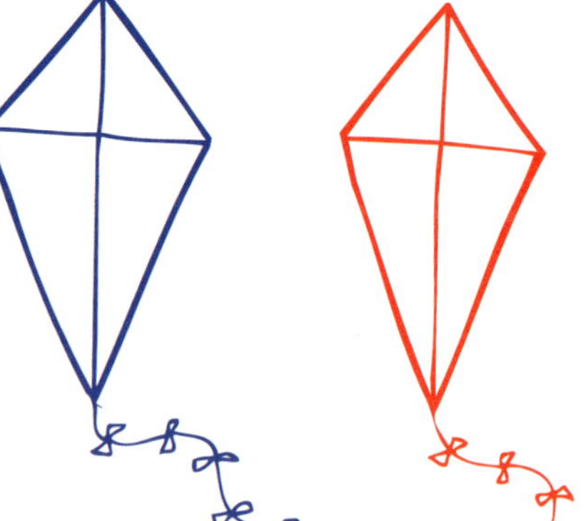

longer

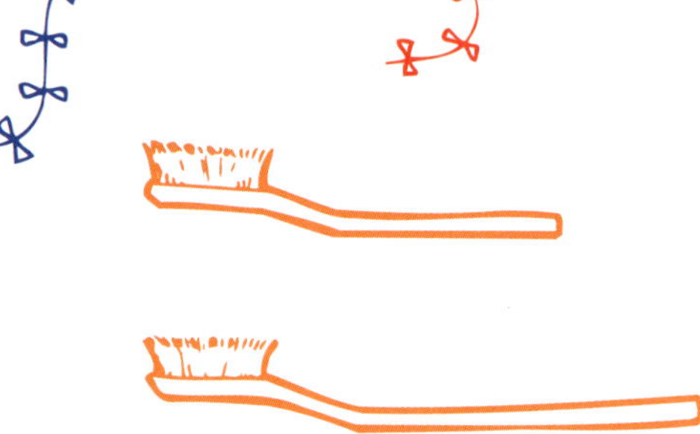

shorter

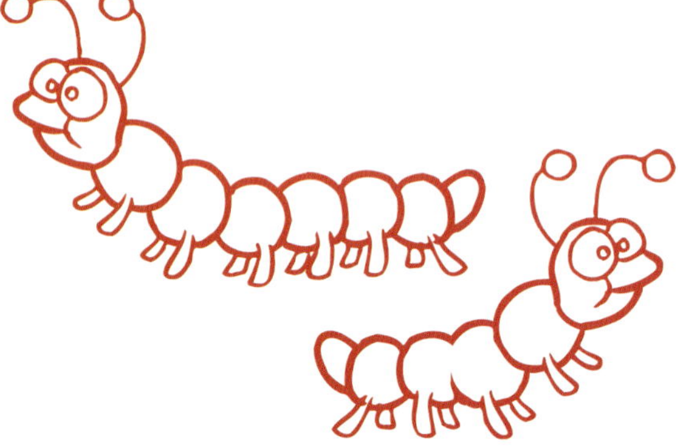

2 Circle the wider television set, the wider glass and the shorter student.

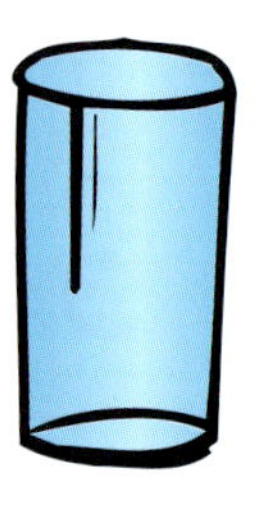

© PEARSON AUSTRALIA 2024 • *AUSTRALIAN SIGNPOST MATHS F* • ISBN 9780655708742

Triangles

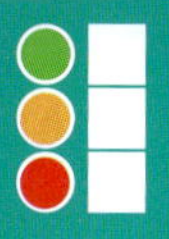

CONCEPT

A triangle has
3 straight sides.

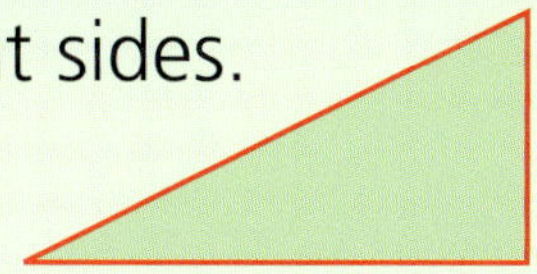

1 Trace the triangles in these pictures.

triangle

2 Colour the triangles. Discuss.

3 Trace the triangles.

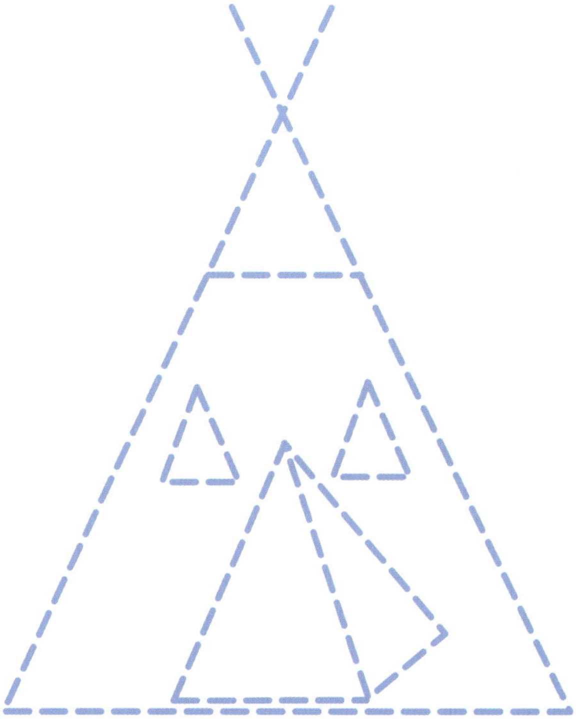

FUN SPOT

Draw a picture using triangles.

This is my triangle picture.

© PEARSON AUSTRALIA 2024 • *AUSTRALIAN SIGNPOST MATHS F* • ISBN 9780655708742

10A Adding two groups

1 Draw a picture to show how many altogether.

a  and  makes 

b  and  makes 

c 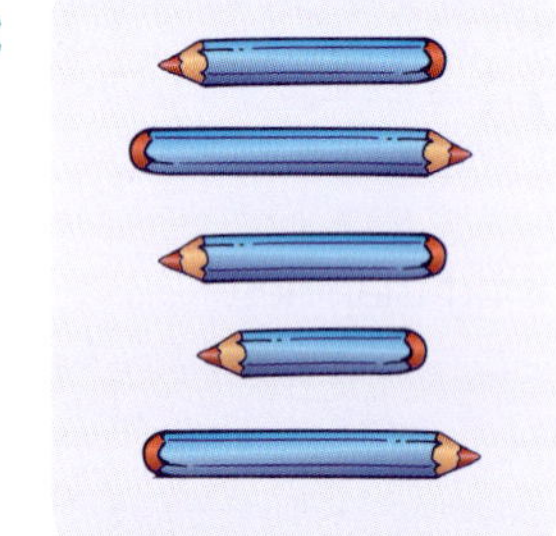 and 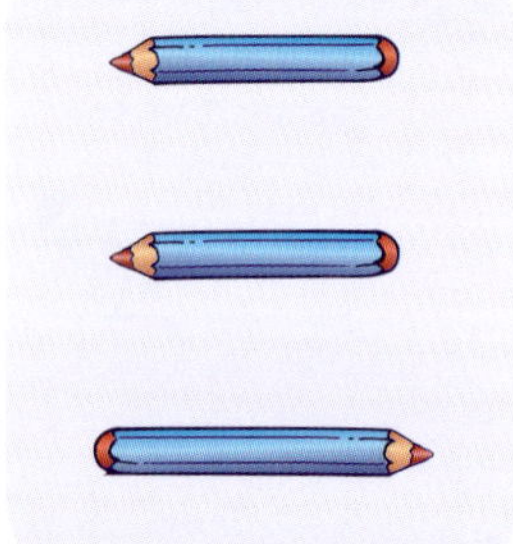 makes 

2

☐ fish and  fish makes  fish altogether.

© PEARSON AUSTRALIA 2024 • *AUSTRALIAN SIGNPOST MATHS F* • ISBN 9780655708742

10B Adding two groups

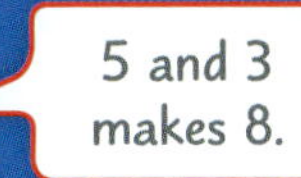

1 Draw a picture to show how many altogether.

 and  makes

 and  makes

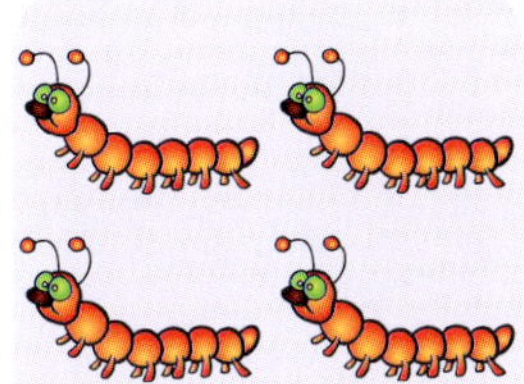 and 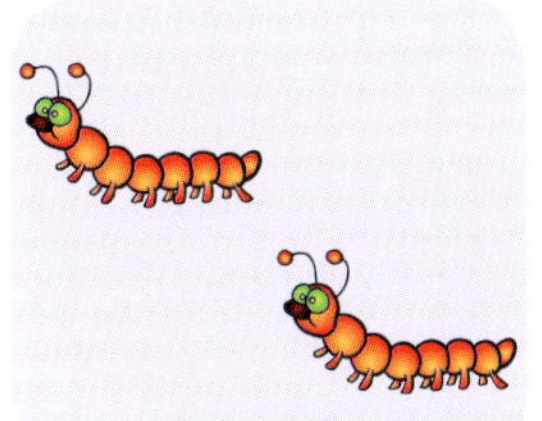 makes

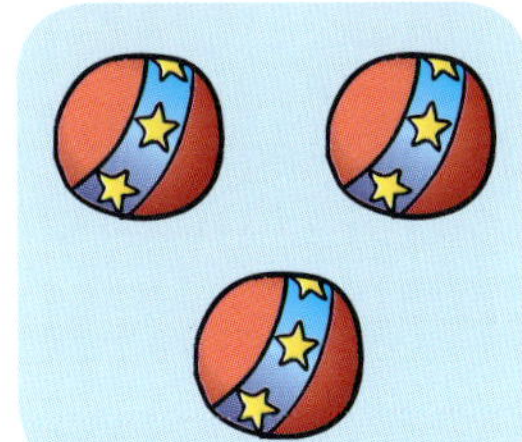 and 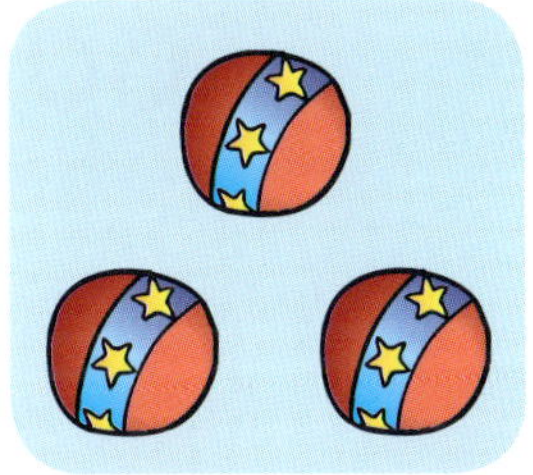 makes

2 Draw:

3 apples

4 apples

Explain what you have done.

a How many altogether?

apples

b 3 apples and 4 apples makes ☐ apples.

© PEARSON AUSTRALIA 2024 • *AUSTRALIAN SIGNPOST MATHS F* • ISBN 9780655708742

10C Cutting shapes

ACTIVITY

- Cut and paste a circle.

circle

- Cut and paste a square.

square

- Cut and paste a triangle.

triangle

- Cut and paste a rectangle.

rectangle

© PEARSON AUSTRALIA 2024 • *AUSTRALIAN SIGNPOST MATHS F* • ISBN 9780655708742

Numbers to 12

1 Write the numbers.

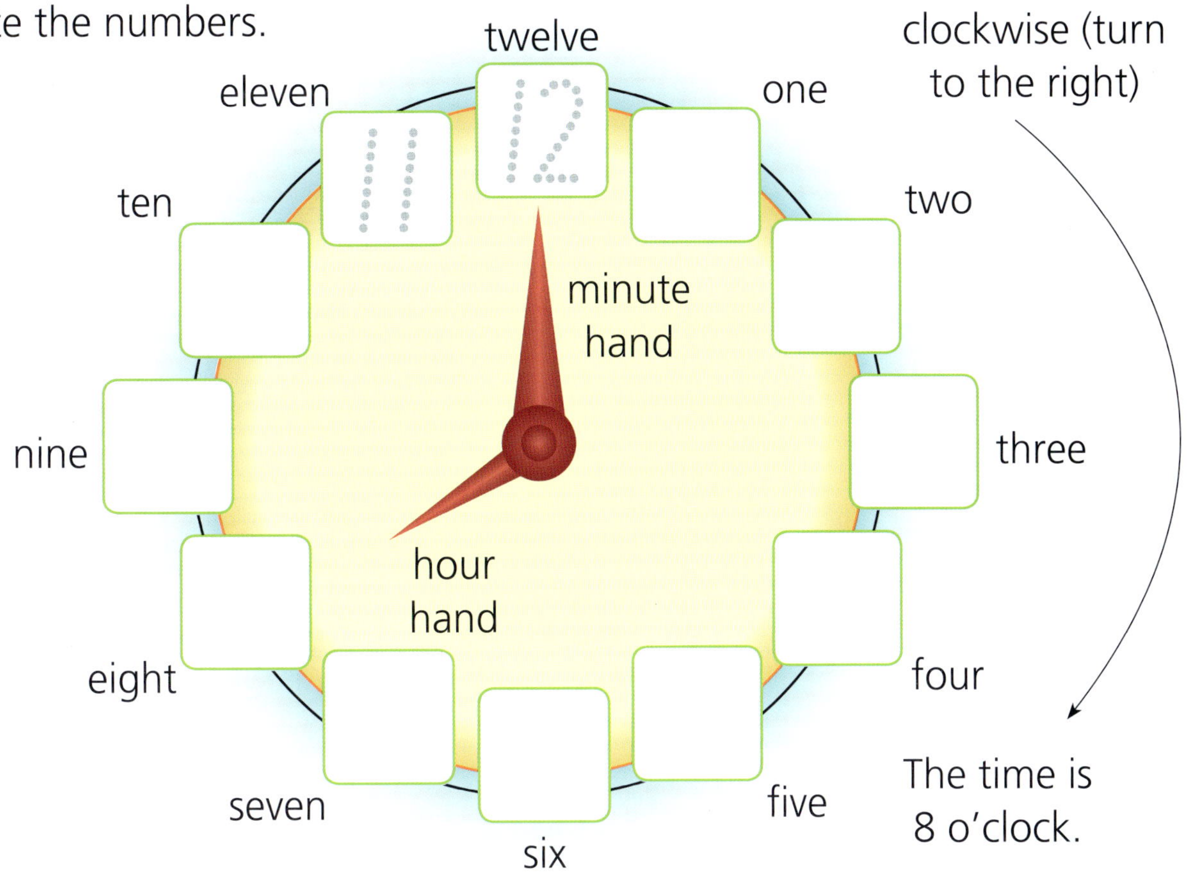

twelve
12
one
two
three
four
five
six
seven
eight
nine
ten
eleven
11

minute hand

hour hand

clockwise (turn to the right)

The time is 8 o'clock.

2 Write the words.

12 twelve
1
2
3
4
5
6
7
8
9
10
11 eleven

11A Numbers 13 to 20

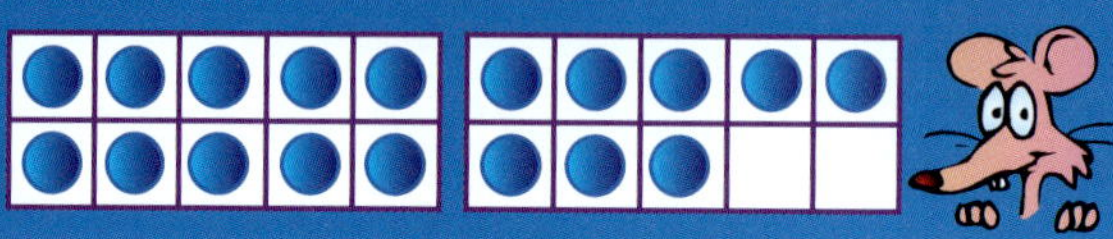

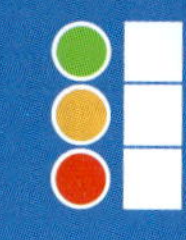

1 Trace over the numerals and words.

13 thirteen (1 ten and 3 ones)

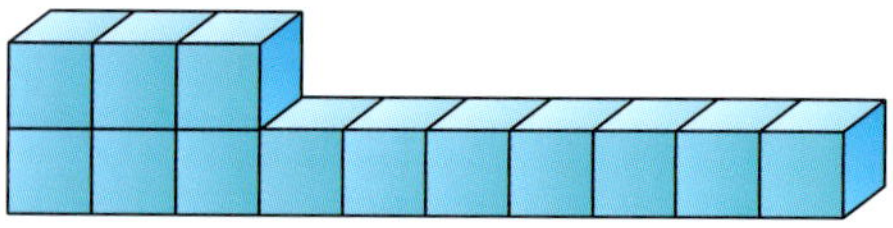

14 fourteen (1 ten and 4 ones)

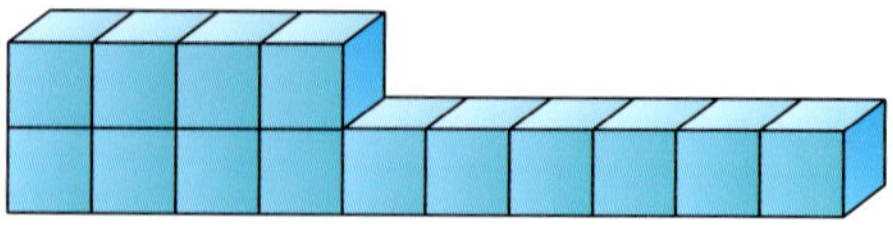

15 fifteen (1 ten and 5 ones)

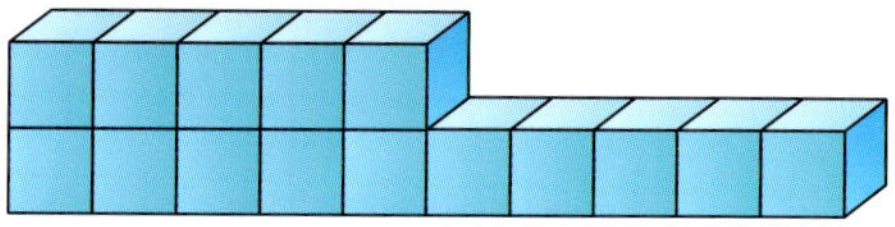

16 sixteen (1 ten and 6 ones)

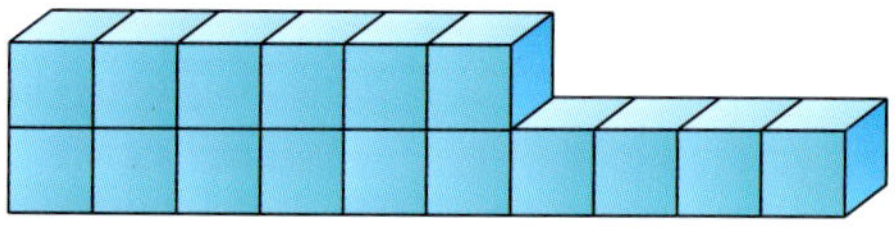

17 seventeen (1 ten and 7 ones)

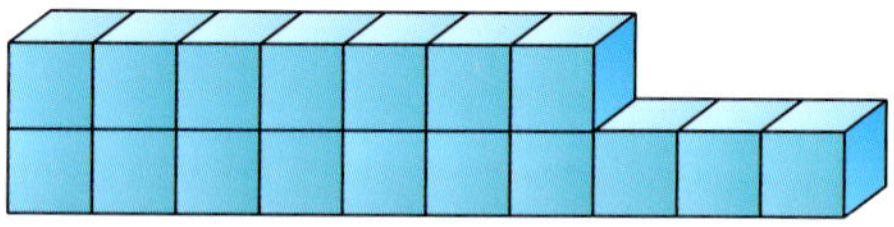

18 eighteen (1 ten and 8 ones)

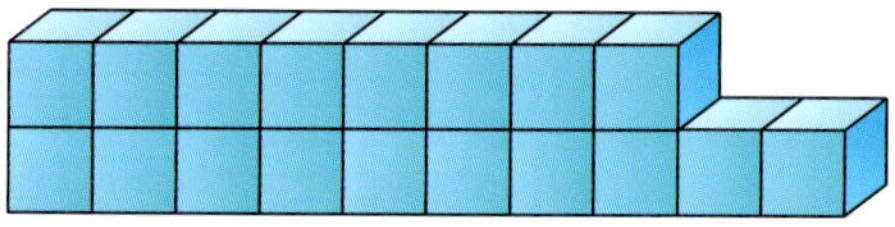

19 nineteen (1 ten and 9 ones)

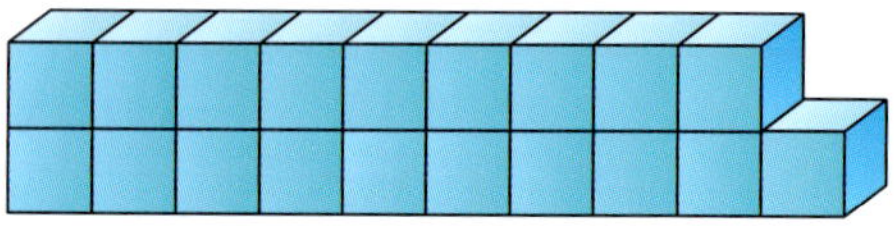

20 twenty (2 tens)

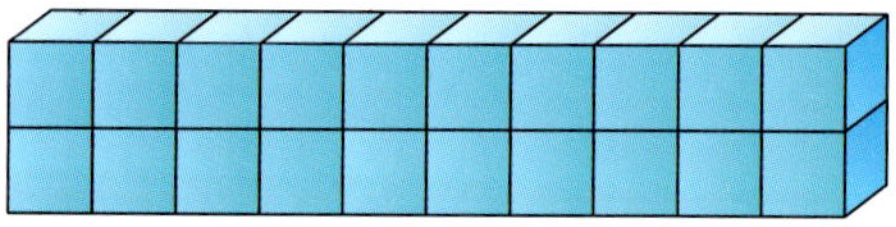

© PEARSON AUSTRALIA 2024 • *AUSTRALIAN SIGNPOST MATHS F* • ISBN 9780655708742

11B Numbers 11 to 20

Thirteen is 1 ten and 3 ones.

Thirty is 3 tens and 0 ones.

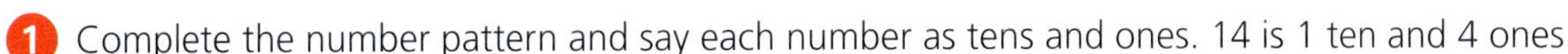

1 Complete the number pattern and say each number as tens and ones. 14 is 1 ten and 4 ones.

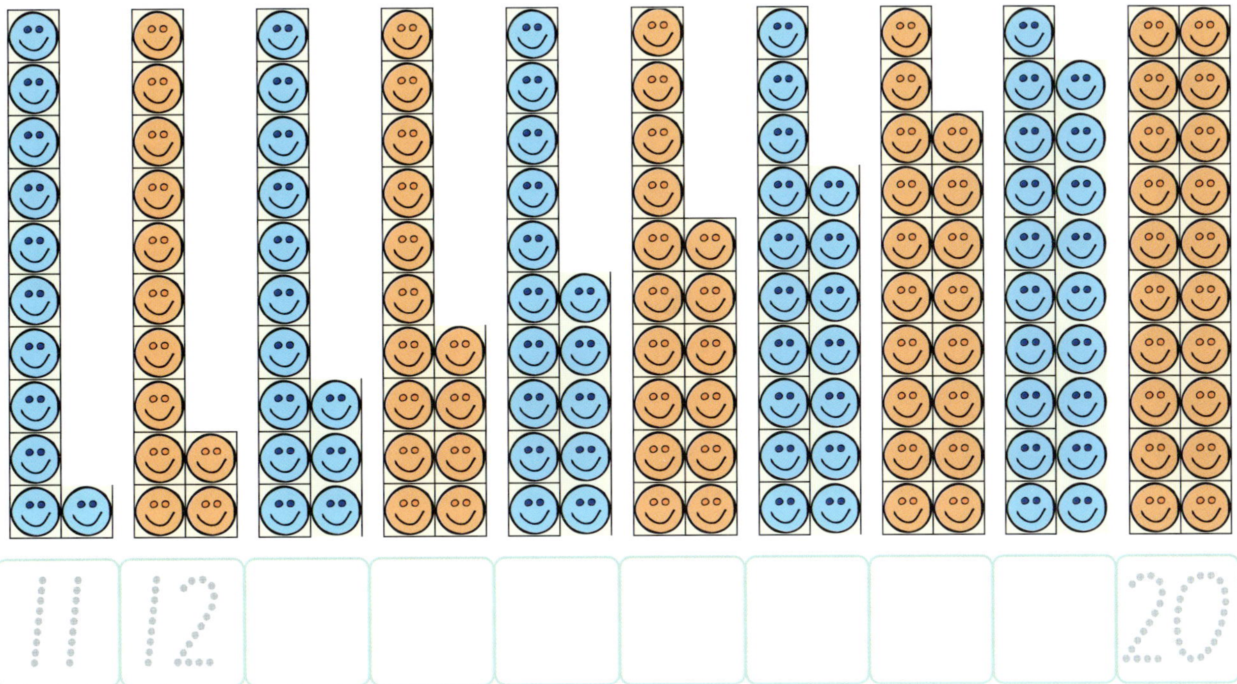

11	12								20

The pattern rule is add .

Talk about numbers before and after a chosen number.

2 Complete the number patterns and talk about them.

3 Make a list of the "teen" numbers.

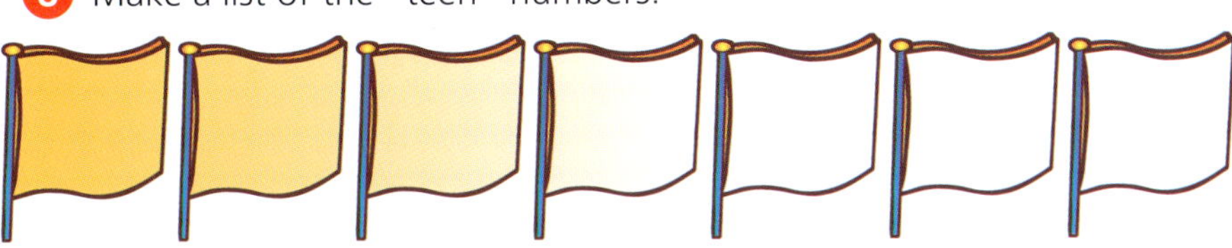

4 Put these numbers in order: 19, 16, 18, 15, 13, 17, 14.

© PEARSON AUSTRALIA 2024 • *AUSTRALIAN SIGNPOST MATHS F* • ISBN 9780655708742

11C Shape pictures

1 Discuss the picture. Colour the shapes at the side with the same colours that are used in the picture.

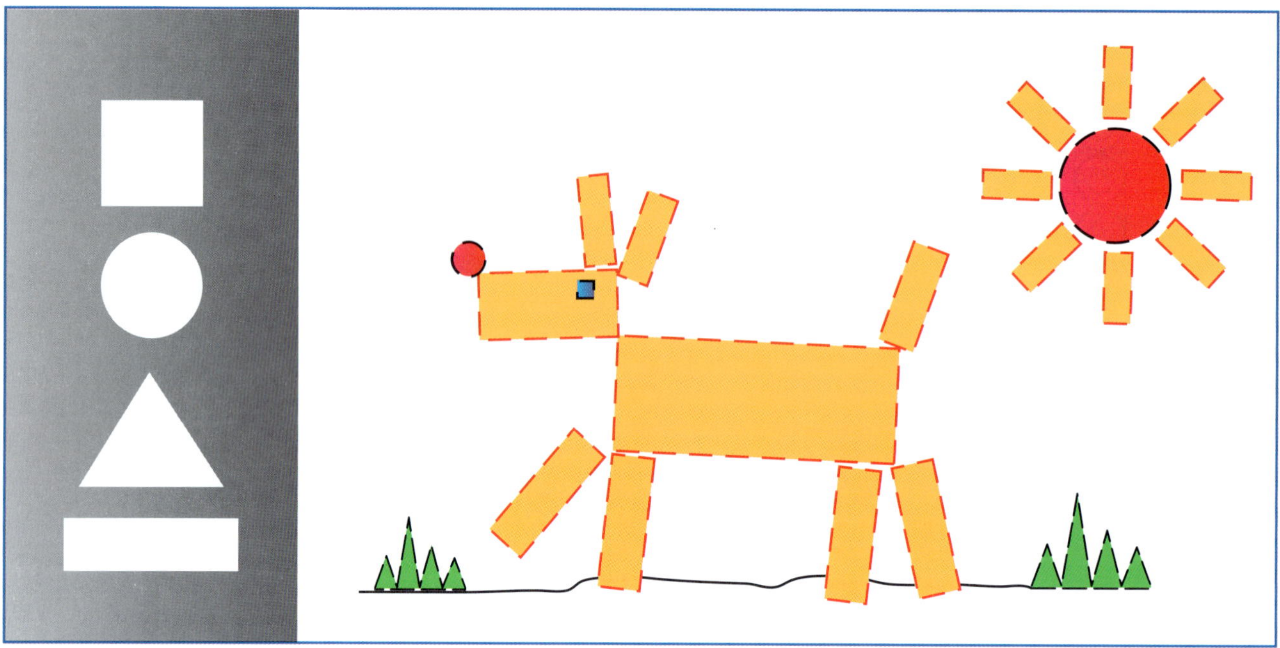

2 Use circles, triangles and rectangles to make a flower.

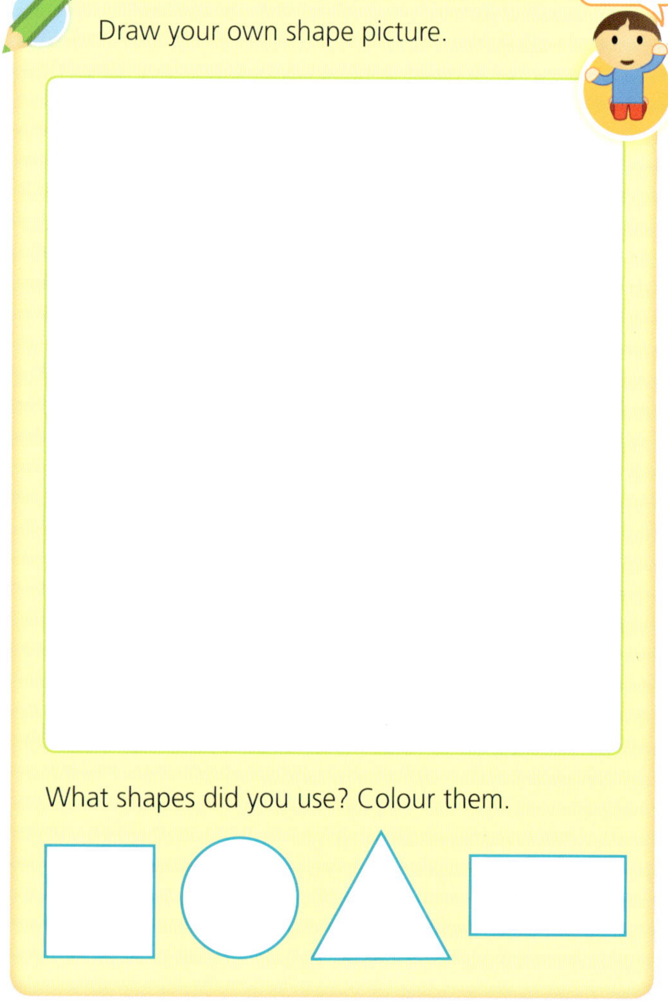

© PEARSON AUSTRALIA 2024 • *AUSTRALIAN SIGNPOST MATHS F* • ISBN 9780655708742

3D objects

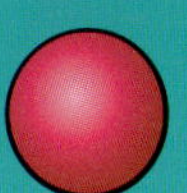

1 Pam found objects the same shape as the yellow blocks. Describe and name each object, then match each block to the correct object. Tick the objects that can stack.

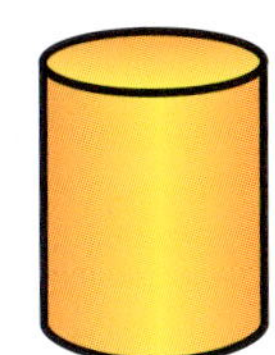

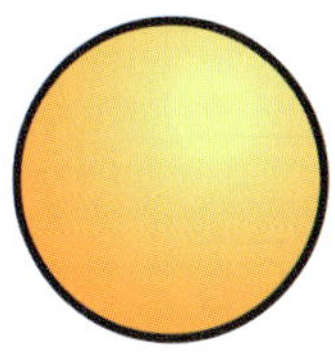

2 Trace each block. Draw lines from each word to the matching blocks.

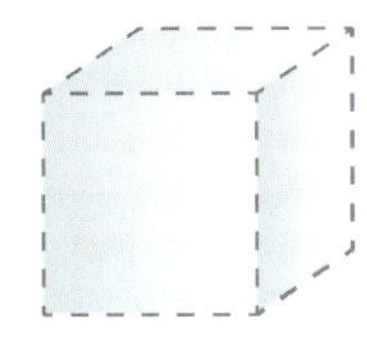

curved

straight

pointy

round

flat

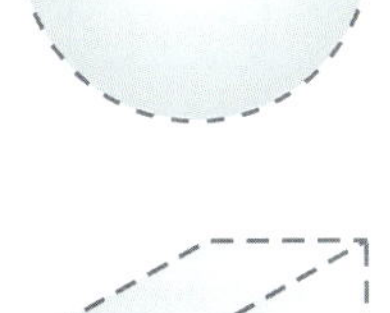

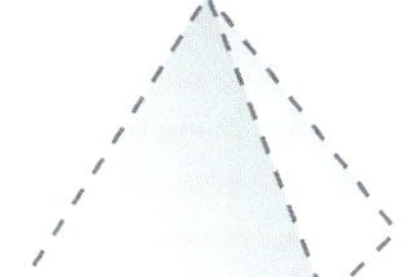
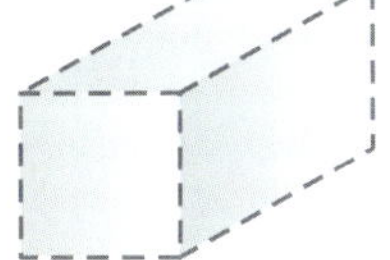
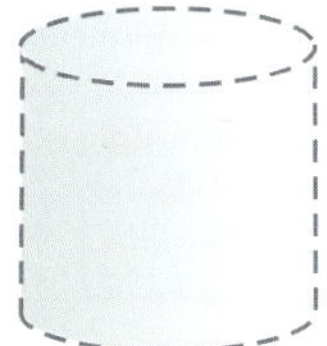
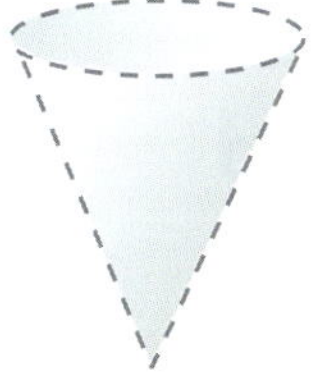

ACTIVITY

Sort a collection of objects into groups.
Discuss how each group was sorted.

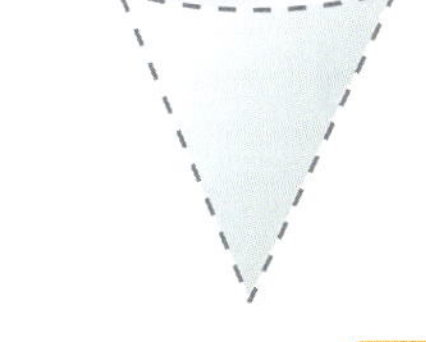

12A Adding dots

1 Complete each number sentence. 6 is 1 and 5.

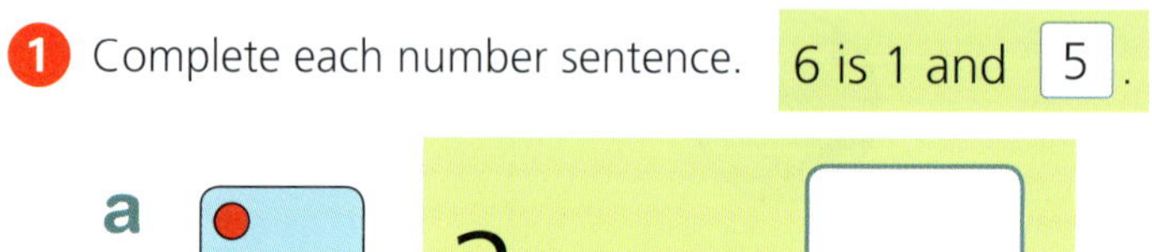

a 2 is 1 and ☐.

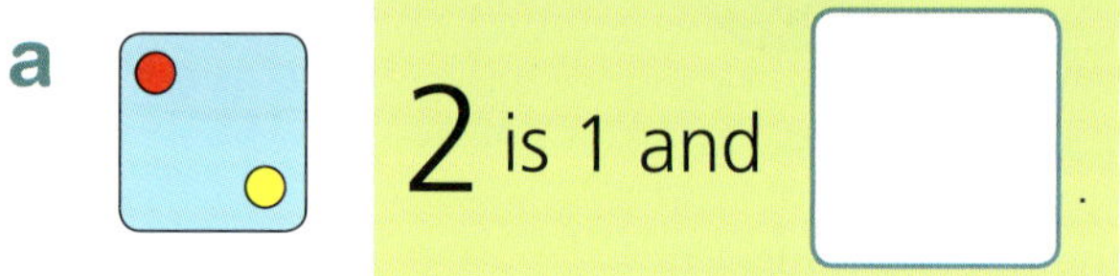

b 3 is 2 and ☐. or 1 and ☐.

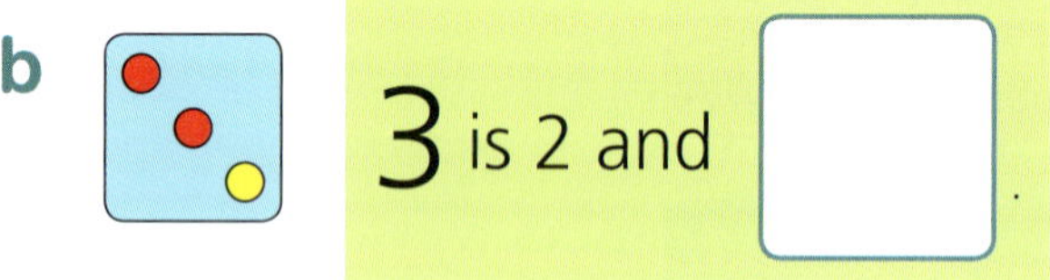

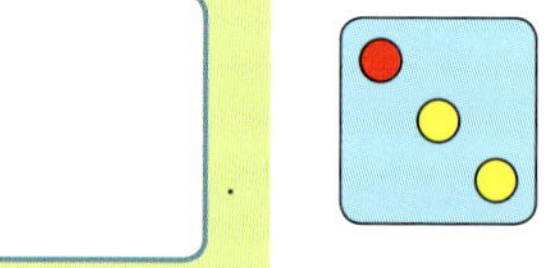

c 4 is 2 and ☐. or 3 and ☐.

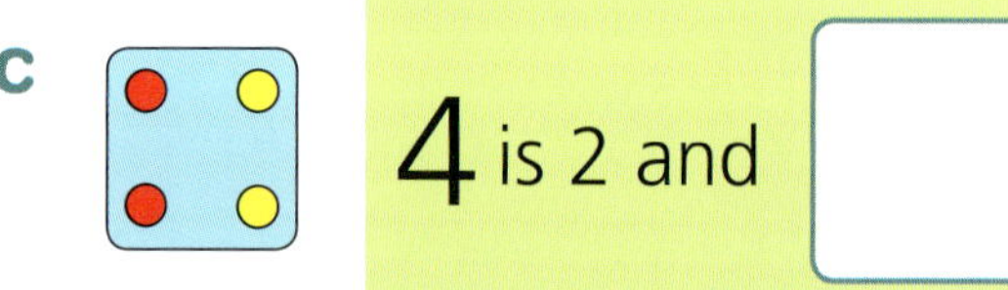
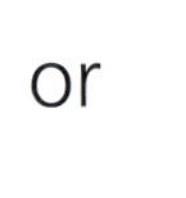

d 5 is 3 and ☐. or 4 and ☐.

e 5 is 2 and ☐. or 1 and ☐.

f 6 is 5 and ☐. or 3 and ☐.

© PEARSON AUSTRALIA 2024 • *AUSTRALIAN SIGNPOST MATHS F* • ISBN 9780655708742

12B Using five to form numbers

1 Try to write these numbers by counting on from 5.

 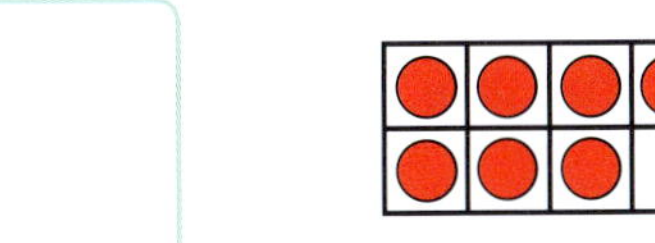 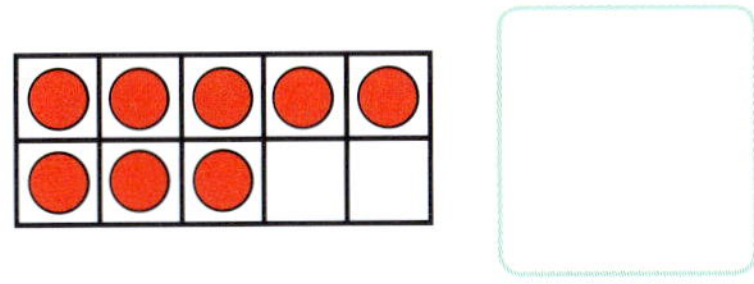

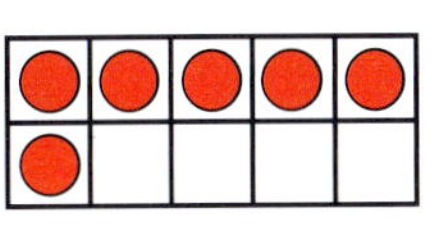   

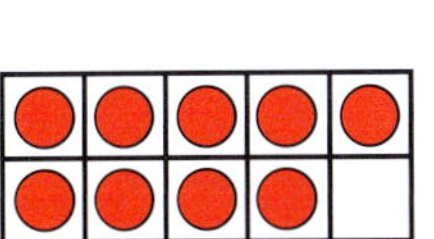  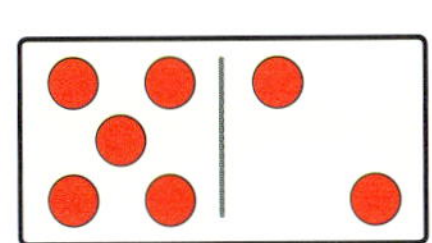  

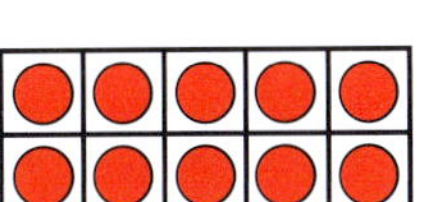  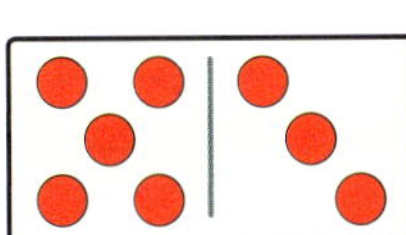  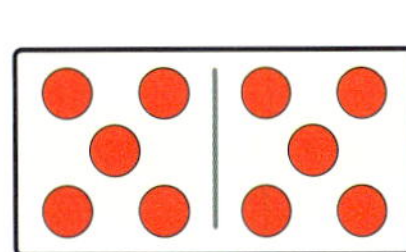 

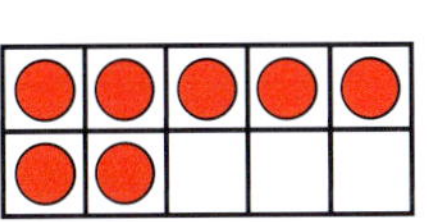  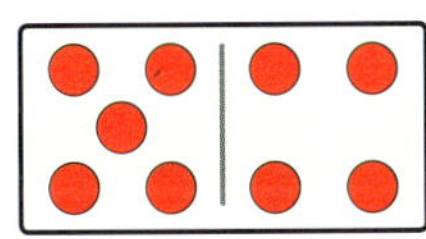  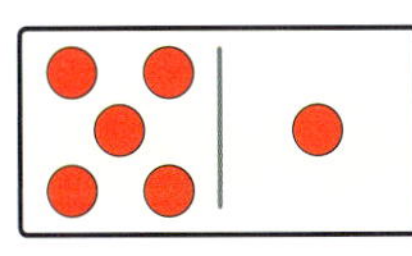 

2 Use these ten frames to show the numbers.

6 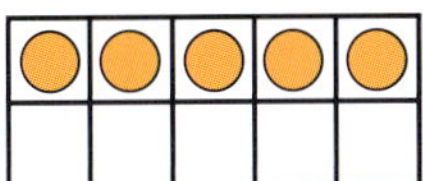 9 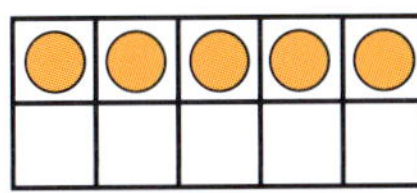

7 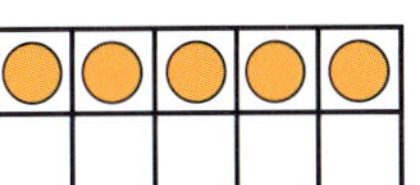 10 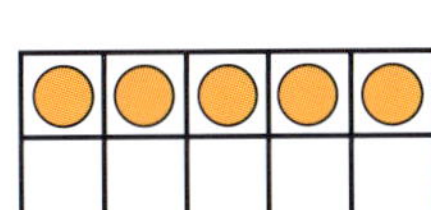

8 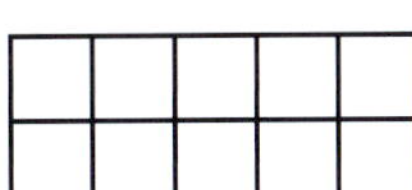 5 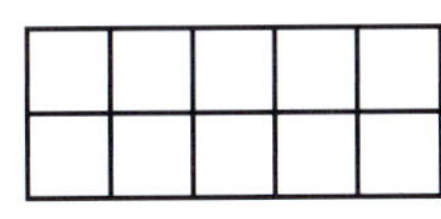

3 Use the dominoes to show the numbers.

6 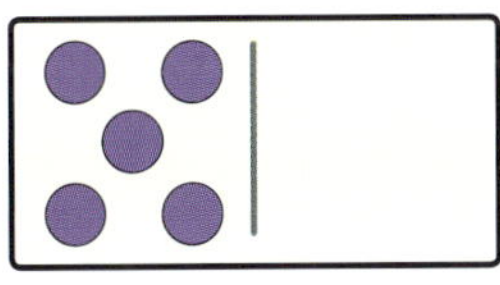 9 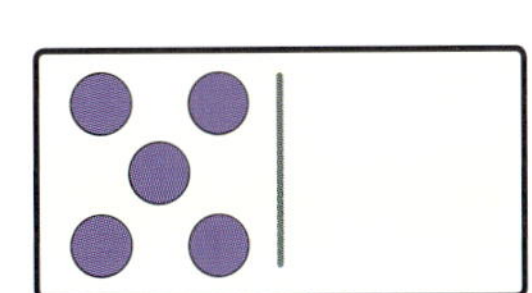 8 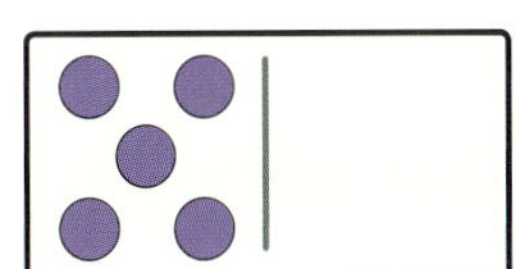

© PEARSON AUSTRALIA 2024 • *AUSTRALIAN SIGNPOST MATHS F* • ISBN 9780655708742

12C Rolling, sliding and stacking

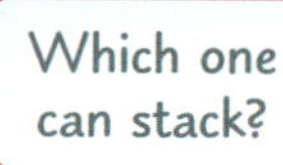

1. Discuss which objects you think will roll, slide or stack. Give reasons for your choice. Test your predictions using objects below.

2. Colour the things that roll. **Circle** things that slide. ✔ Tick the things that stack.

Curved objects can  r___ . Flat objects can 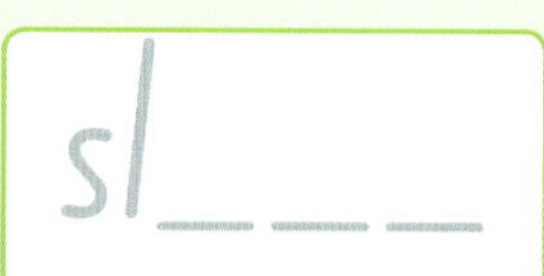 sl___ .

3. Draw an object that can roll. Draw an object that can slide. Draw an object that can stack.

© PEARSON AUSTRALIA 2024 • *AUSTRALIAN SIGNPOST MATHS F* • ISBN 9780655708742

Stacking and packing

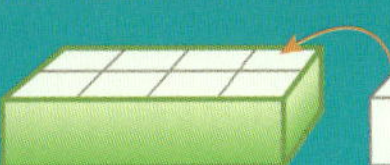

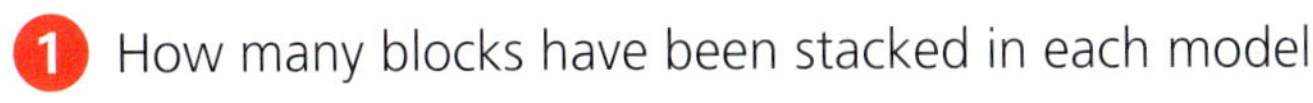

1 How many blocks have been stacked in each model?

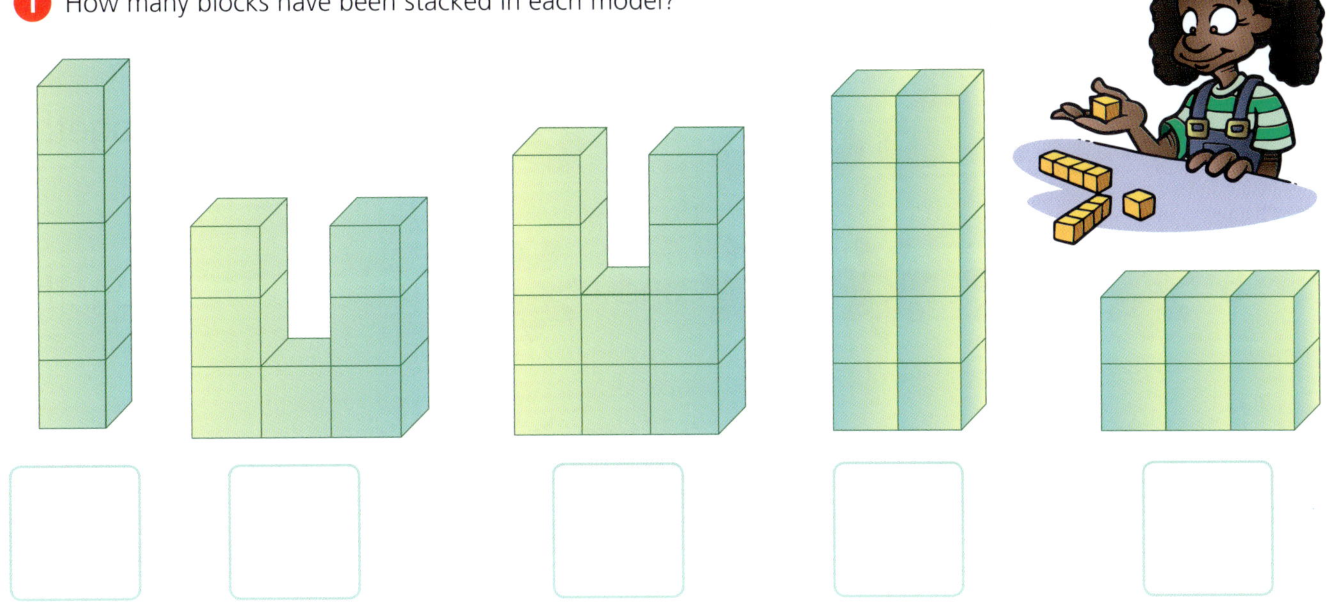

Build each model using blocks. Did you use the same number of blocks?

✔ Tick the two models that use the same number of blocks.

2 How many blocks have been packed into each box?

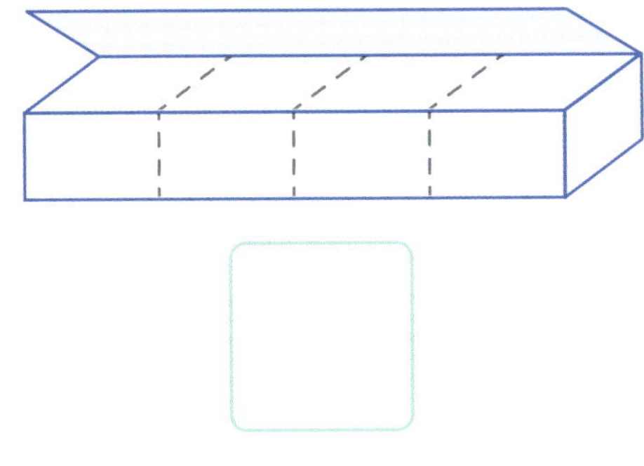
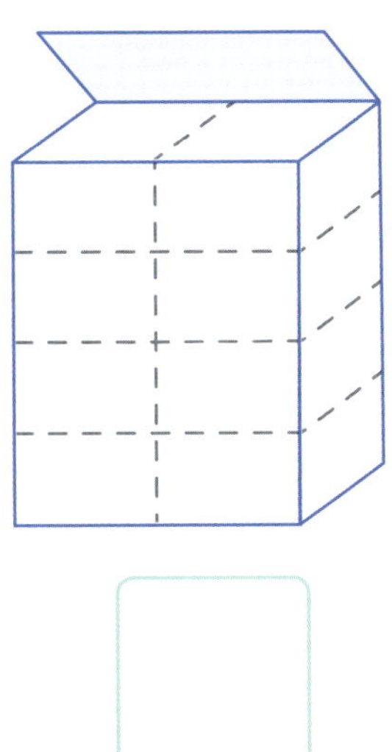
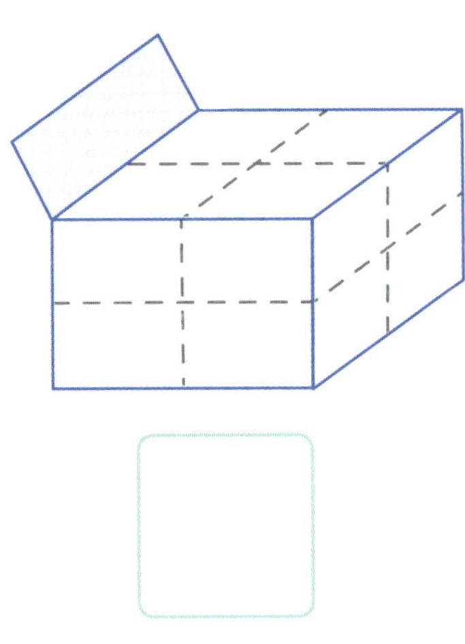

✔ Tick the two boxes that hold the same amount.

Pack blocks into a box.

How many blocks did you use?

13A Adding two groups

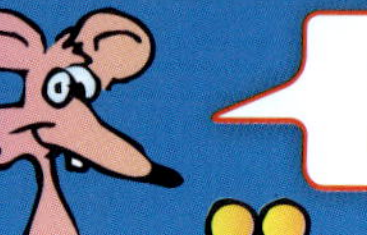

1 Talk about and complete these story problems.

a and  ☐ altogether

b and  ☐ altogether

c

☐ fish and ☐ fish makes ☐ fish.

d

☐ coins and ☐ coins makes ☐ coins.

e

☐ apples and ☐ apples makes ☐ apples.

ACTIVITY

Make your own question. Talk about it.

☐ balls and ☐ balls makes ☐ balls.

© PEARSON AUSTRALIA 2024 • *AUSTRALIAN SIGNPOST MATHS F* • ISBN 9780655708742

13B Adding two groups

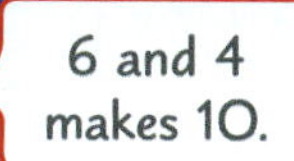

1 Complete these number sentences.

a       ☐ and ☐ makes ☐

b       ☐ and ☐ makes ☐

c         ☐ and ☐ makes ☐

d   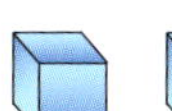  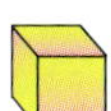 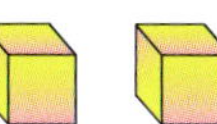   ☐ and ☐ makes ☐

e  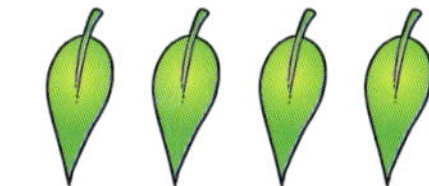 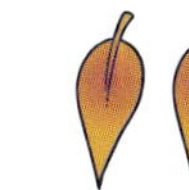 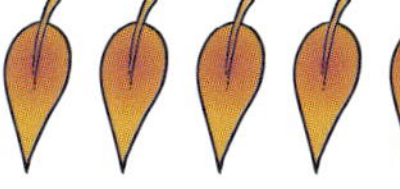   ☐ and ☐ makes ☐

2 Colour 2 green 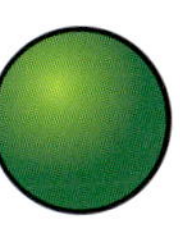 and 5 orange 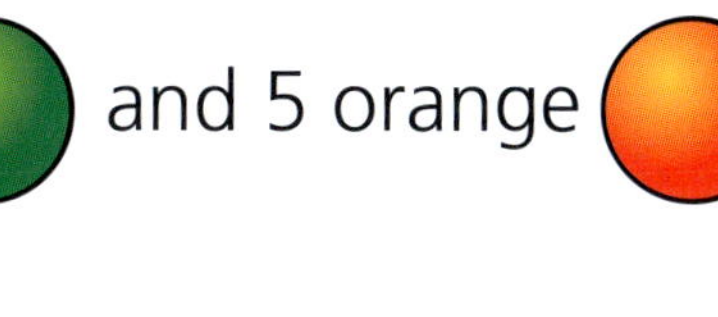.

2 and 5 makes ☐

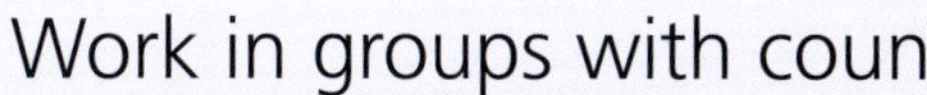

Work in groups with counters.

- Take 10 counters. Separate them into 2 groups.
- Record what you have done using a number sentence.
- Explain what you did. Do this again and again.

© PEARSON AUSTRALIA 2024

13C Ball-shaped objects

Curved objects can roll.

CONCEPT

This is a ball-shaped object. It is round. It has no pointy parts. It can roll.

2 Circle the ball-shaped objects.

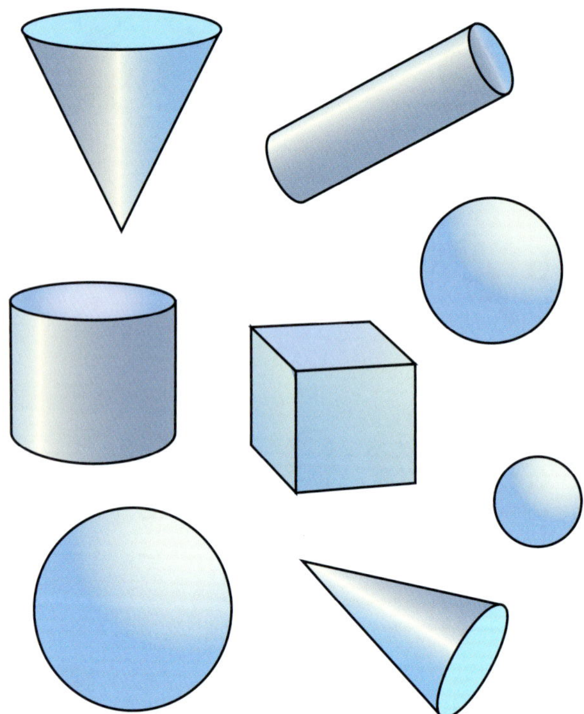

1 Trace this ball-shaped object.

3 Circle the ball-shaped objects in this picture.

Talk about these objects using the words round, pointy, curved, straight, flat, rolls, slides and stacks.

ACTIVITY

Use playdough to make a model of a ball-shaped object. Draw your model here.

© PEARSON AUSTRALIA 2024 • *AUSTRALIAN SIGNPOST MATHS F* • ISBN 9780655708742

13D Box-shaped objects

Box-shaped objects can stack.

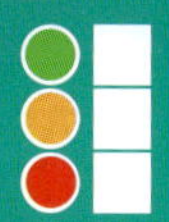

CONCEPT

This is a box-shaped object. It has flat parts and sharp corners. It has straight edges and it can slide.

1 Trace.

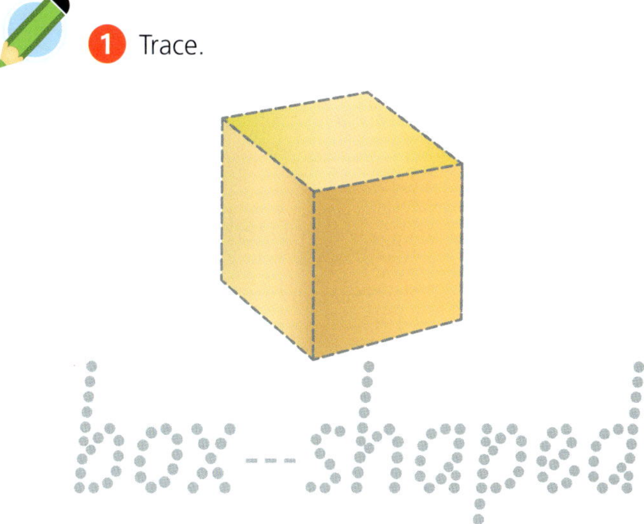

If all faces are squares, it is a cube.

2 **Circle** the box-shaped objects.

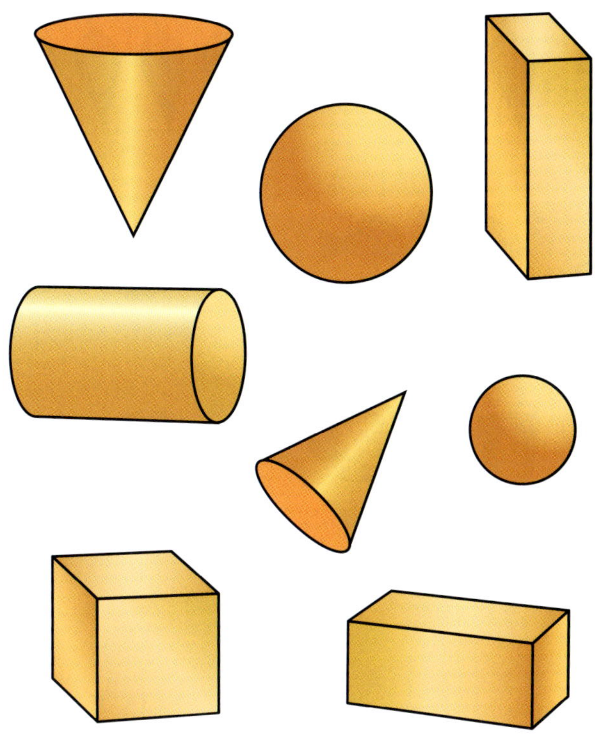

3 **Circle** the box-shaped objects in this picture.

Talk about these objects using the words round, pointy, curved, straight, flat, rolls, slides and stacks.

ACTIVITY

Use playdough to make a model of a box-shaped object.
Draw your model here.

© PEARSON AUSTRALIA 2024 • *AUSTRALIAN SIGNPOST MATHS F* • ISBN 9780655708742

14A Adding two groups

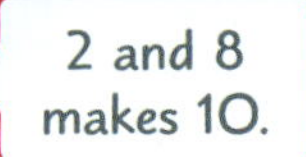

1 Complete these number sentences.

a ☐ and ☐ makes ☐

b ☐ and ☐ makes ☐

c ☐ and ☐ makes ☐

d ☐ and ☐ makes ☐

e ☐ and ☐ makes ☐

ACTIVITY

Draw pictures to create your own addition stories. Complete the number sentences. Explain.

- ☐ and ☐ makes ☐
- ☐ and ☐ makes ☐
- ☐ and ☐ makes ☐

© PEARSON AUSTRALIA 2024 • *AUSTRALIAN SIGNPOST MATHS F* • ISBN 9780655708742

14B Addition

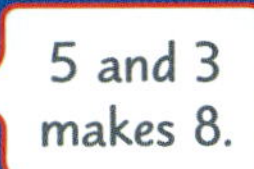

We can combine 2 groups to make a larger one.

2 and 3 makes 5.

1 Count how many altogether.

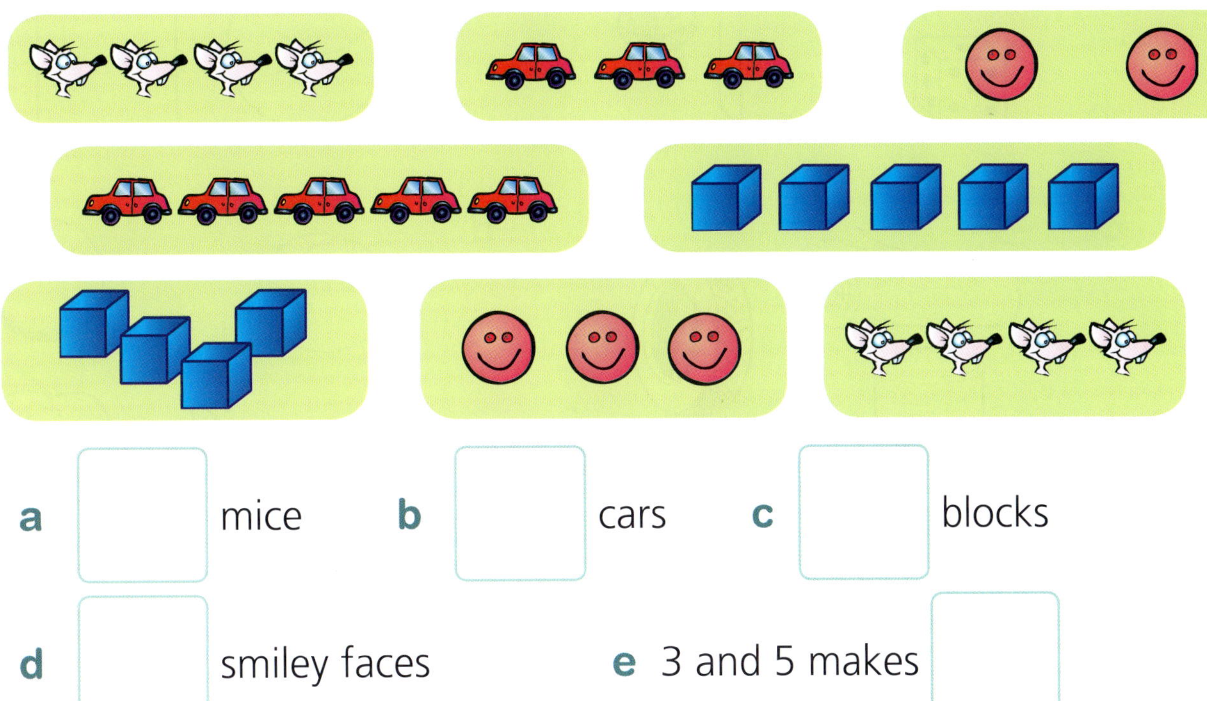

a ☐ mice b ☐ cars c ☐ blocks

d ☐ smiley faces e 3 and 5 makes ☐

2 Colour and count.

2 red
4 green

☐ mushrooms

ACTIVITY

- Put some counters in box A. Count them.
- Put one counter in box B. How many altogether?
- Put another counter in box B. How many now?

Repeat this activity again and again with a different number of counters in box A.

© PEARSON AUSTRALIA 2024 • *AUSTRALIAN SIGNPOST MATHS F* • ISBN 9780655708742

Sorting objects

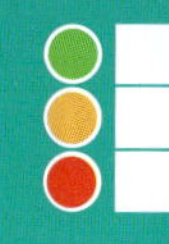

1 Colour three objects that belong together. Discuss.

a

b

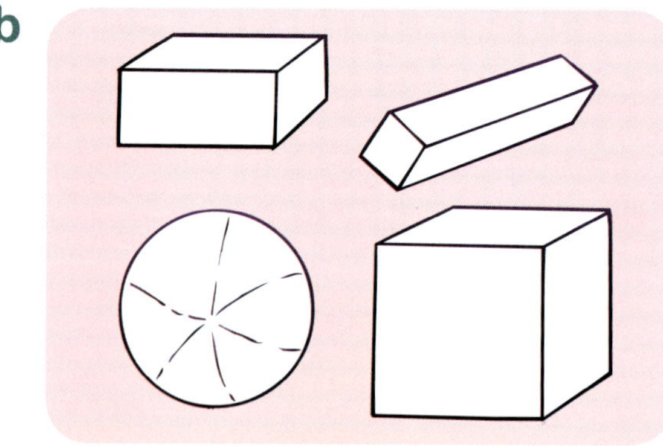

c

d

2 **Circle** the objects that do not belong. Discuss.

3 Colour to match objects that are the same. **Circle** two objects that can stack. Give reasons for your answers.

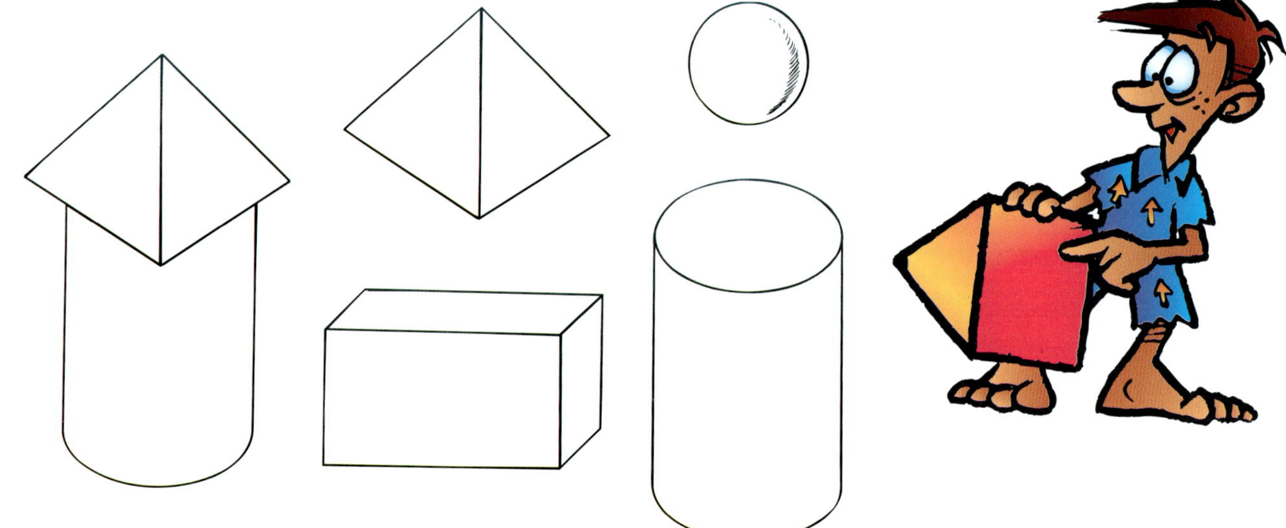

© PEARSON AUSTRALIA 2024 • *AUSTRALIAN SIGNPOST MATHS F* • ISBN 9780655708742

14D Using data displays

Could lunch boxes be other colours?

1 Lunch boxes

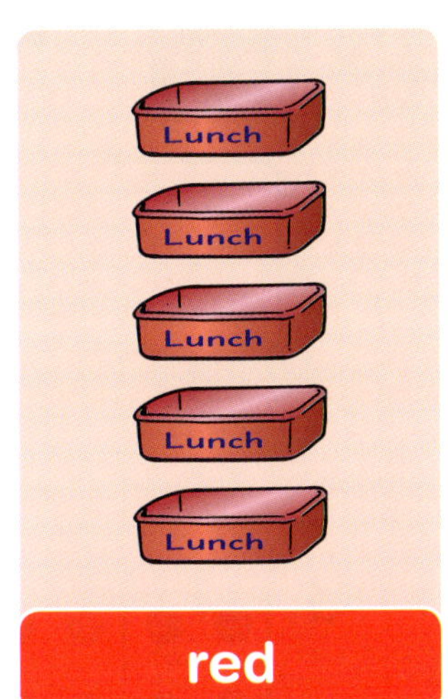

red | blue | green | yellow

a How many 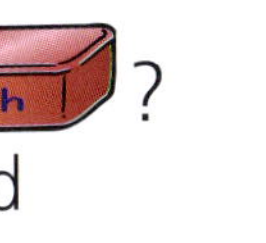 ? red

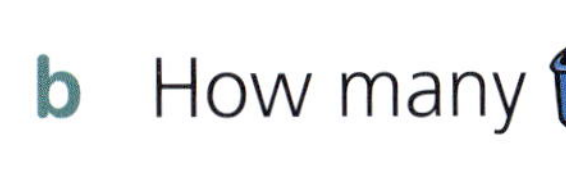

b How many 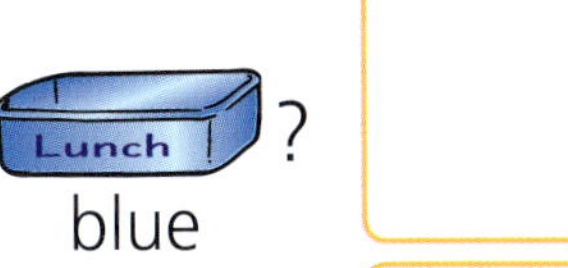 ? blue

c How many ? green

d How many ? yellow

e How many lunch boxes altogether?

f Are there more red than green? **Circle** yes or no.

g Ask a friend a question about the graph.

2 Place counters or ones blocks on this display to show how many students brought these to school today, then draw faces on the display to show the results.

15A Dominoes and dice

5 and 1 ☐

How many altogether?

4 and 2 ☐

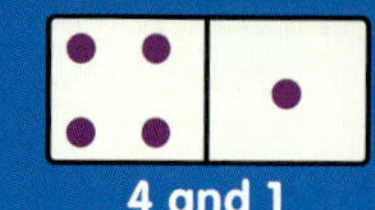

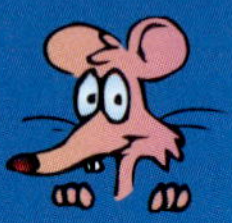

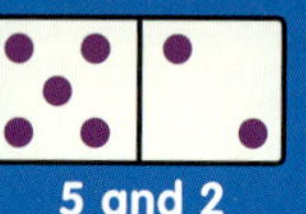

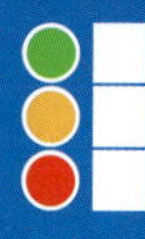

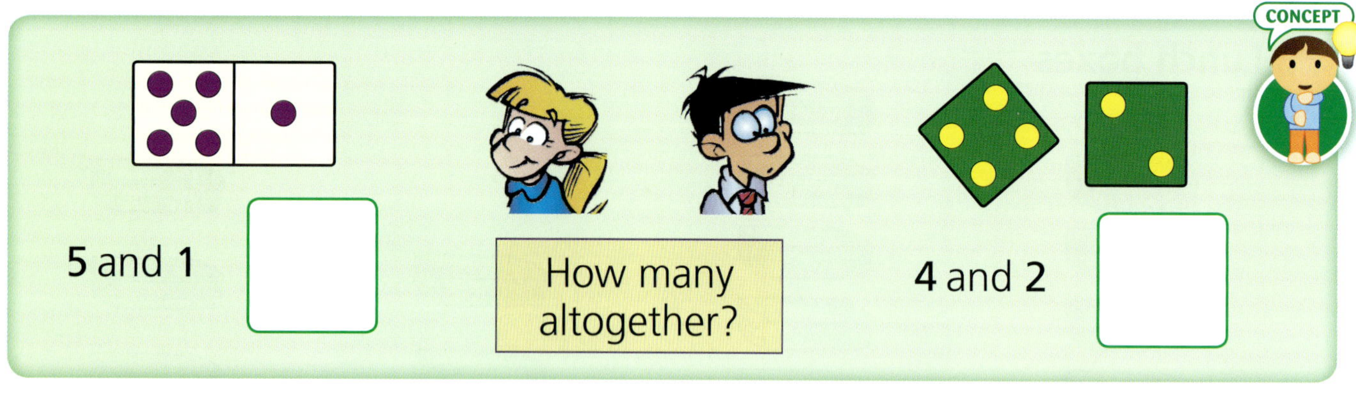

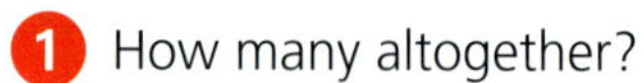

1 How many altogether?

a
1 and 1 ☐

b
2 and 2 ☐

c
3 and 3 ☐

d
4 and 4 ☐

e
4 and 2 ☐

f
3 and 5 ☐

g
2 and 6 ☐

h
5 and 5 ☐

i
6 and 4 ☐

j
3 and 6 ☐

k
5 and 4 ☐

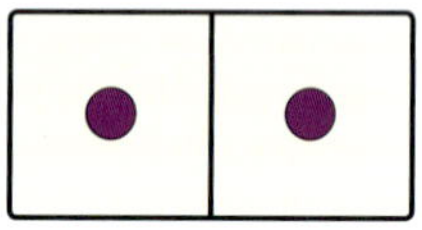

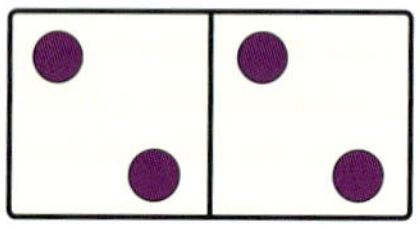

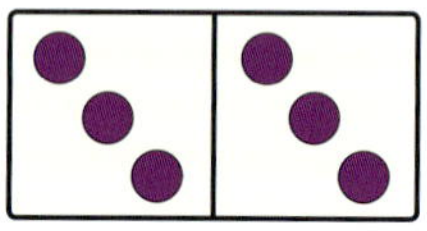

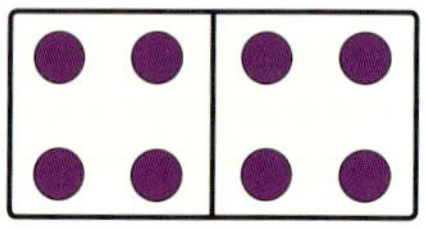

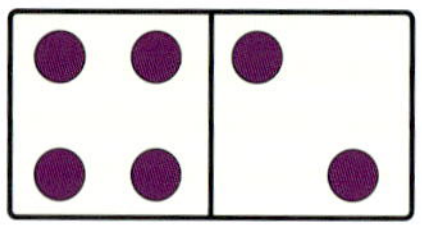

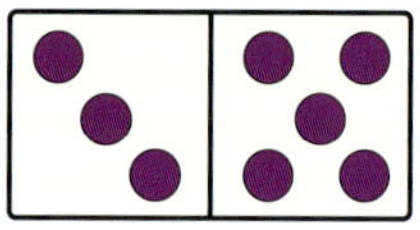

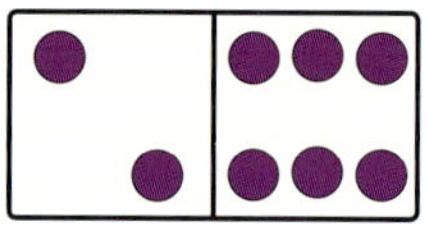

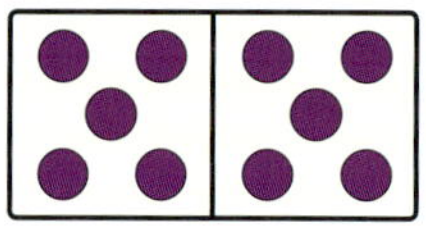

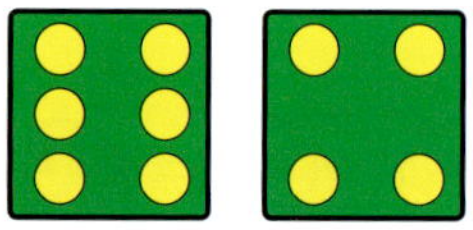

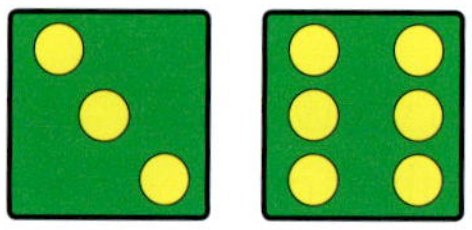

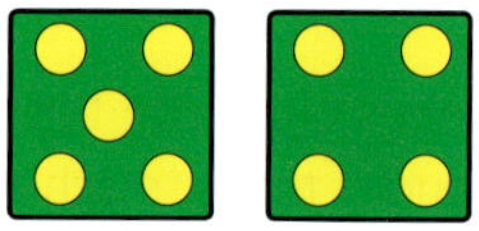

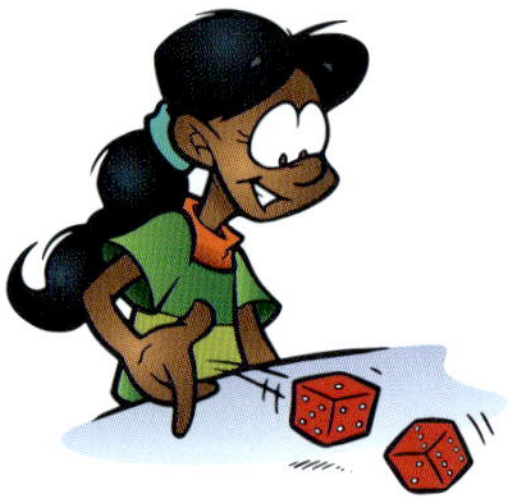

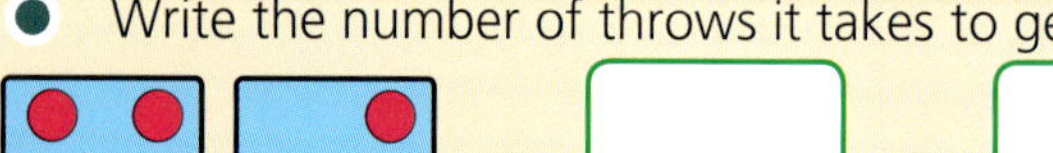

- Write the number of throws it takes to get:

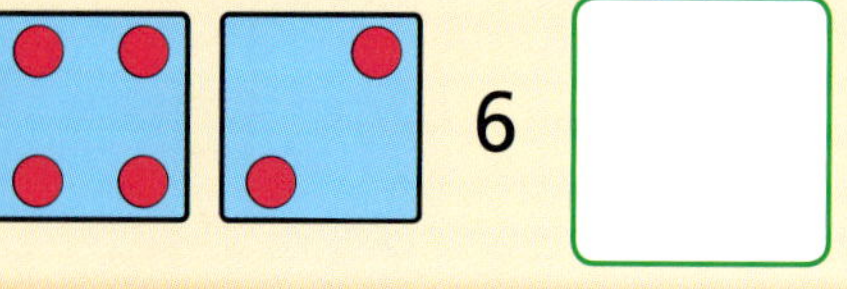

6 ☐ 7 ☐ 8 ☐

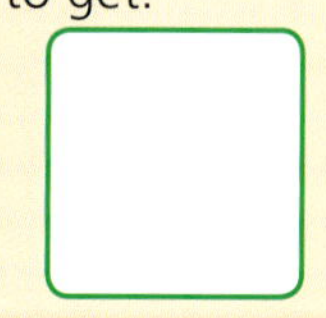

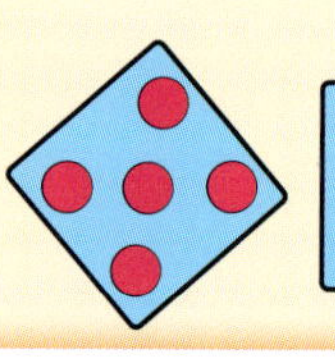

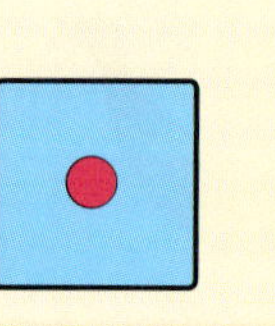

© PEARSON AUSTRALIA 2024 • *AUSTRALIAN SIGNPOST MATHS F* • ISBN 9780655708742

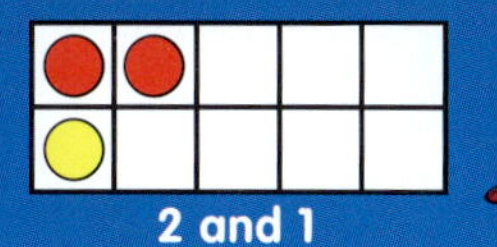

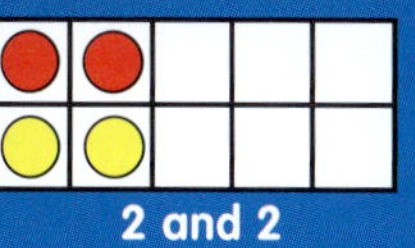

CONCEPT

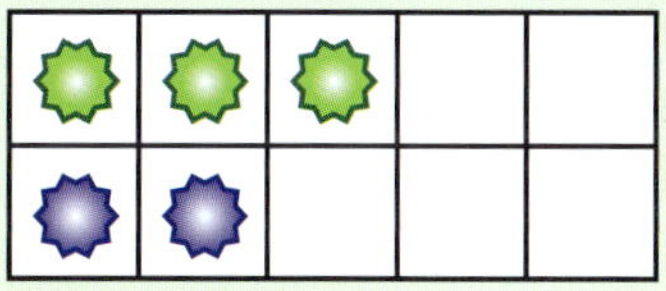

3 and 2 ☐

3 and 2 more makes 5.

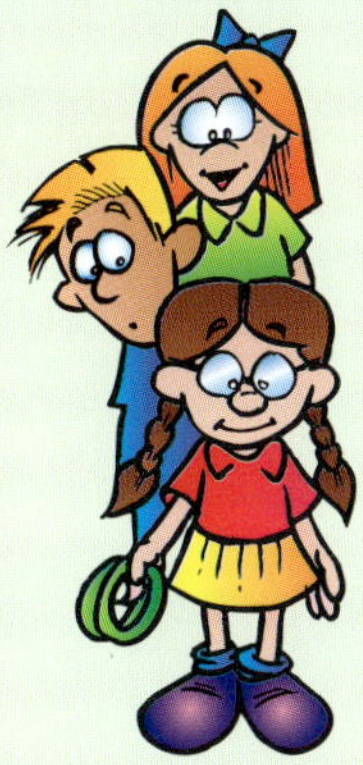

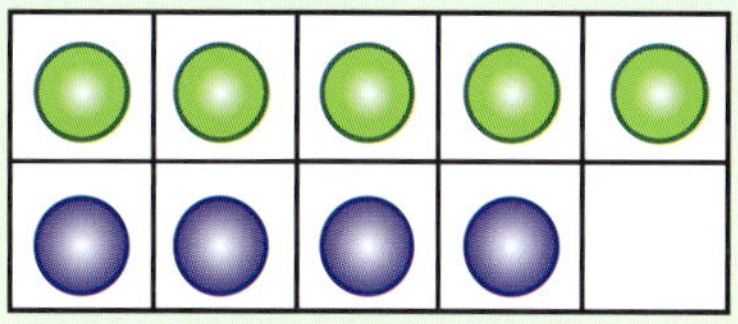

5 and 4 ☐

5 and 4 more makes 9.

1 a 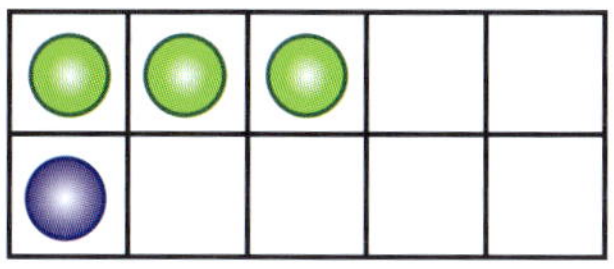 3 and 1 ☐

b 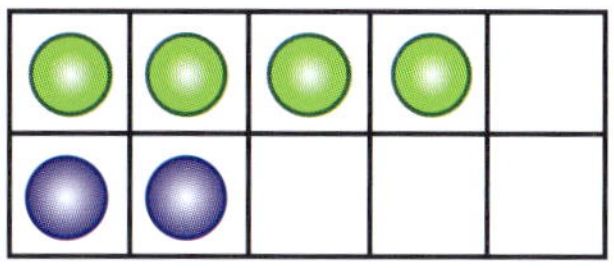 4 and 2 ☐

c 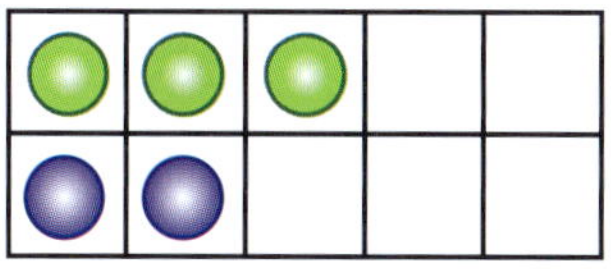 3 and 2 ☐

d 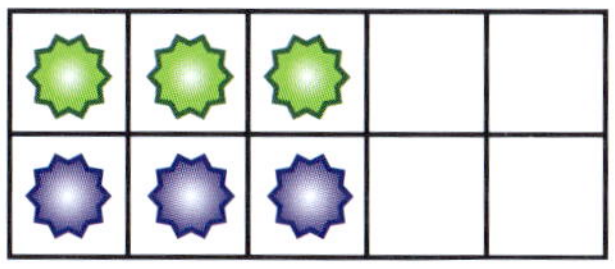 3 and 3 ☐

e 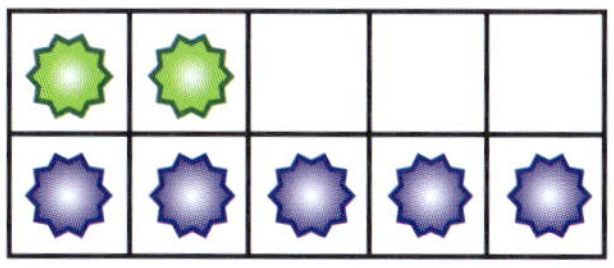 2 and 5 ☐

f 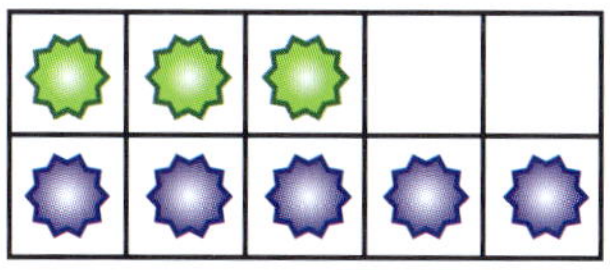 3 and 5 ☐

g 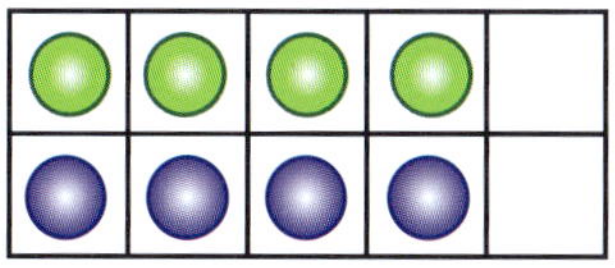 4 and 4 ☐

h 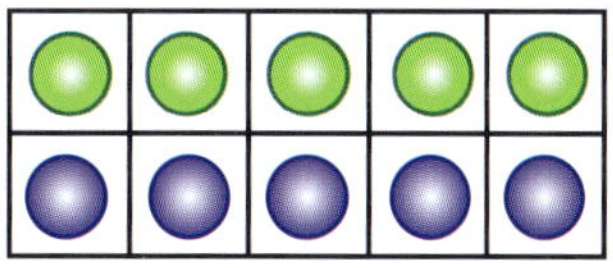 5 and 5 ☐

i 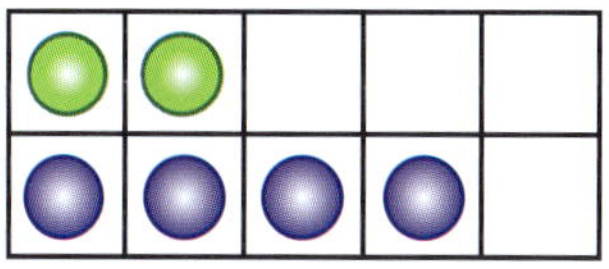 2 and 4 ☐

2 a Show 5 and 1

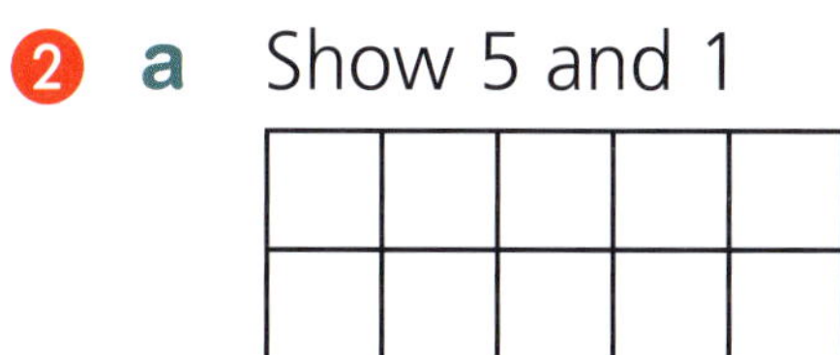

b Show 2 and 3

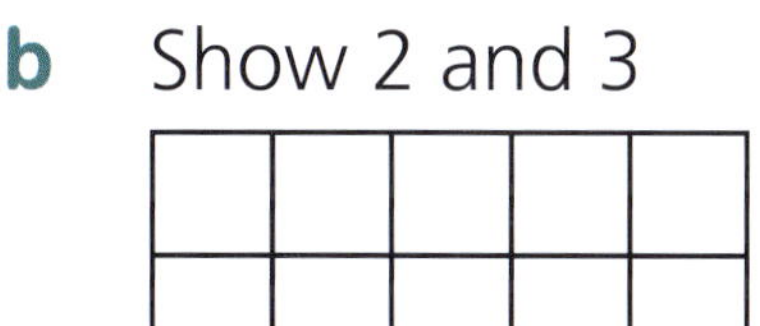

c Show 4 and 5

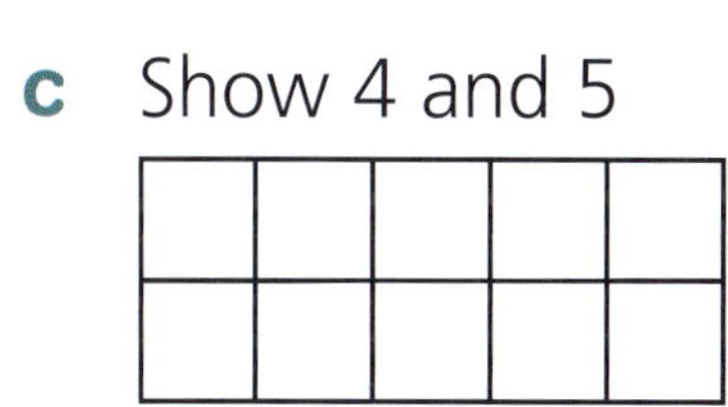

15C Sequencing events in a day

1 Discuss the pictures.  Draw what you do at different times in the day.

My day

morning

afternoon

night

2 Use 1 to 4 to put these events in order.

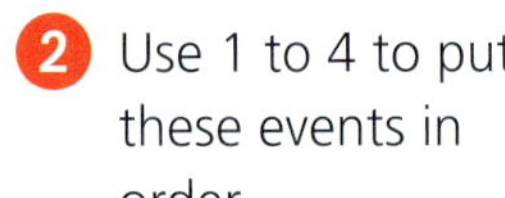

Blinky has a rest after his meal. ☐

Blinky wakes up. ☐

Blinky goes to sleep. ☐

Blinky eats his meal. ☐

3 Put these events in order, using 1 to 3.

eating the food ☐ cooking the food ☐ washing the dishes ☐

© PEARSON AUSTRALIA 2024 • *AUSTRALIAN SIGNPOST MATHS F* • ISBN 9780655708742

15D Days of the week

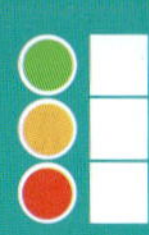

CONCEPT

There are 7 days in a week. Practise saying the days.

1 **Circle** the day it is today. Colour the school days red. Draw lines to join a picture to a day.

- Sunday
- Monday
- Tuesday
- Wednesday
- Thursday
- Friday
- Saturday

The days of the week repeat to make a pattern.

2 Draw something you did yesterday.

3 Draw something you might do tomorrow.

16A Adding groups

2 and 2 and 3 makes 7.

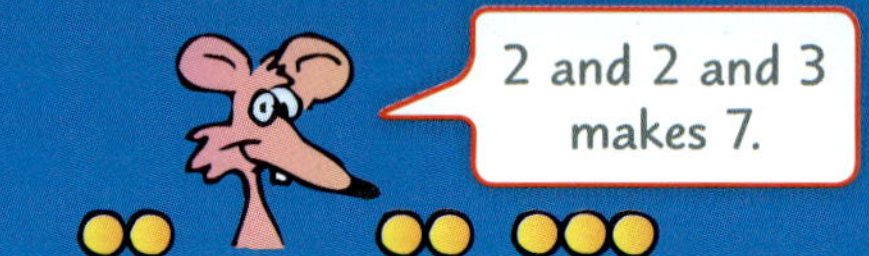

1 Count and complete.

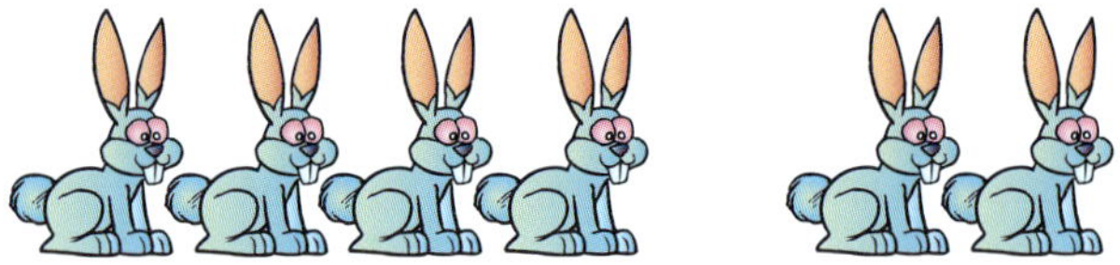

a ☐ and ☐ makes ☐

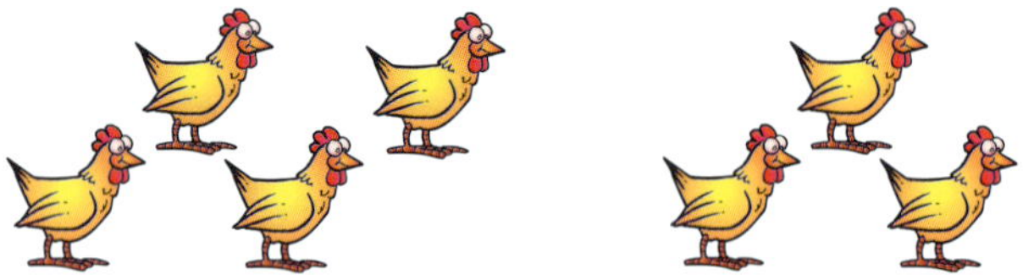

b ☐ and ☐ makes ☐

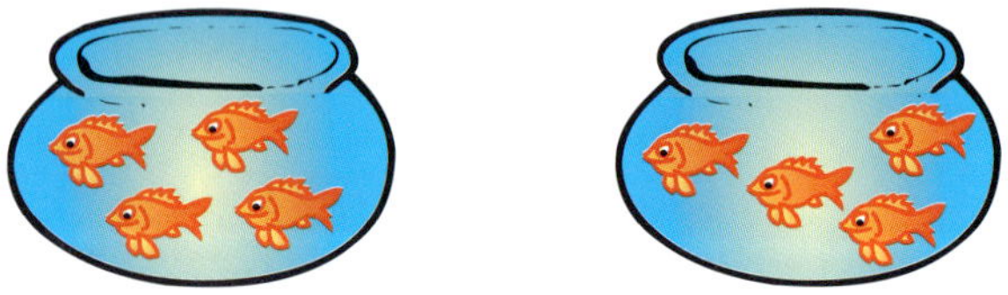

c ☐ and ☐ makes ☐

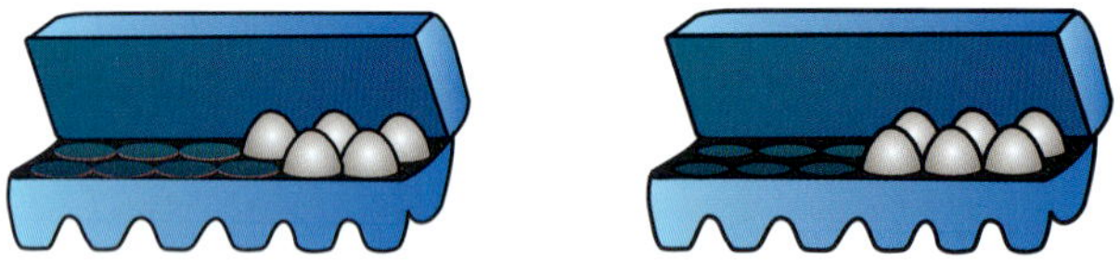

d ☐ and ☐ makes ☐

2 **a** Draw 2 circles for Hamid. Draw 5 circles for Mina.

☐ and ☐ makes ☐ circles altogether.

b Matt drew 3 squares. Fiona drew 4 squares. Lanh drew 2 squares.

☐ and ☐ and ☐ makes ☐ squares altogether.

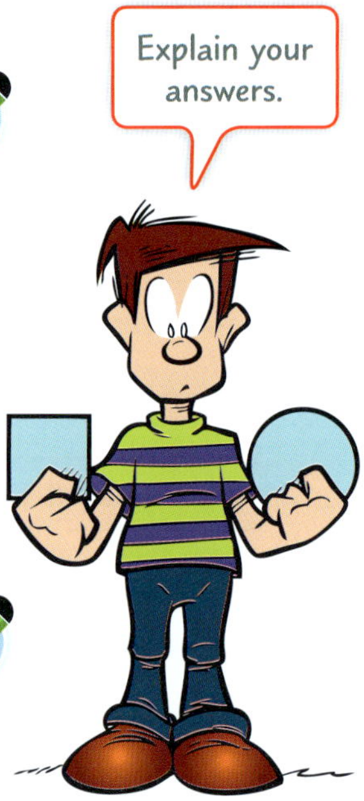
Explain your answers.

© PEARSON AUSTRALIA 2024 • *AUSTRALIAN SIGNPOST MATHS F* • ISBN 9780655708742

Adding rows of dots

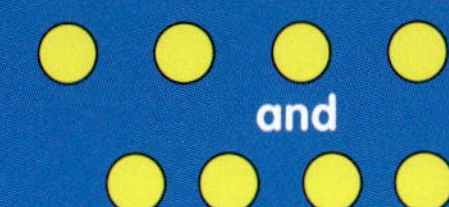

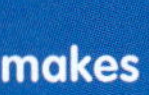

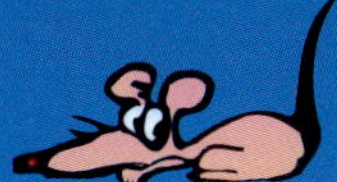

1 How many altogether?

a
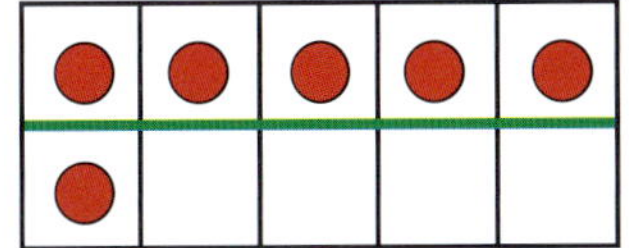
5 and 1 more

makes  .

b
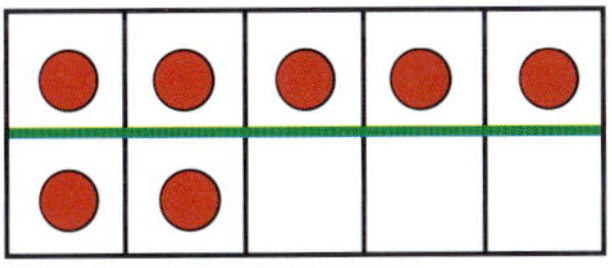
5 and 2 more

makes  .

c
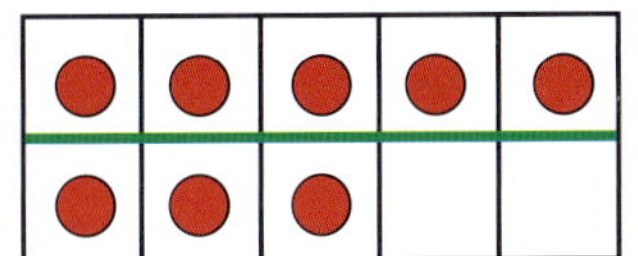
5 and 3 more

makes  .

d
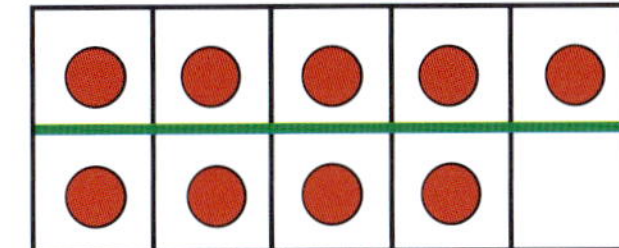
5 and 4 more

makes  .

e
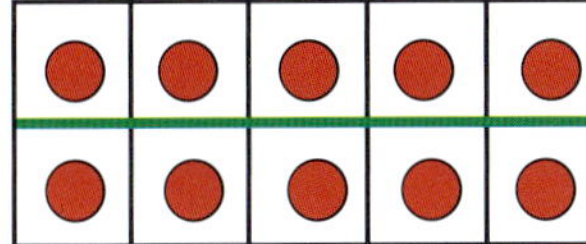
5 and 5 more

makes  .

2 How many altogether?

a
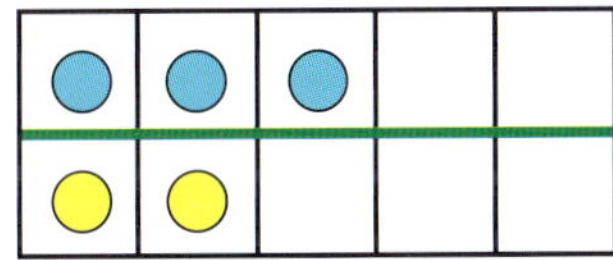
3 and 2 more

makes  .

b
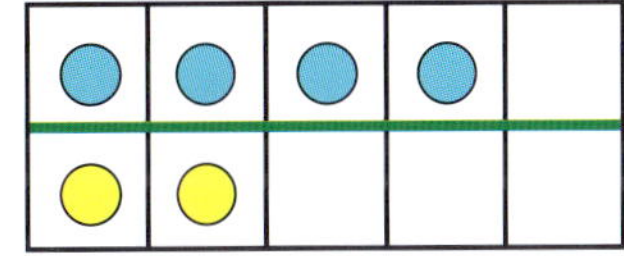
4 and 2 more

makes  .

c
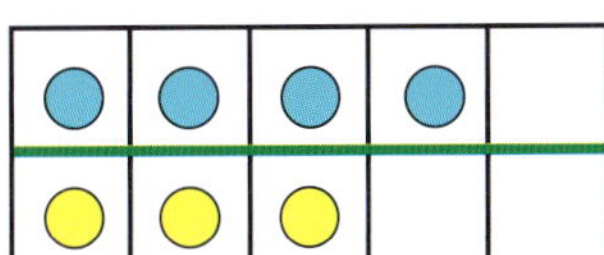
4 and 3 more

makes ☐ .

d
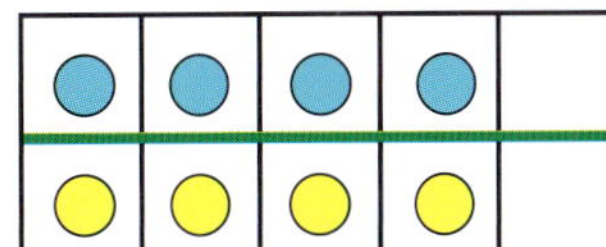
4 and 4 more

makes ☐ .

e
3 and 3 more

makes ☐ .

16C Cone-shaped objects

Slide

You can slide on flat surfaces.

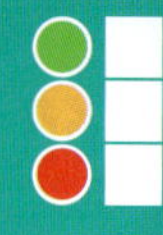

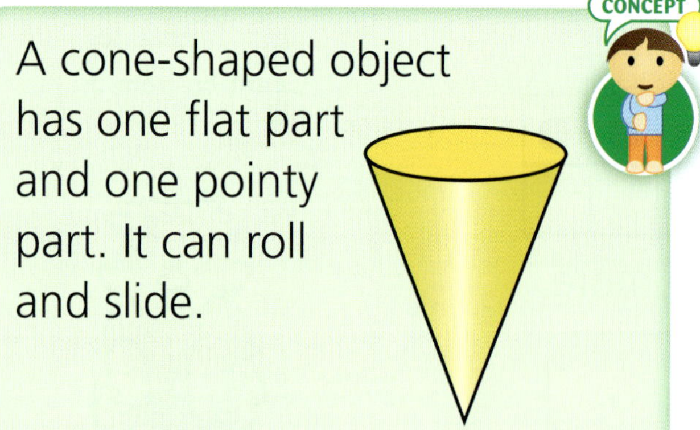

A cone-shaped object has one flat part and one pointy part. It can roll and slide.

1 Trace this cone-shaped object.

3 Circle the cone-shaped objects in this picture.

Talk about these objects using the words round, pointy, curved, straight, flat, rolls, slides and stacks.

2 Circle the cone-shaped objects.

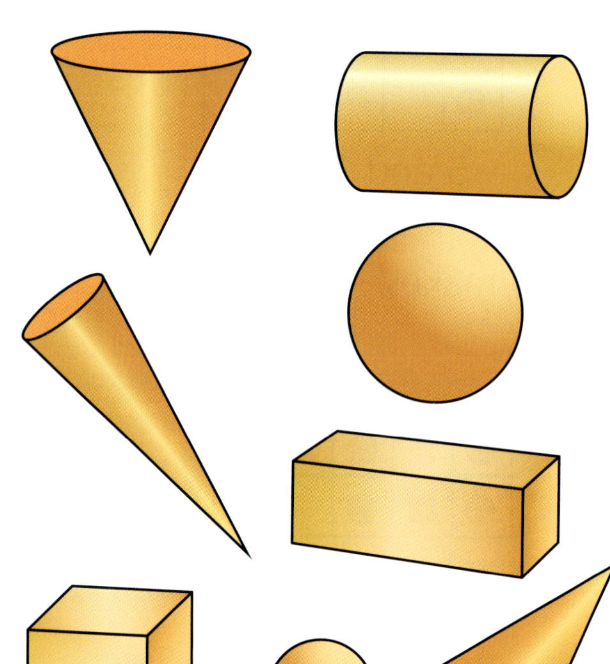

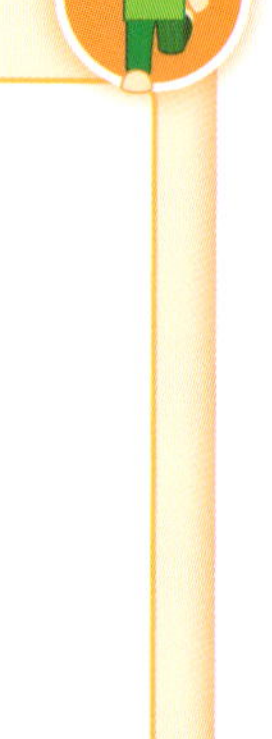

Use playdough to make a model of a cone-shaped object.
Draw your model here.

© PEARSON AUSTRALIA 2024 • *AUSTRALIAN SIGNPOST MATHS F* • ISBN 9780655708742

16D Using data displays

1

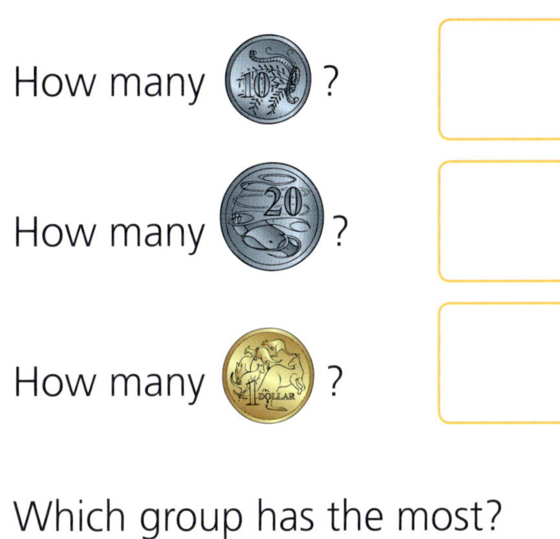

Which group has the most?

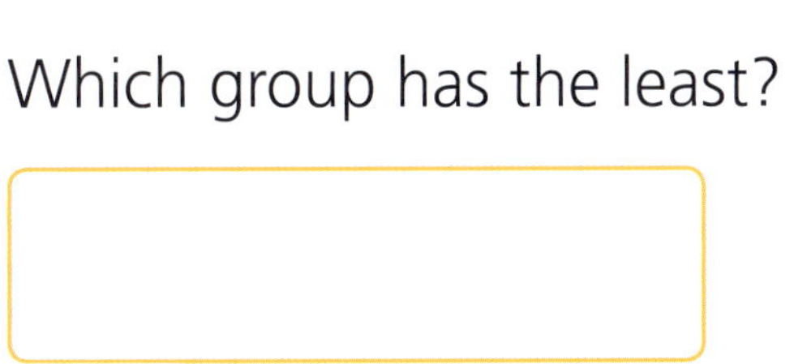

Which group has the least?

How many coins altogether?

2 Use counters to make your own data display.
Draw a circle for each.

fish	cars	balls

17A Adding groups

1 Discuss the picture.

a		and		makes		horses altogether.
b		and		makes		dogs altogether.
c		and		makes		pigs altogether.
d		and		makes		cows altogether.
e		and		makes		trees altogether.

2 Make up your own number sentences.

© PEARSON AUSTRALIA 2024 • *AUSTRALIAN SIGNPOST MATHS F* • ISBN 9780655708742

Ordinal numbers

1 Complete:

first second third

2 Write the position of the kangaroo above that is:

a wearing shorts

b the shortest

c carrying a bottle

d waving

e wearing a hat

f the tallest

3 Circle 1st place and 3rd place. ✔ Tick 2nd place and 7th place.

Put a box around 4th place and 6th place.

© PEARSON AUSTRALIA 2024 • *AUSTRALIAN SIGNPOST MATHS F* • ISBN 9780655708742

17C Can-shaped objects

CONCEPT

This is a can-shaped object. It has a round part and 2 flat parts. It can roll, slide and stack.

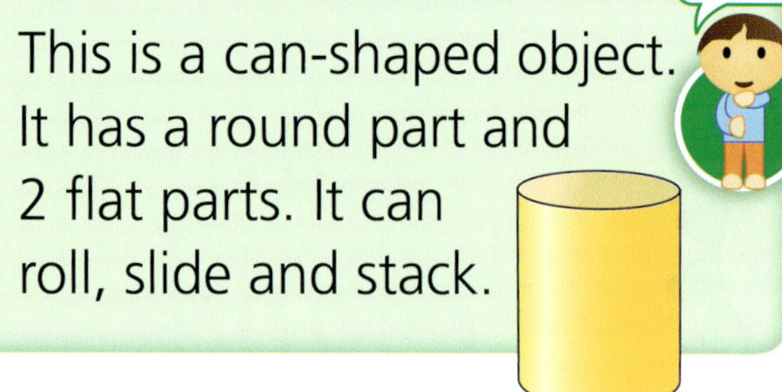

1 Trace this can-shaped object.

3 **Circle** the can-shaped objects in this picture.

Talk about these objects using the words round, pointy, curved, straight, flat, rolls, slides and stacks.

2 **Circle** the can-shaped objects.

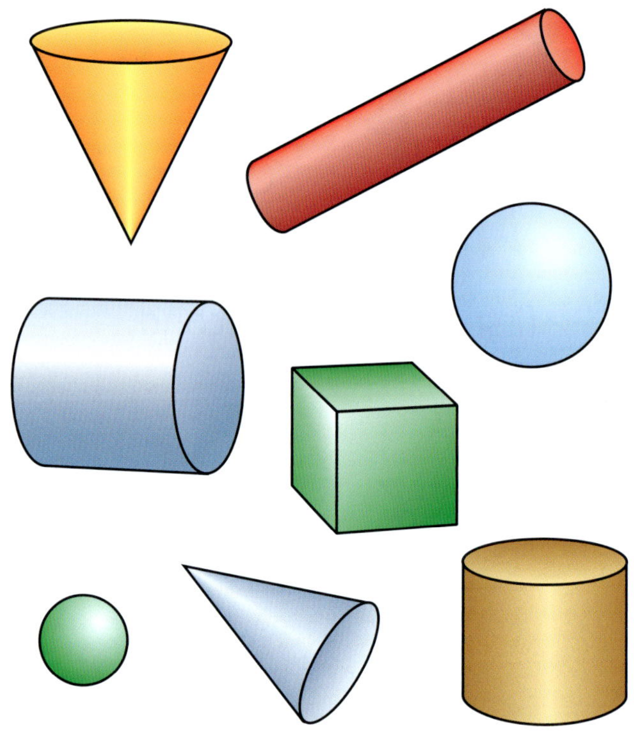

FUN SPOT

Use playdough to make a model of a can-shaped object. Draw your model here.

© PEARSON AUSTRALIA 2024 • *AUSTRALIAN SIGNPOST MATHS F* • ISBN 9780655708742

Duration of events

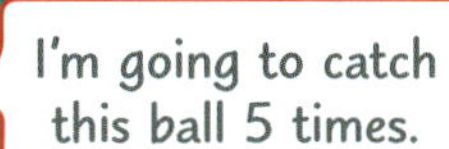

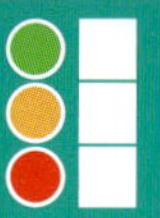

1. Two students start spinning a spinner at the same time.
   Keep a record of whose spinner spins longer.
   Do this five times.

Player A	
Player B	

2. Spin a spinner while another student counts how many claps it takes before the spinner stops.
   Record the number of claps taken for your best two spins.

   ☐ claps ☐ claps

3. Balloons are placed on the heads of two students (A and B).
   They can only use their heads to keep the balloons off the ground.
   Keep a record of who goes longer. Do this five times.

Player A	
Player B	

4. Balance a balloon on your head while your partner counts how many claps it takes before the balloon hits the ground.
   Record your best two goes.

   ☐ claps ☐ claps

5. Throw up a ball and catch it on the full, five times.
   Your partner will count as you do this to give you a score.
   Do this three times.

   score 1: ☐ score 2: ☐ score 3: ☐

© PEARSON AUSTRALIA 2024 • *AUSTRALIAN SIGNPOST MATHS F* • ISBN 9780655708742

18A Looking for patterns

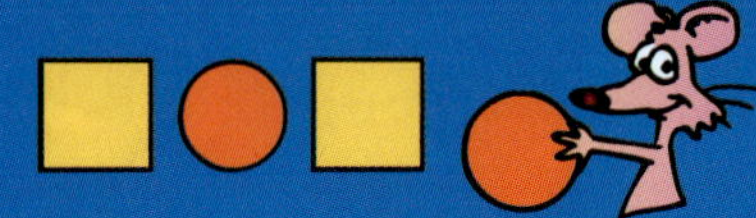

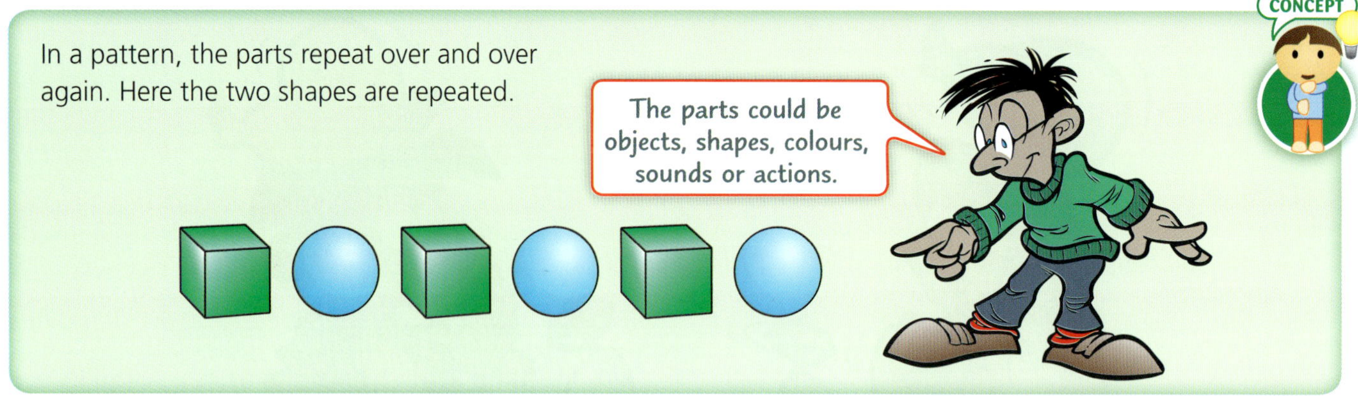

In a pattern, the parts repeat over and over again. Here the two shapes are repeated.

Talk about patterns in this picture. ✔ Tick each pattern.

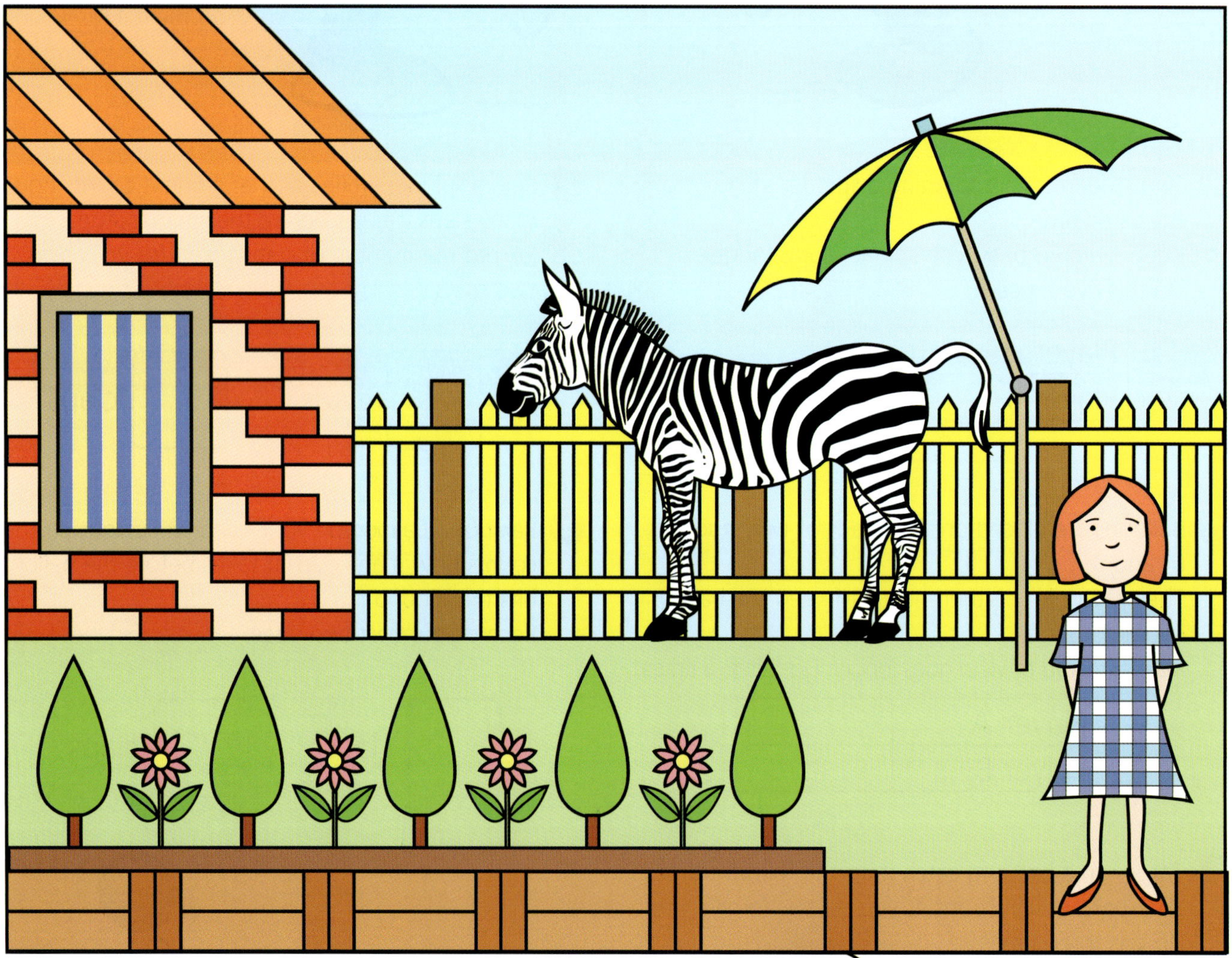

Find patterns in your classroom.

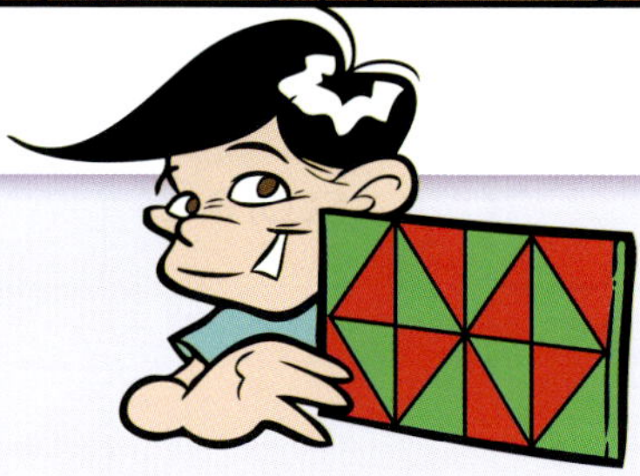

© PEARSON AUSTRALIA 2024 • *AUSTRALIAN SIGNPOST MATHS F* • ISBN 9780655708742

Patterns

CONCEPT

In a pattern, the parts repeat over and over again. Here the three shapes are repeated.

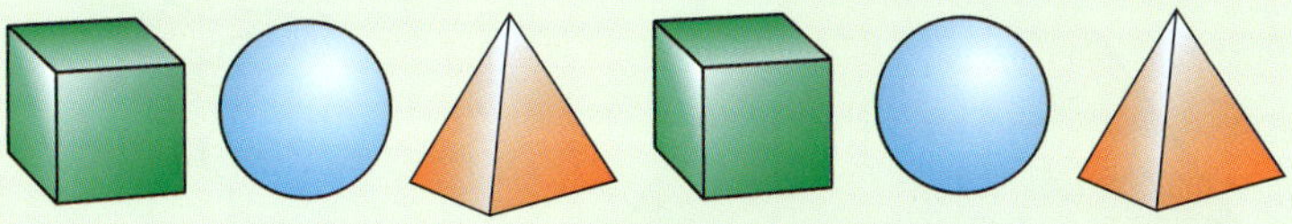

We can make patterns using three objects.

1 Describe these patterns. Complete each pattern.

2 Use two colours to make a pattern. Draw more beads to make more patterns.

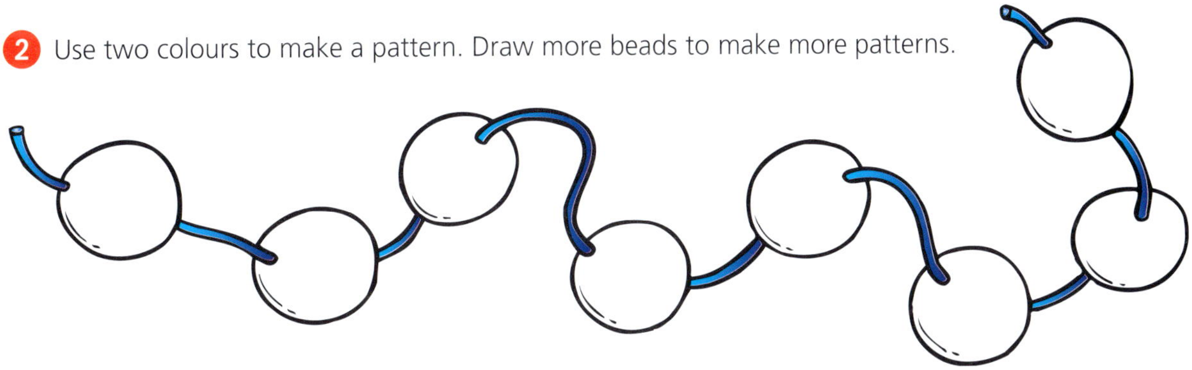

ACTIVITY

Use counters to make these patterns.
Use counters to make patterns of your own.

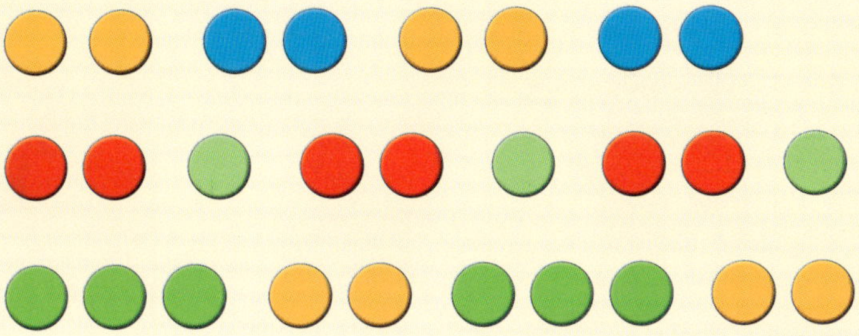

I made this one.

© PEARSON AUSTRALIA 2024 • *AUSTRALIAN SIGNPOST MATHS F* • ISBN 9780655708742

Shapes

1 Use colour to match shapes.

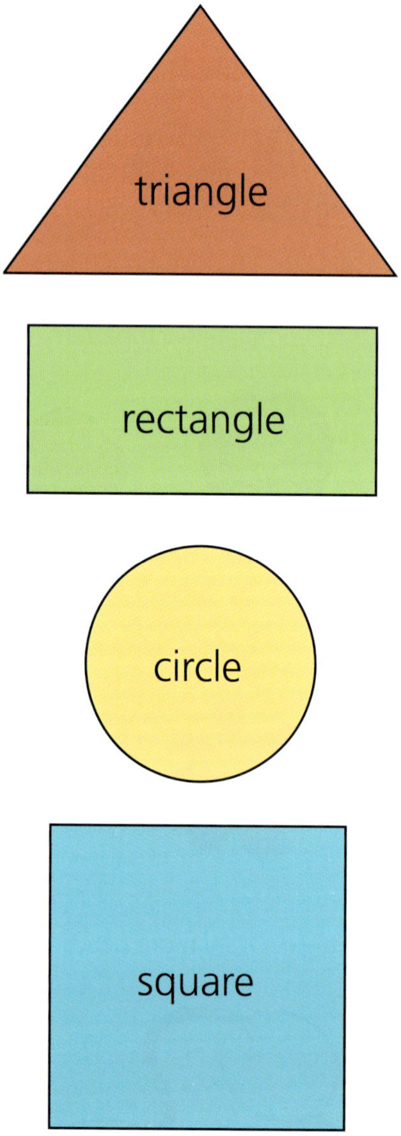

triangle

rectangle

circle

square

2 Continue the pattern of shapes down the rope.

Name these shapes. Talk about each shape. Draw a circle inside each shape.

ACTIVITY

© PEARSON AUSTRALIA 2024 • *AUSTRALIAN SIGNPOST MATHS F* • ISBN 9780655708742

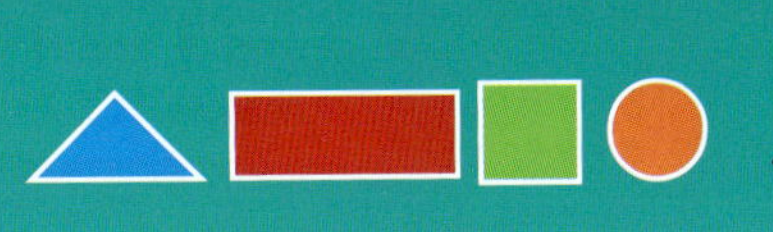

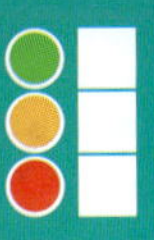

1 Use colour to match shapes. Discuss the features of each shape.

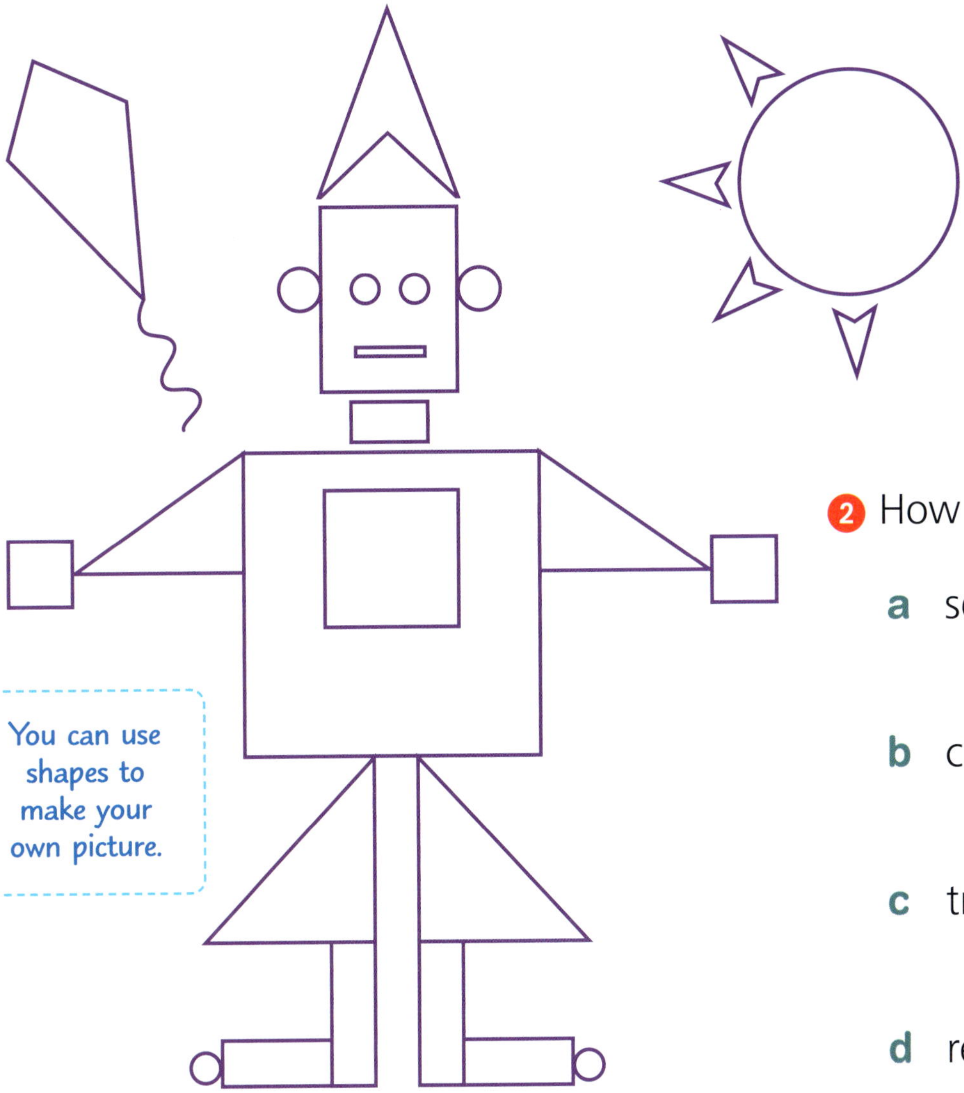

green

blue

orange

red

You can use shapes to make your own picture.

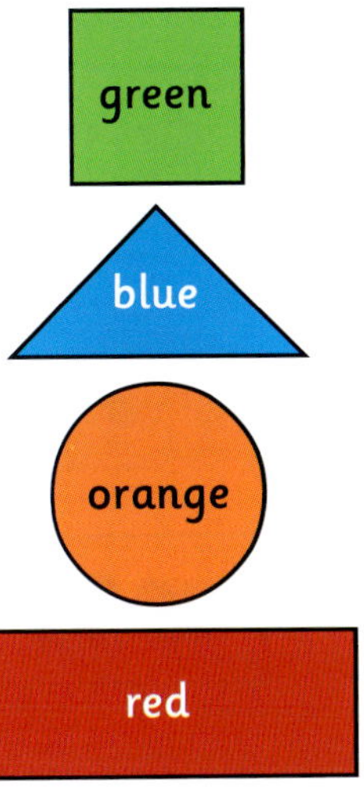

2 How many:

a squares?

b circles?

c triangles?

d rectangles?

ACTIVITY

Use pipe cleaners to make these shapes. Draw your shapes below.

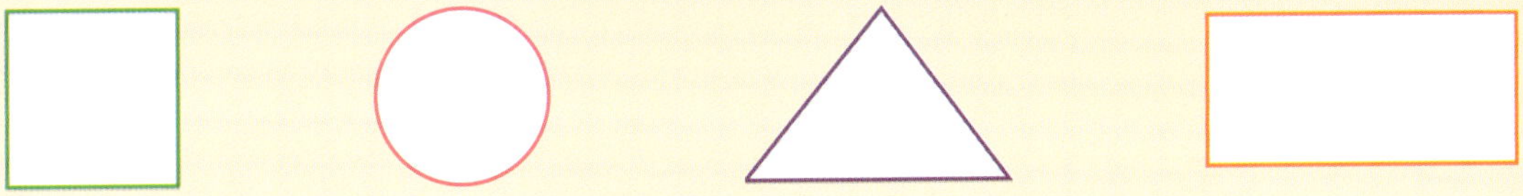

© PEARSON AUSTRALIA 2024 • • ISBN 9780655708742

Adding groups

1 Count and complete.

a

☐ and ☐ and ☐ makes ☐

b

☐ and ☐ and ☐ makes ☐

c

☐ and ☐ and ☐ makes ☐

d

☐ and ☐ and ☐ and ☐ makes ☐

INVESTIGATION

Place 2 or 3 counters in each box. How many in each box? How many altogether?

☐ and ☐ and ☐ makes ☐

© PEARSON AUSTRALIA 2024 • *AUSTRALIAN SIGNPOST MATHS F* • ISBN 9780655708742

19B Counting to 20

1 Discuss this picture. Count the number of flowers, chairs, hoops, windows and students.

a How many blocks? ☐

b How many balls? ☐

c How many chairs? ☐

d How many birds? ☐

e How many students? ☐

f How many hats? ☐

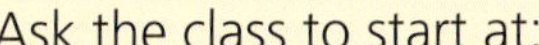

Ask the class to start at:

- 1 and count to 20
- 20 and count backwards to 1
- 8 and count to 18
- 16 and count backwards to 6.

Ask the class:

- What number is one more than 4, 7, 11, 19?
- What number is one less than 4, 7, 11, 19?

Practise counting beyond 20.

1	2	3	4	5
6	7	8	9	10
11	12	13	14	15
16	17	18	19	20

19C Comparing objects

1 **Circle** the objects that are lighter than your lunch box. Explain your reasons.
✔ Tick objects that would be about the same weight as the apple.

Draw pictures of an object that is:

lighter than my book	heavier than my book
longer than my book	shorter than my book

© PEARSON AUSTRALIA 2024 • *AUSTRALIAN SIGNPOST MATHS F* • ISBN 9780655708742

19D Gathering data

1 Ask the members of your class,

"Do you belong to a team?"

Draw a line for each answer, then draw the graph.

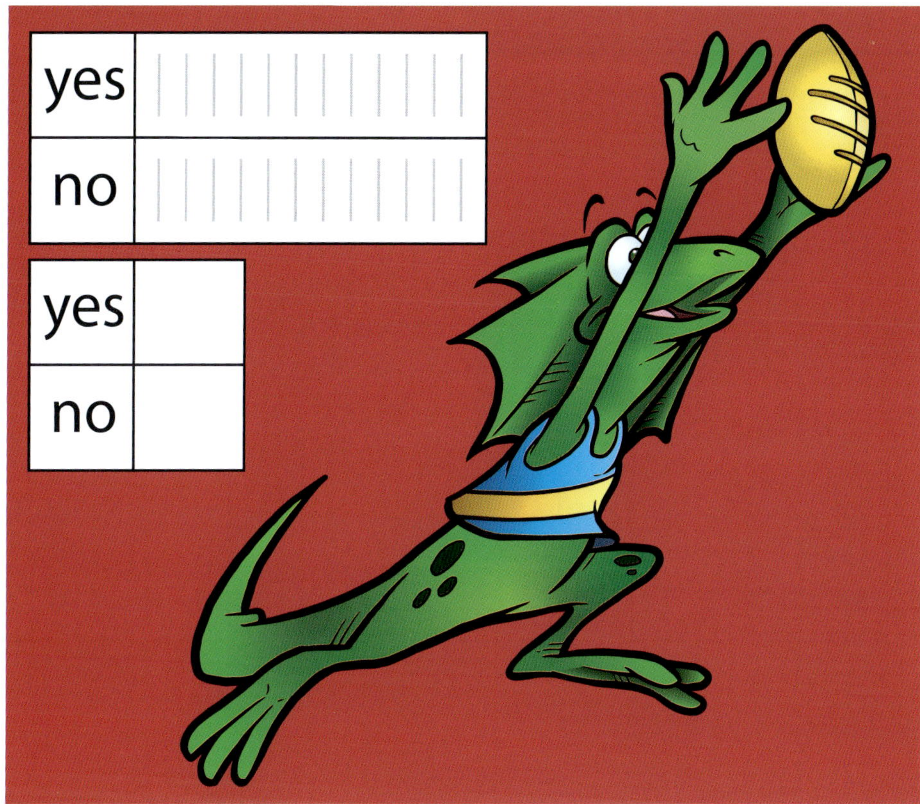

yes	| | | | | | | | | | | |
no	| | | | | | | | | | | |

yes	
no	

Belongs to a team

yes	no

INVESTIGATION

- Make up your own yes / no question to ask some of your classmates.

- After you have collected the data, draw a graph.

Draw a face for each classmate.

yes	| | | | | | | | | | | |
no	| | | | | | | | | | | |

yes													
no													

20A Comparing collections

Fourteen is 1 ten and 4 ones.

Forty is 4 tens and 0 ones.

Sometimes we hear patterns in the way we say numbers. This helps us remember them in order.
Clap when you hear the "teen" part of these numbers:

13, 14, 15, 16, 17, 18 and 19

1 Count each group. Write the number in each box.

✔ Tick the largest group. **Circle** the smallest group.

A

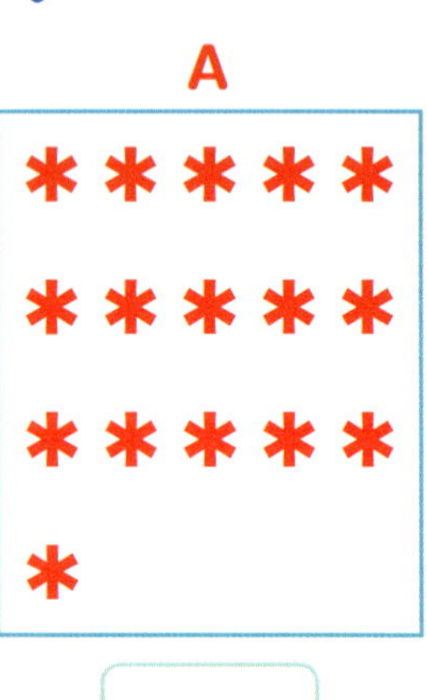

B

C

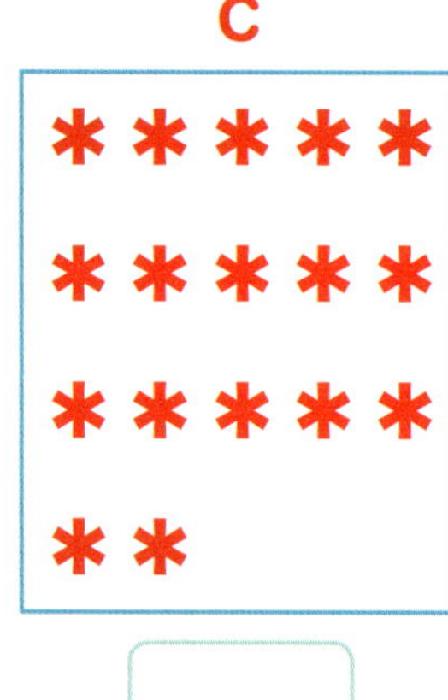

D

2 Discuss the groups above. Write them in order, from smallest to largest.

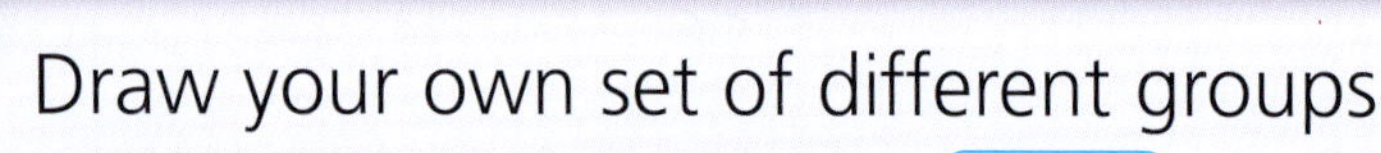

Draw your own set of different groups.
✔ Tick the largest group. **Circle** the smallest group.

© PEARSON AUSTRALIA 2024 • *AUSTRALIAN SIGNPOST MATHS F* • ISBN 9780655708742

20B Counting to 30

1

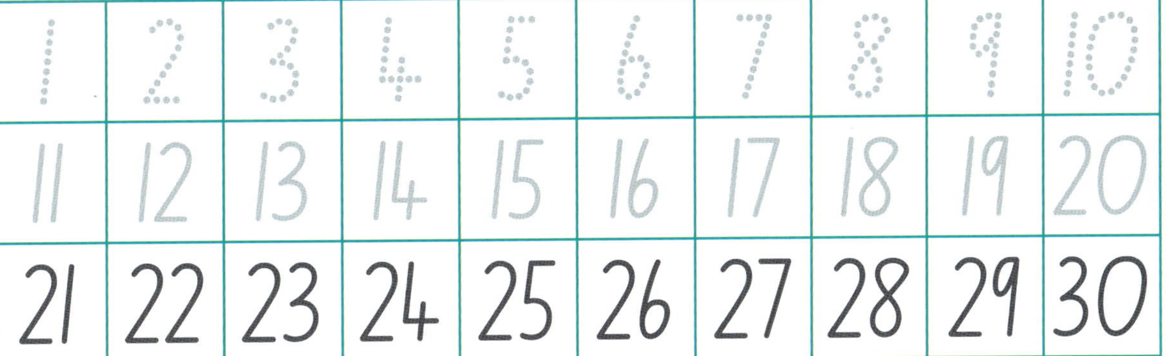

1	2	3	4	5	6	7	8	9	10
11	12	13	14	15	16	17	18	19	20
21	22	23	24	25	26	27	28	29	30

- Point to the numbers as you count them. Count from 1 to 30.
- Start at 30 and count backwards.
- Start at 13 and count to 27.
- Trace over the numbers 1 to 10.
- **Circle** every second number. Say them aloud.

- Colour **red** the numbers that have a **5** in them.
- Colour **blue** the numbers that have a **0** in them.

2 Write the number one more than:

a 13 ☐ b 9 ☐ c 15 ☐

d 18 ☐ e 11 ☐ f 17 ☐

13 is one ten and three ones.

3 Write the number one less than:

a 18 ☐ b 13 ☐ c 16 ☐

d 15 ☐ e 19 ☐ f 10 ☐

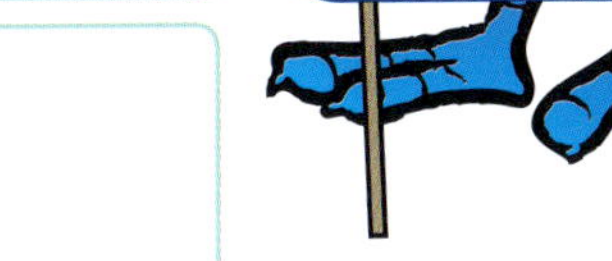

INVESTIGATION

The Wurundjeri people have a counting system that uses parts of the body to represent numbers.

1

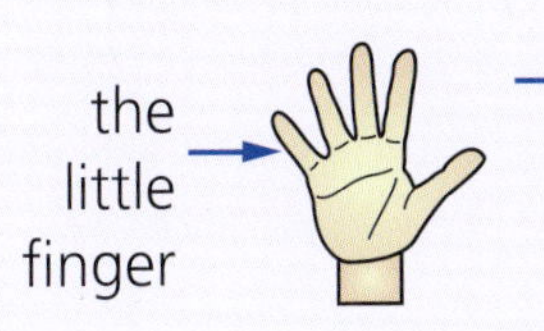

2

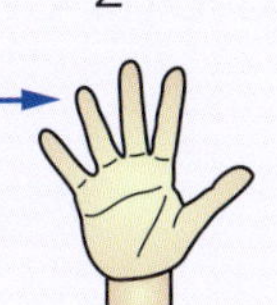

3

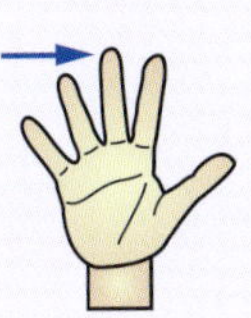

4

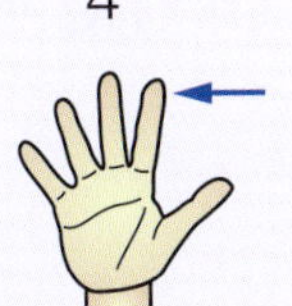

5

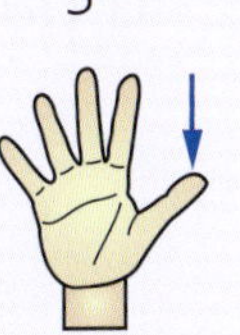

6

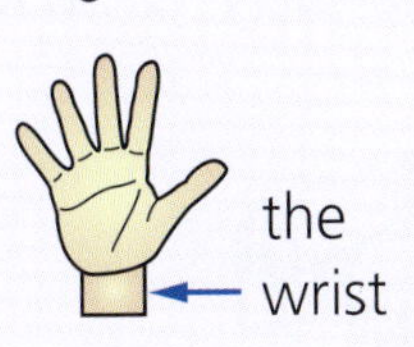

20C Sequencing events

1 Draw lines to show the order.

2 Draw something you do before school.

Draw something you do after school.

before

after

3 Read the days of the week. Fill in the empty boxes. Colour the school days. How many days in a week?

Sunday	Monday	Tuesday	Wednesday	Thursday	Friday	Saturday
1st	2nd					

What day is: the 2nd day of the week? the 6th day of the week?

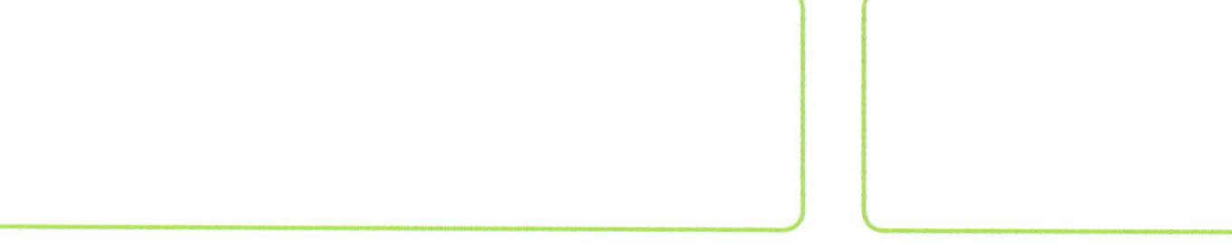

© PEARSON AUSTRALIA 2024 • *AUSTRALIAN SIGNPOST MATHS F* • ISBN 9780655708742

20D Days of the week

1 Help John find his way to the waterhole by following the days of the week. Draw the route he takes. Colour the days of the weekend red and the weekdays blue.

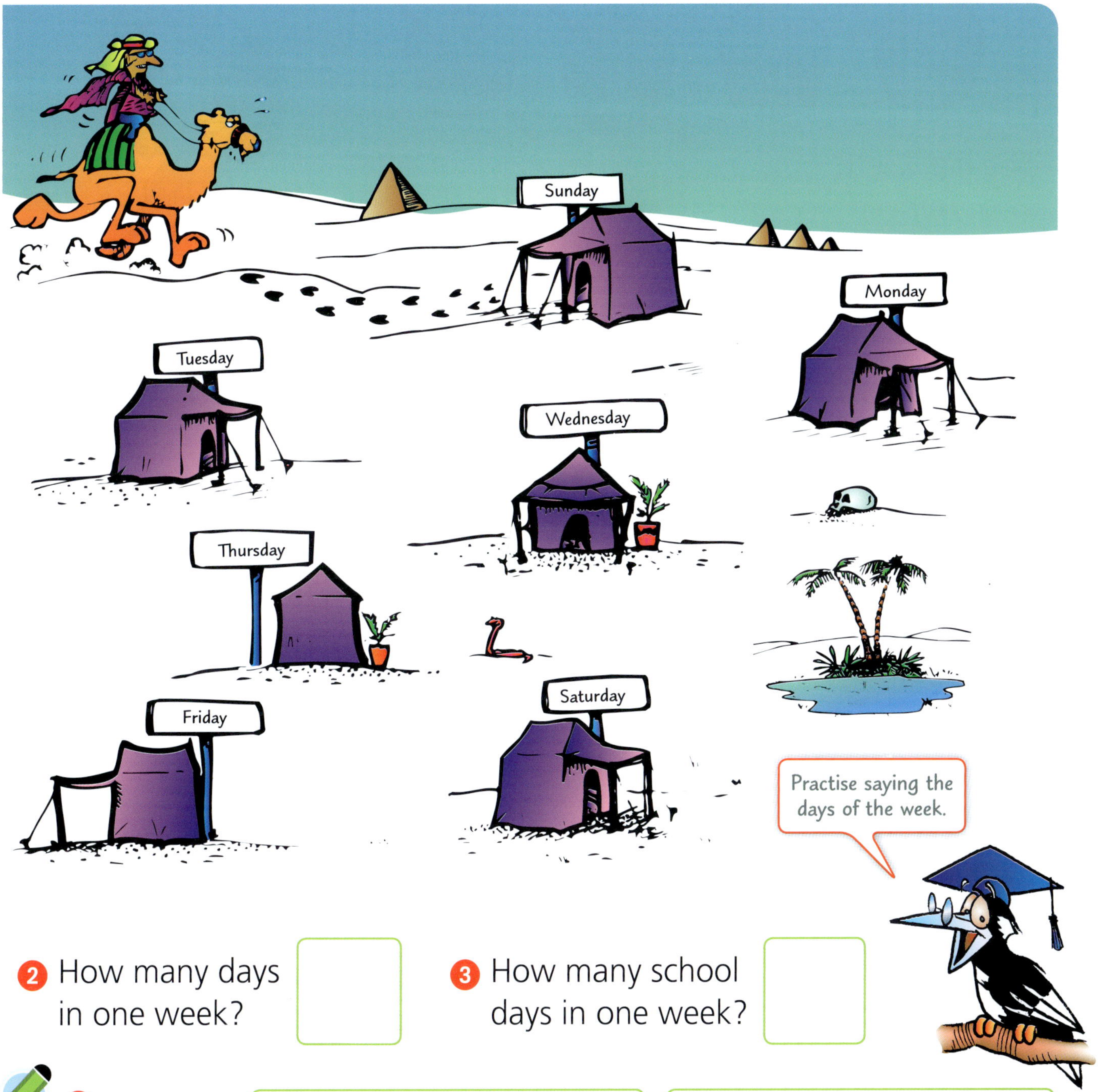

Sunday
Monday
Tuesday
Wednesday
Thursday
Friday
Saturday

Practise saying the days of the week.

2 How many days in one week? ☐

3 How many school days in one week? ☐

4 Draw a picture of something you do on the weekend.

Saturday	Sunday

21A Taking objects away

Jo started with 4 cupcakes. She gave 2 away.

She has 2 left.

1 How many are left?

a Three dogs, one walked away.

☐ left

b Four frogs, one hopped away.

☐ left

c Six grubs, two fell off.

☐ left

d Eight birds, three flew away.

☐ left

e Ten rabbits, four hopped away.

☐ left

f Seven apples, two were eaten.

☐ left

© PEARSON AUSTRALIA 2024 • *AUSTRALIAN SIGNPOST MATHS F* • ISBN 9780655708742

Taking away

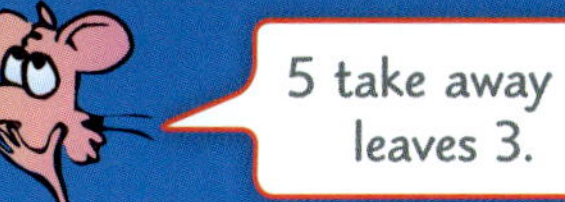

1 Complete each number sentence.

a 8 cakes take away 3 leaves ☐.

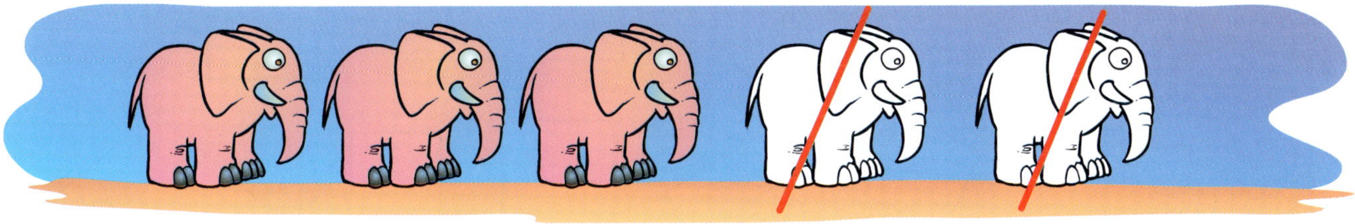

b ☐ elephants take away ☐ leaves ☐.

c ☐ ducks take away ☐ leaves ☐.

d ☐ boats take away ☐ leaves ☐.

ACTIVITY

In pairs, collect a group of 8 objects. Take turns to take some away and have your partner find how many are left. Talk about this using the number sentence below.

☐ objects take away ☐ leaves ☐.

© PEARSON AUSTRALIA 2024 • *AUSTRALIAN SIGNPOST MATHS F* • ISBN 9780655708742

21C Classifying 2D shapes

1 Colour the matching shapes in each row.

Describe these shapes.

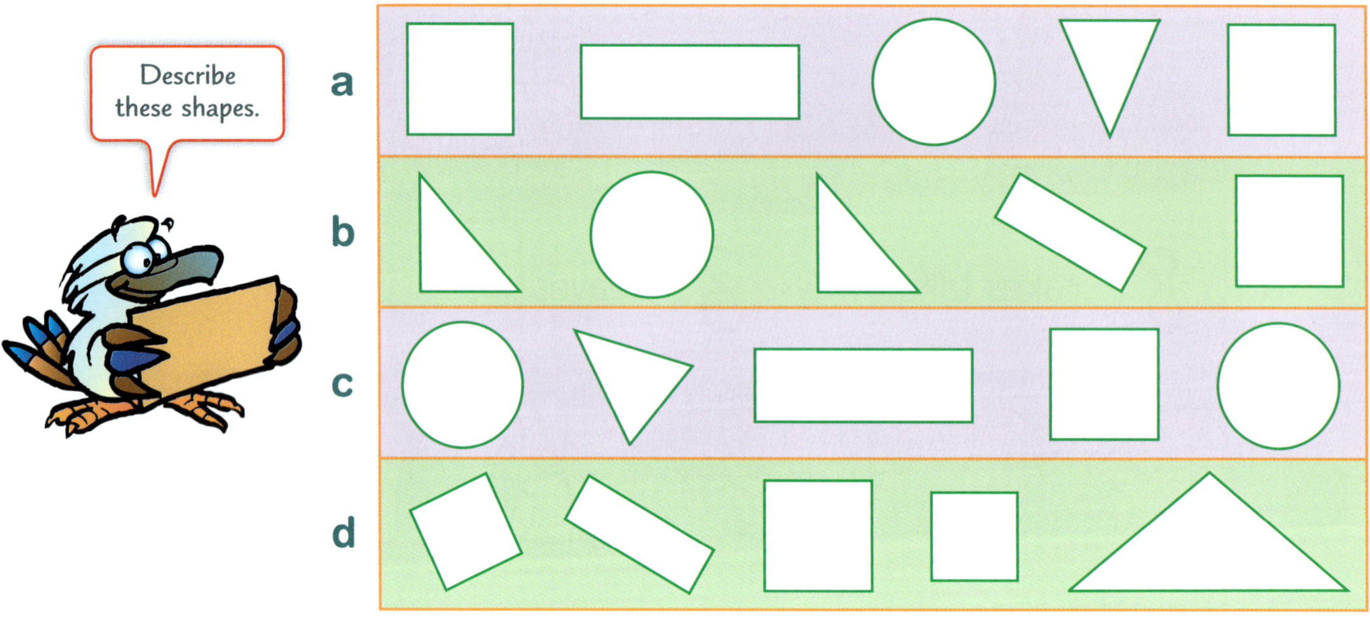

2 Complete:

a A square has ☐ straight sides.

b A triangle has ☐ straight sides.

c A rectangle has ☐ straight sides.

d Is the side of a circle straight or curved? ☐

Making shapes

INVESTIGATION

How many craft sticks do you need to make a:

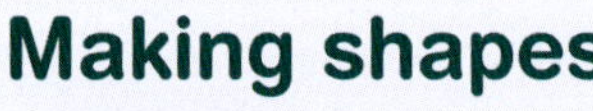

- square? ☐
- triangle? ☐

Can you make a circle? yes no Discuss.

© PEARSON AUSTRALIA 2024 • *AUSTRALIAN SIGNPOST MATHS F* • ISBN 9780655708742

21D Describing objects in our world

Discuss the shape of the objects in the picture.

1 Draw objects from the picture above that have:

a 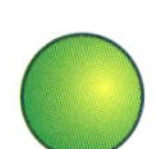 a ball shape (sphere)

b  a can shape (cylinder)

c 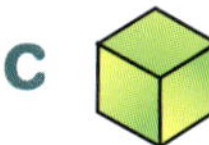 a box shape (prism)

d 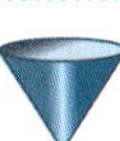 a cone shape (cone)

Predict then test which of the objects in question 1 will stack.

Find ball-shaped, can-shaped, box-shaped and cone-shaped objects in your classroom.

Use playdough to make ball-shaped, can-shaped, box-shaped and cone-shaped objects.

22A Taking away

1 Cross off two objects in each row. Write how many are left. Colour them in.

a         left

b   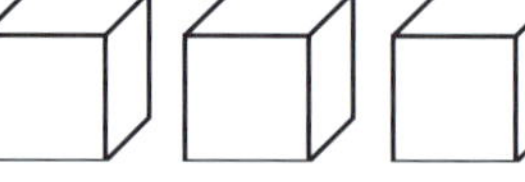   left

c         left

d         left

2 Complete each number sentence.

a        

7 stars take away 2 leaves  ☐.

b 

☐ butterflies take away  ☐ leaves  ☐.

c       

☐ frogs take away ☐ leaves   ☐.

© PEARSON AUSTRALIA 2024 • *AUSTRALIAN SIGNPOST MATHS F* • ISBN 9780655708742

22B Taking away

CONCEPT

1 Complete these number sentences, then explain what you did.

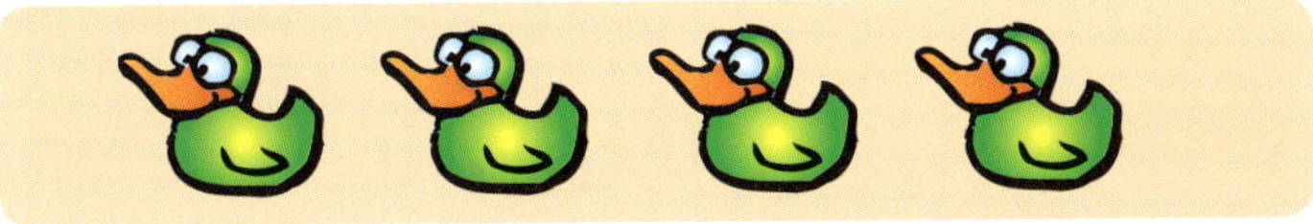

a 4 take away 1 leaves ☐

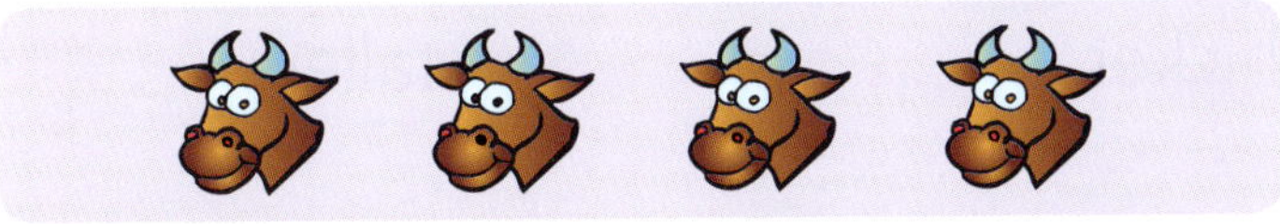

b 4 take away 3 leaves ☐

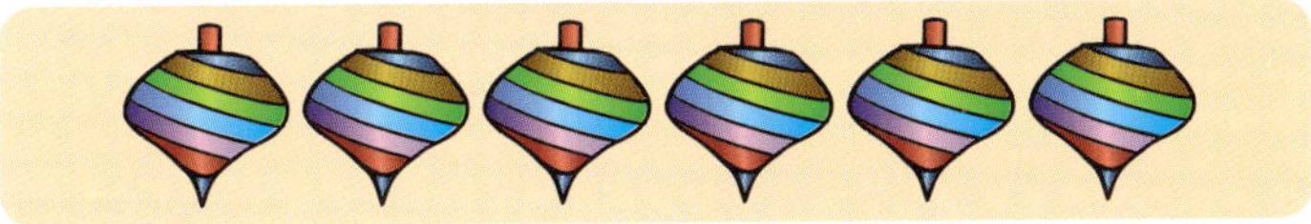

c 6 take away 4 leaves ☐

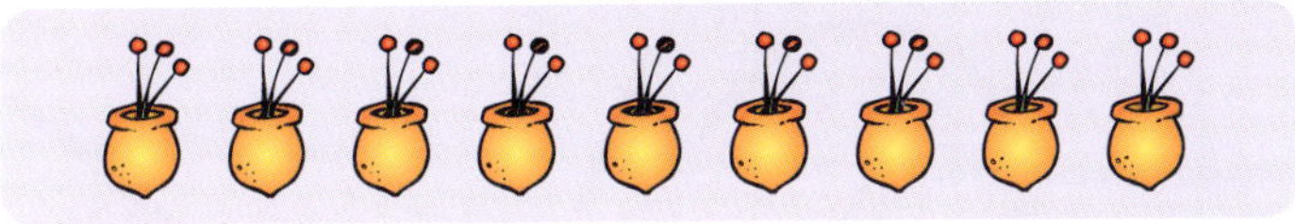

d 9 take away 2 leaves ☐

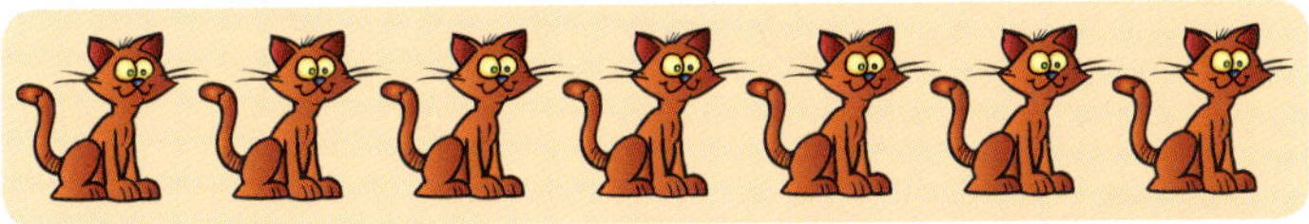

e 7 take away 4 leaves ☐

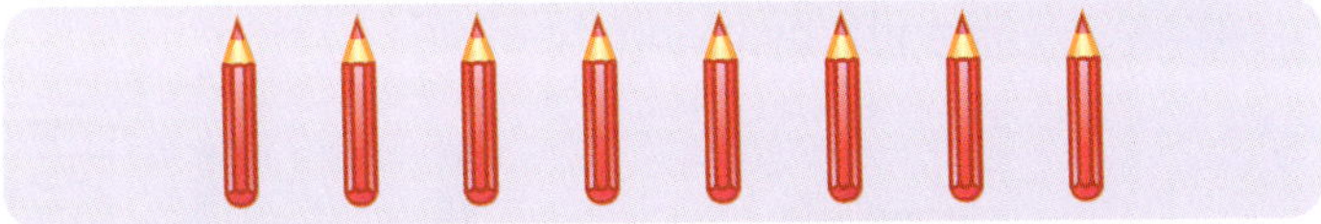

f 8 take away 3 leaves ☐

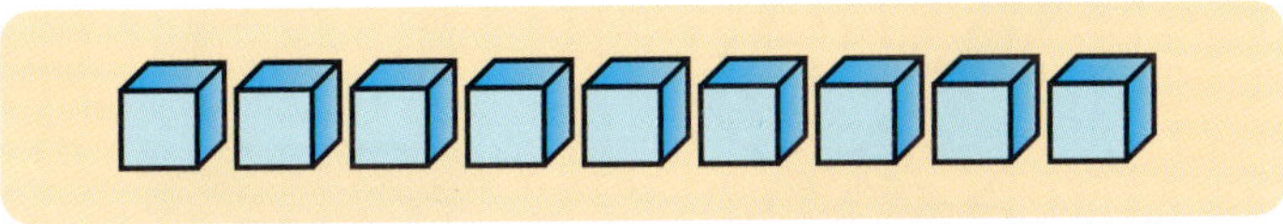

g 9 take away 0 leaves ☐

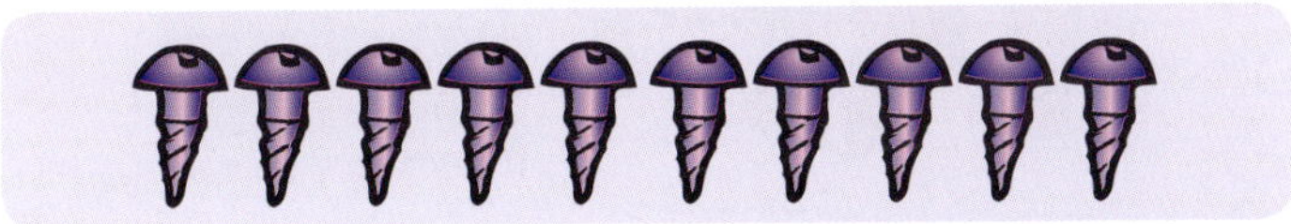

h 10 take away 8 leaves ☐

22C Comparing two lengths

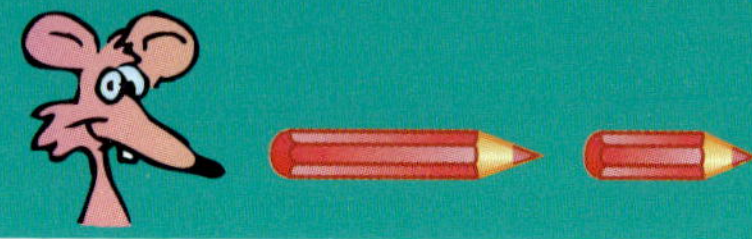

1 **Circle** the one that is:

deeper

thinner

lower

higher

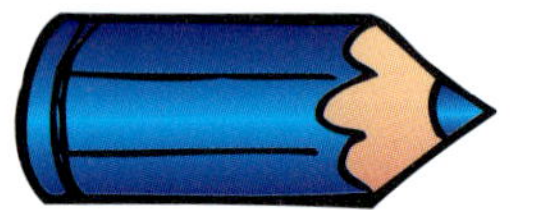

thicker

taller

2 To compare objects, place them side by side with ends matching. Colour the longer objects.

a 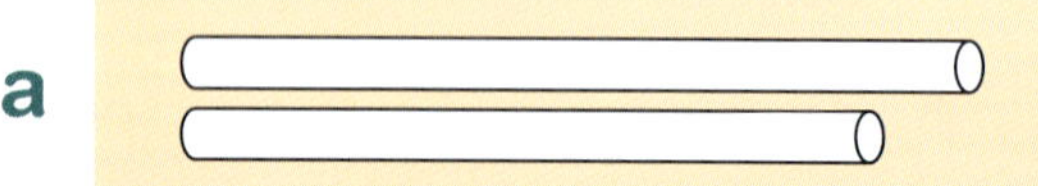

b 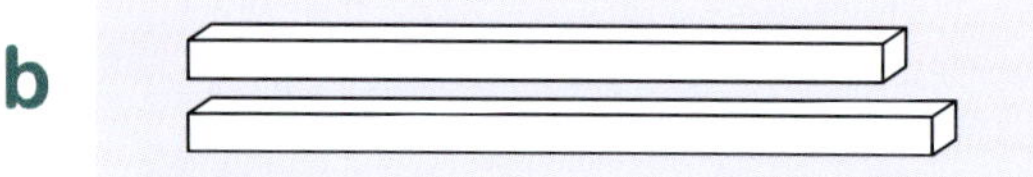

c 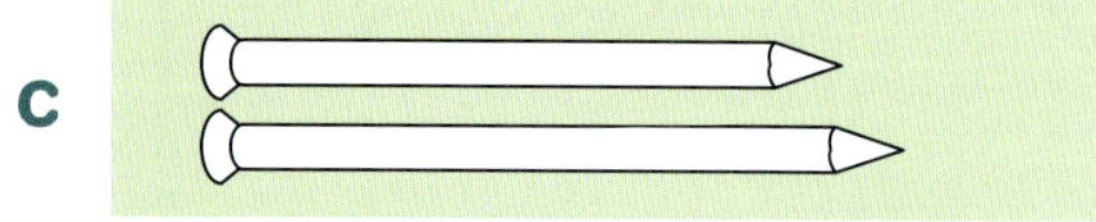

3 Do you think that these pieces of string have the same length? Discuss your answer.

4 Cut three lengths of string. Compare their lengths by laying them side by side.

INVESTIGATION

Choose an object you can carry.

Compare the length of the object to the length of other objects.

Place the objects side by side and match the ends.

© PEARSON AUSTRALIA 2024 • *AUSTRALIAN SIGNPOST MATHS F* • ISBN 9780655708742

22D Position and length

Discuss this picture.
Draw a circle around: the lowest kite, the tallest bush, the highest bird, the longest snake, the longer truck, the house further away, the flower to the right of the bin, the echidna closer to the bin, the duck halfway across the pond, the cats side by side, the shortest dog, the lowest cloud, the flowers between the rocks, the cars parked end to end, the flower to the left of the cow.

© PEARSON AUSTRALIA 2024 • *AUSTRALIAN SIGNPOST MATHS F* • ISBN 9780655708742

23A Taking away

1 How many are left?

a

9 take away 3 leaves  cows.

b

8 take away 3 leaves  coins.

c

10 take away 5 leaves  fish.

2 Draw counters to find the answers. Talk about these.

a 6 take away 4 leaves ☐.

If you put back 4 what happens?

b 10 take away 7 leaves 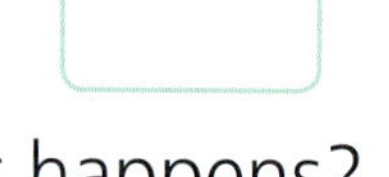.

If you put back 7 what happens?

© PEARSON AUSTRALIA 2024 • *AUSTRALIAN SIGNPOST MATHS F* • ISBN 9780655708742

Taking away

1 Cross off three objects in each row. How many are left?

a

b

c

Discuss what happens when the objects are added back on.

2 Cross off four objects in each row. How many are left?

a
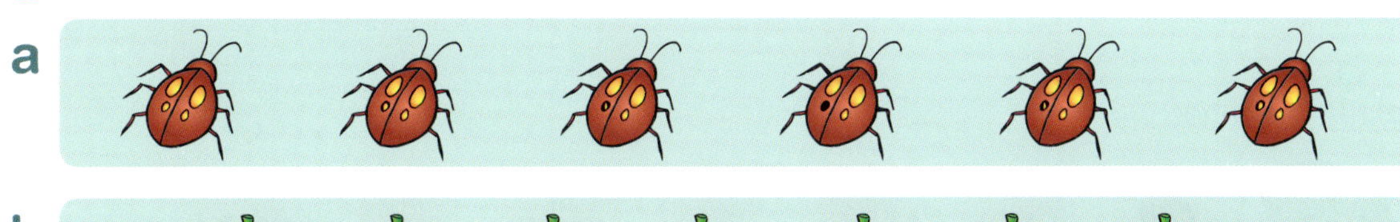

b

c
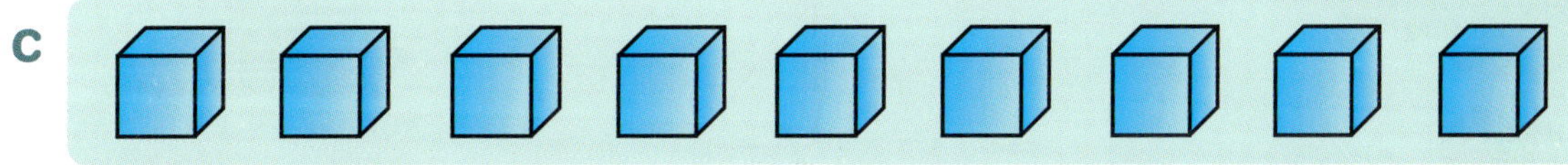

d

Draw and complete.

- 9 fish, take away 5.

How many are left?

- 8 balls, take away 6.

How many are left?

23C Left and right

CONCEPT

The cat is on the **left**.

The dog is on the **right**.

We can make an L with our left hand.

1. Talk about objects that are on your left-hand side and those on your right.
2. Talk about the picture below using the words "left" and "right".
3. Colour the boat on the the left. Colour the cloud on the right.
   Colour the island on the left. Colour the bucket on the right.

4. Circle the left hands.

5. Circle your answer. "I hold my pencil in my **right** / **left** hand."

© PEARSON AUSTRALIA 2024 • *AUSTRALIAN SIGNPOST MATHS F* • ISBN 9780655708742

23D Giving and following directions

1 Trace each path with your finger.
To go to **D** your finger could pass through 2, 6 and 7 or 1, 3 and 7 .

Begin at **Start**. Write the numbers your finger passes through to reach:

A ______ **B** ______ **C** ______ **D** ______

E ______ **F** ______ **G** ______

Start

How would you go to the ice-cream shop **H**? ______

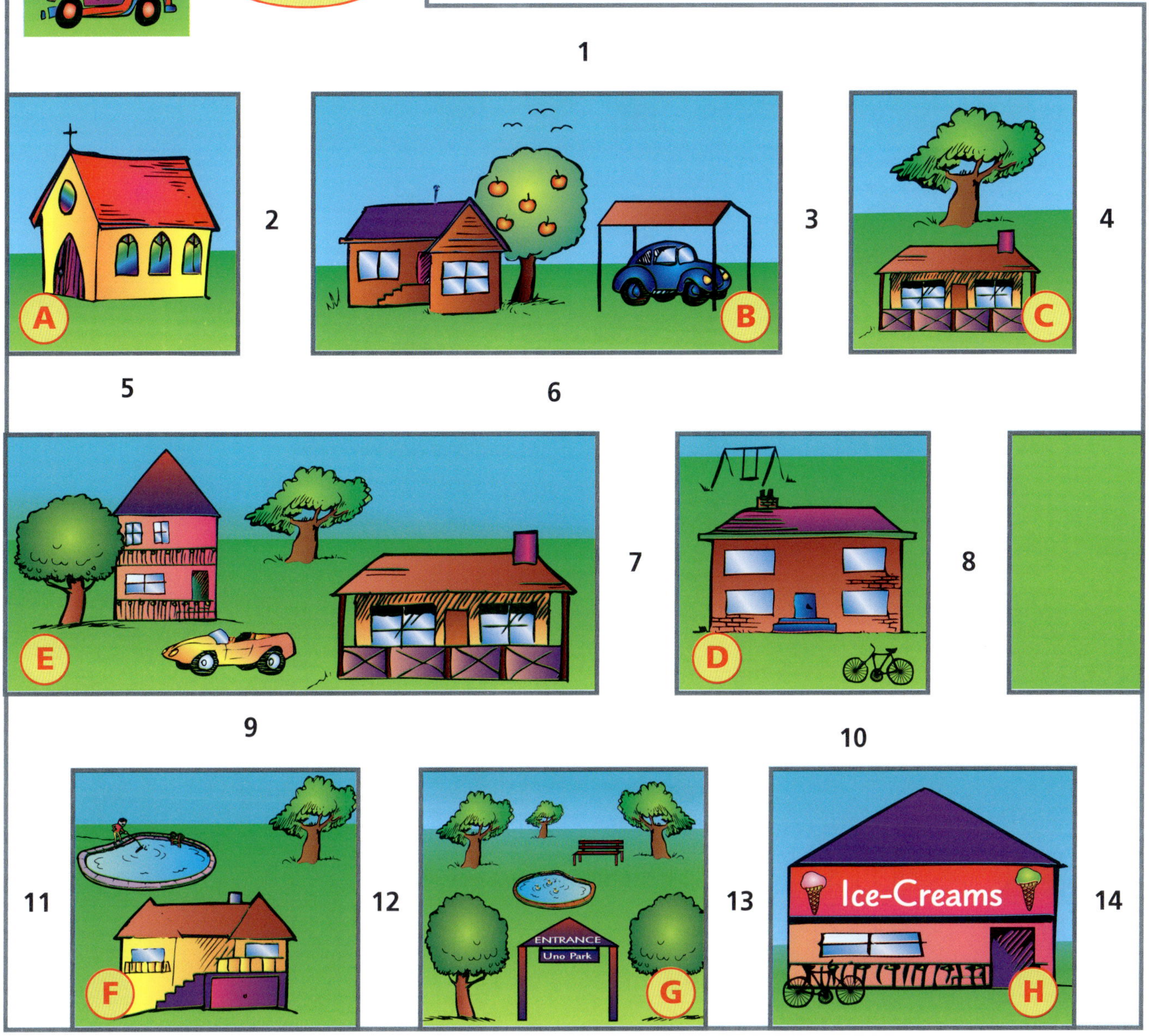

1

A 2 B 3 C 4

5 6

E 7 D 8

9 10

11 F 12 G 13 H 14

ENTRANCE
Uno Park

Ice-Creams

24A Separating a number into parts

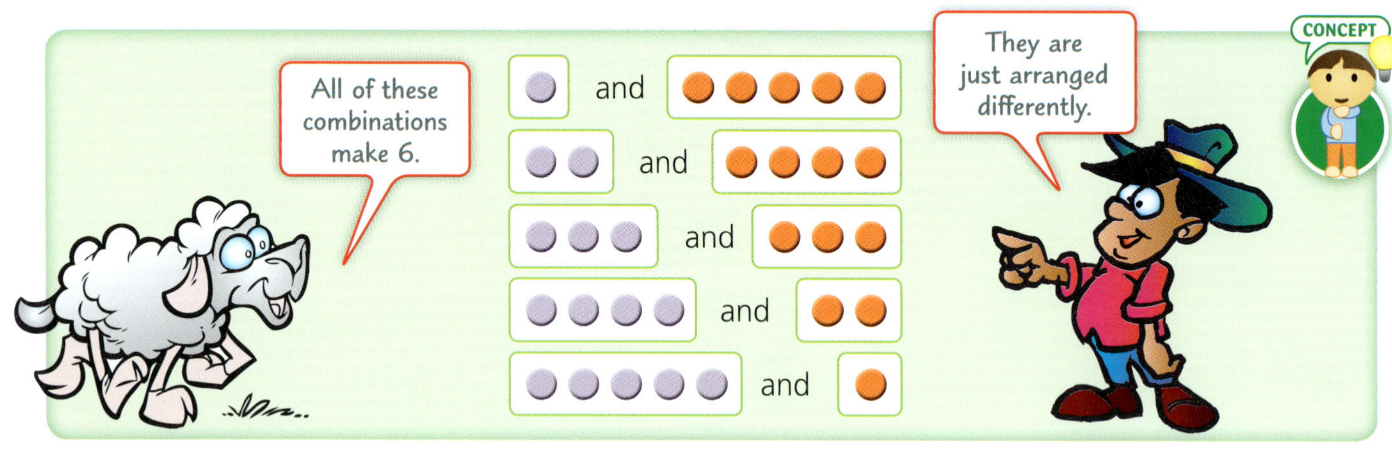

1 Discuss and complete the sentences.

 and    makes ☐

  and    makes ☐

   and   makes ☐

    and  makes ☐

     and  makes ☐

Learn what makes **6** by saying the pairs of numbers in the **6** house.

1 and 5 makes 6 2 and 4 makes 6

3 and 3 makes 6 4 and 2 makes 6

5 and 1 makes 6

3	
1	2
2	1

4	
1	3
2	2
3	1

5	
1	4
2	3
3	2
4	1

6	
1	5
2	4
3	3
4	2
5	1

7	
1	6
2	5
3	4
4	3
5	2
6	1

8	
1	7
2	6
3	5
4	4
5	3
6	2
7	1

© PEARSON AUSTRALIA 2024 • *AUSTRALIAN SIGNPOST MATHS F* • ISBN 9780655708742

24B Separating a number into parts

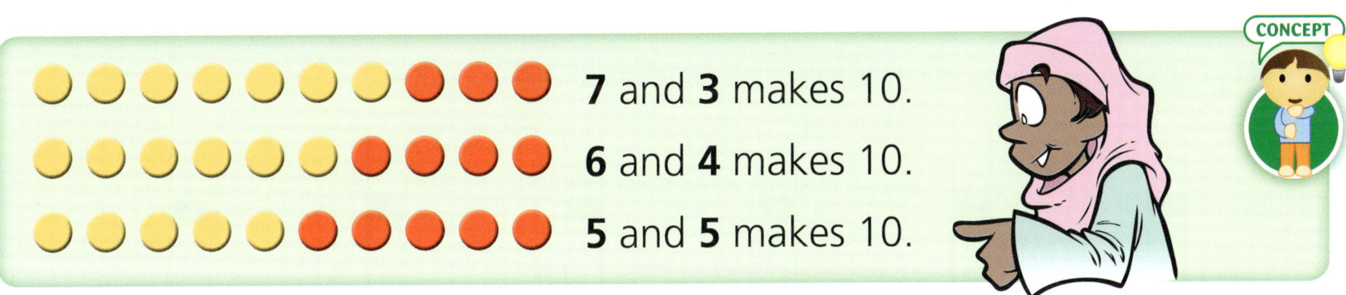

1 Complete the number sentence for each picture.

a 

☐ and ☐ makes 9.

b 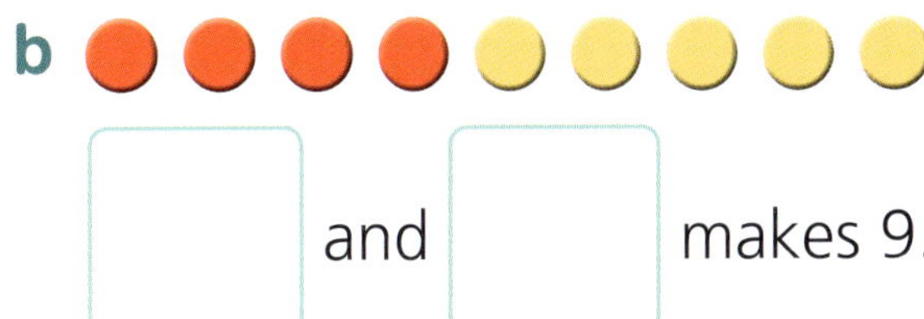

☐ and ☐ makes 9.

c 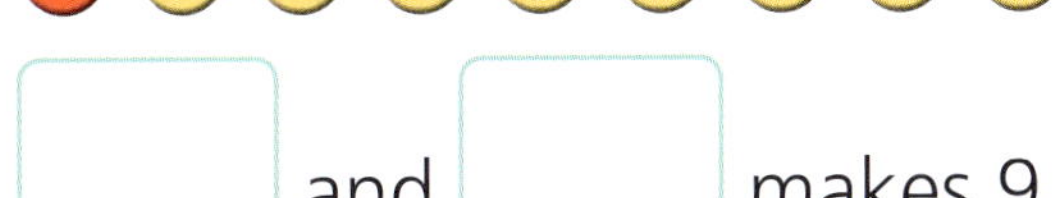

☐ and ☐ makes 9.

d 

☐ and ☐ makes 9.

e 

☐ and ☐ makes 9.

f 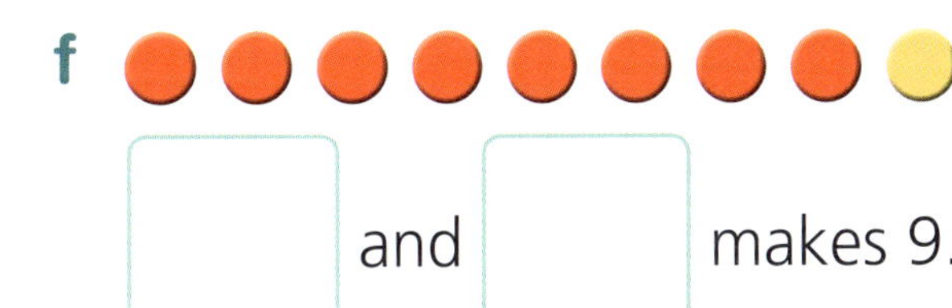

☐ and ☐ makes 9.

g 

☐ and ☐ makes 9.

h 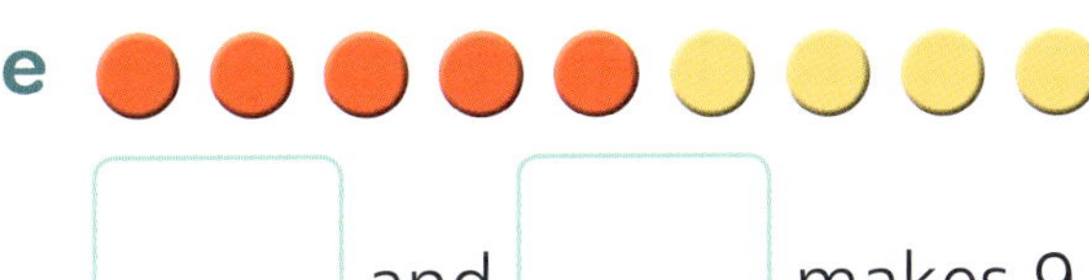

☐ and 0 makes 9.

i 

☐ and ☐ makes 9.

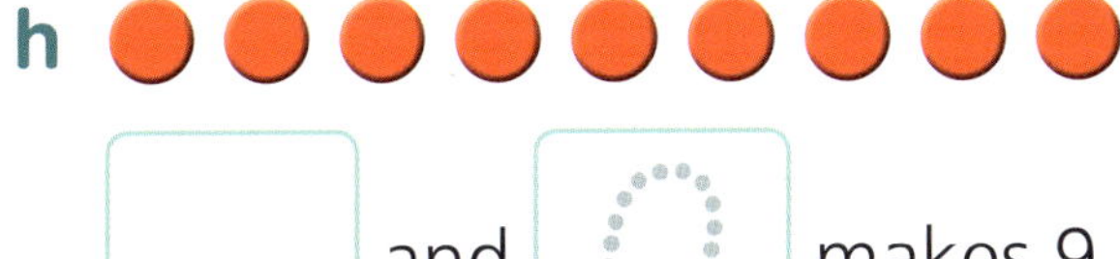

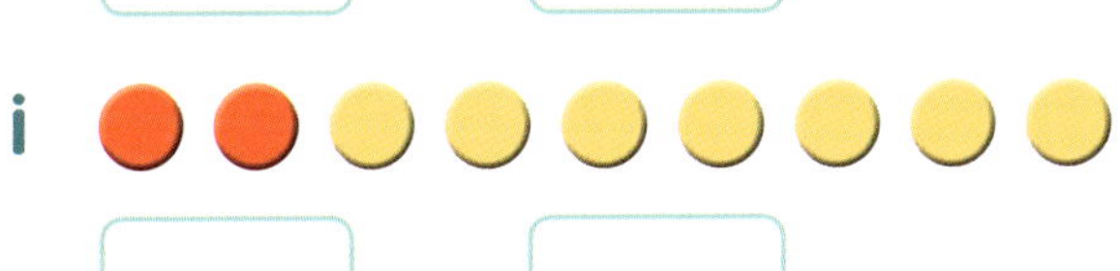

Learn what makes 10.

The friends of 10

1 and 9 makes 10
2 and 8 makes 10
3 and 7 makes 10
4 and 6 makes 10
5 and 5 makes 10
6 and 4 makes 10
7 and 3 makes 10
8 and 2 makes 10
9 and 1 makes 10

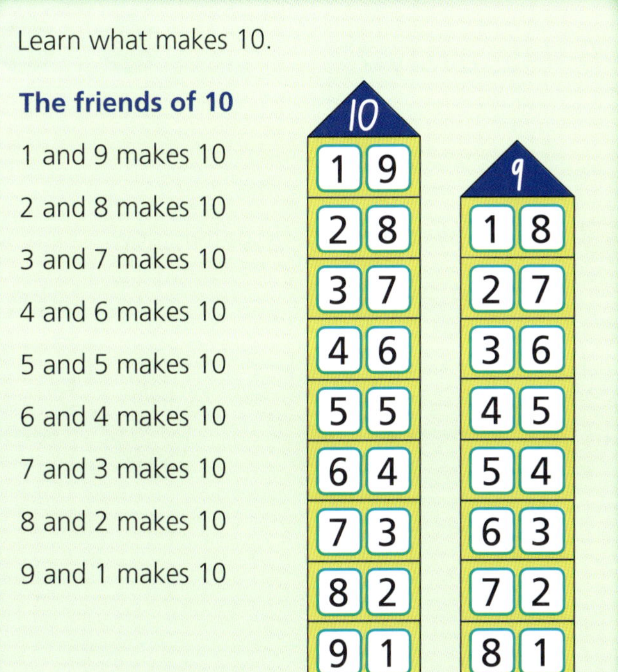

© PEARSON AUSTRALIA 2024

24C Adding on and counting back

 and 

1 Use counters to add by counting on. Put extra counters on the line, one at a time.

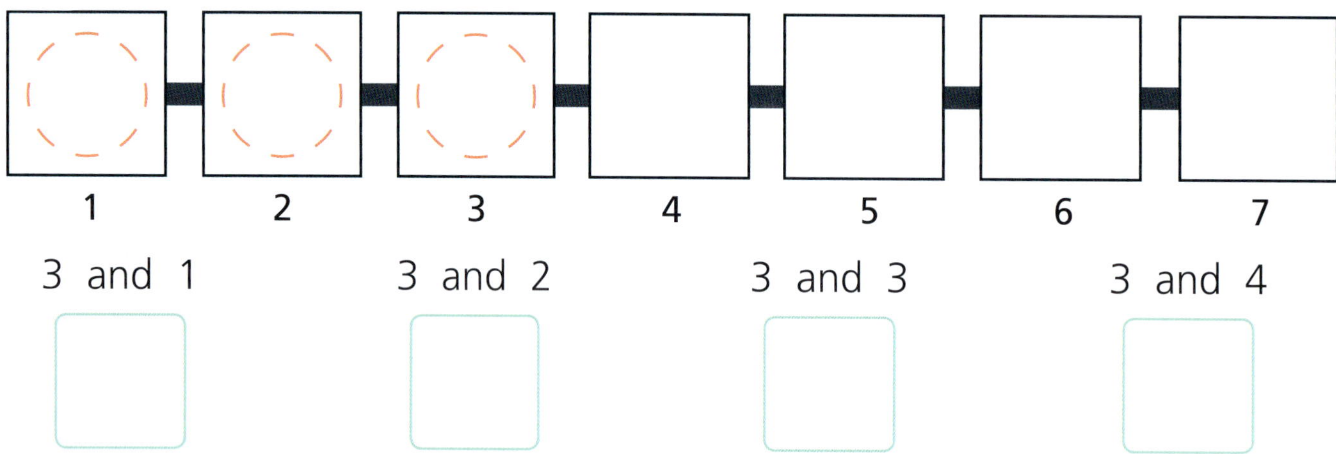

1 2 3 4 5 6 7

3 and 1 | 3 and 2 | 3 and 3 | 3 and 4

2 Add by counting on, lifting one finger at a time.

5 and 2 — 5 … 6, 7

4 and 3 — 4 … 5, 6, 7

5 and 3 — 5 … 6, 7, 8

Use the counting line above to subtract, by taking away one counter at a time.

6 take away 2

3 Subtract by counting back, putting down one finger at a time.

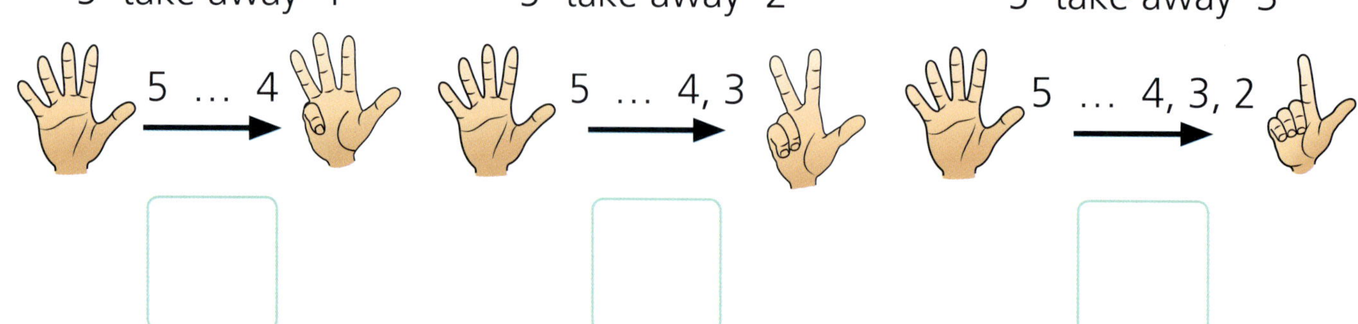

5 take away 1 — 5 … 4

5 take away 2 — 5 … 4, 3

5 take away 3 — 5 … 4, 3, 2

© PEARSON AUSTRALIA 2024 • *AUSTRALIAN SIGNPOST MATHS F* • ISBN 9780655708742

24D 2D shapes

1 Join the dots using straight lines. Say the name of each shape and write the number of sides.

a

☐ sides

b

☐ sides

c

☐ sides

2 Draw 3 different squares.

3 Draw 4 different triangles.

ACTIVITY

Use playdough, craft sticks, paper or string to make these shape pictures. Make a picture of your own.

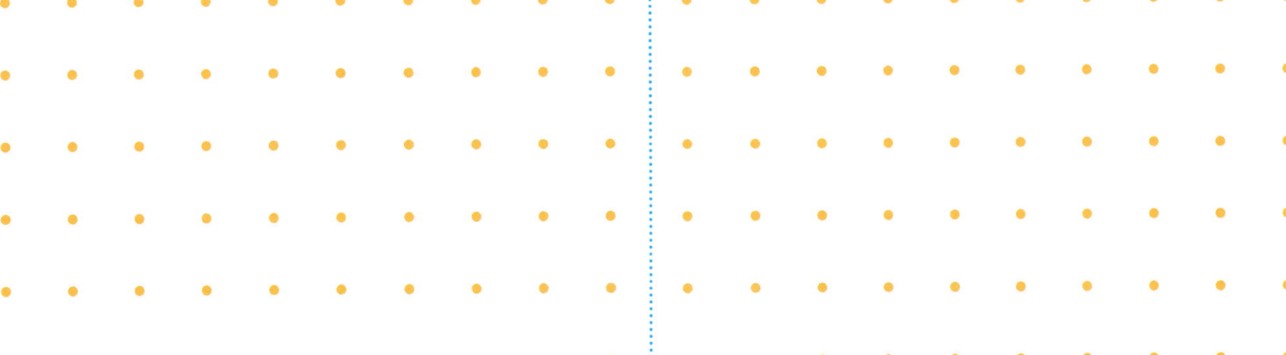

© PEARSON AUSTRALIA 2024 • *AUSTRALIAN SIGNPOST MATHS F* • ISBN 9780655708742

Everyday patterns

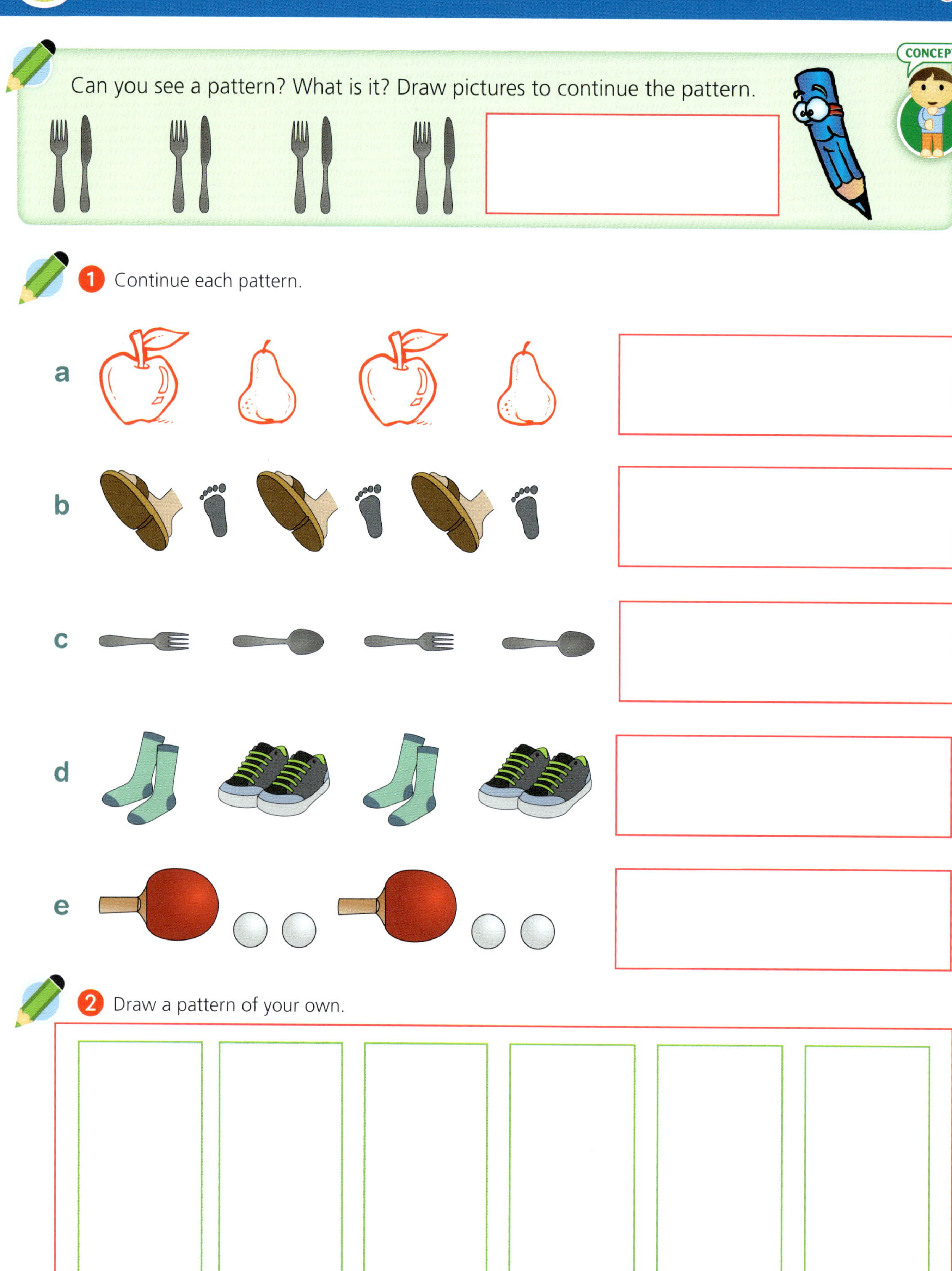

Can you see a pattern? What is it? Draw pictures to continue the pattern.

1 Continue each pattern.

a

b

c

d

e

2 Draw a pattern of your own.

© PEARSON AUSTRALIA 2024 • *AUSTRALIAN SIGNPOST MATHS F* • ISBN 9780655708742

25B Making patterns

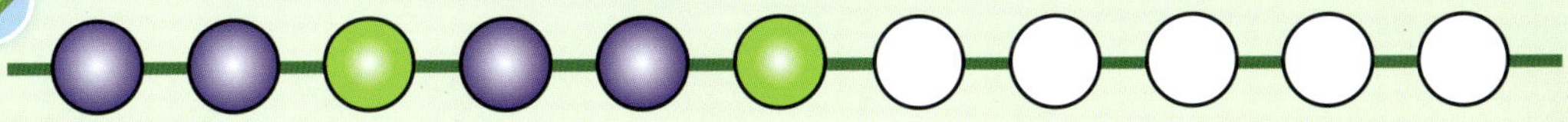

CONCEPT

Can you see a pattern? What is it?

Colour more beads to carry on the pattern.

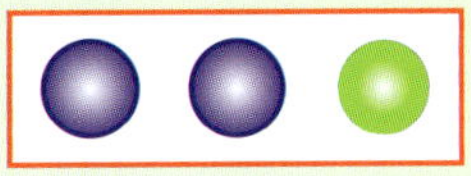

3 beads repeat.

1 Use colours to continue each pattern.

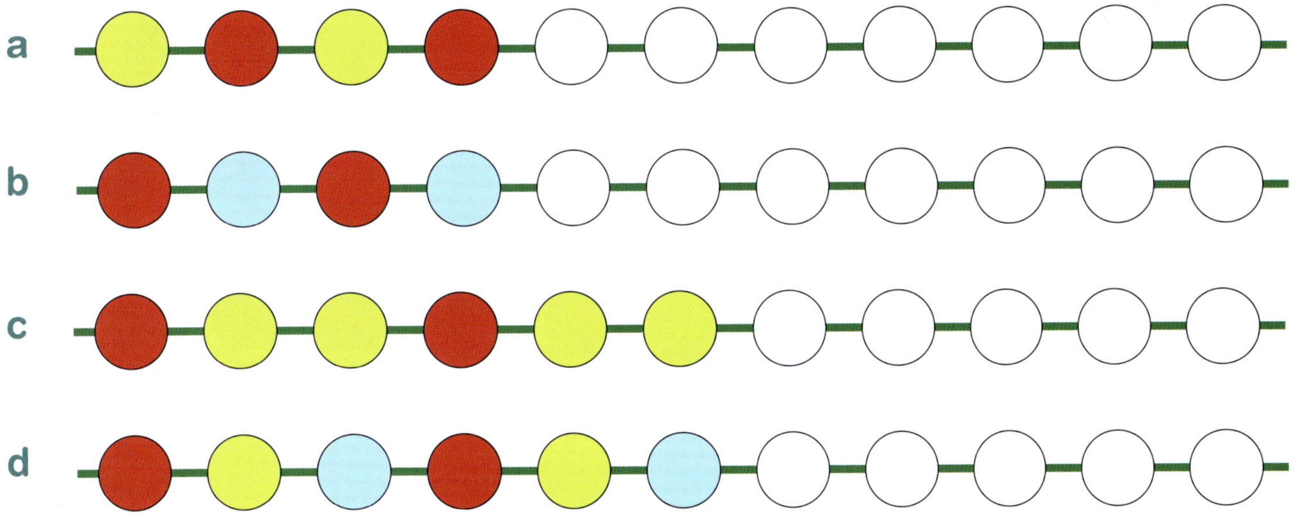

a

b

c

d

2 Continue each pattern.

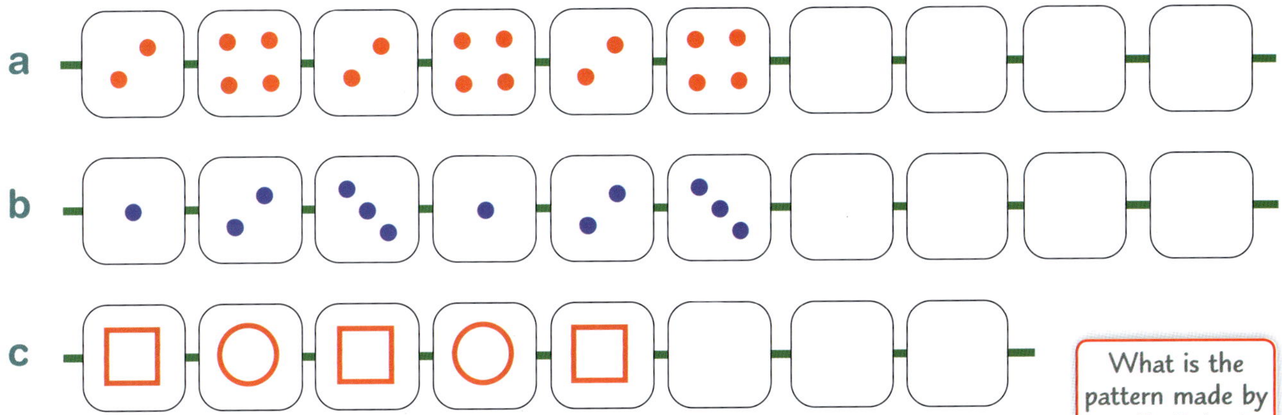

a

b

c

What is the pattern made by traffic lights?

3 Make colour patterns of your own.

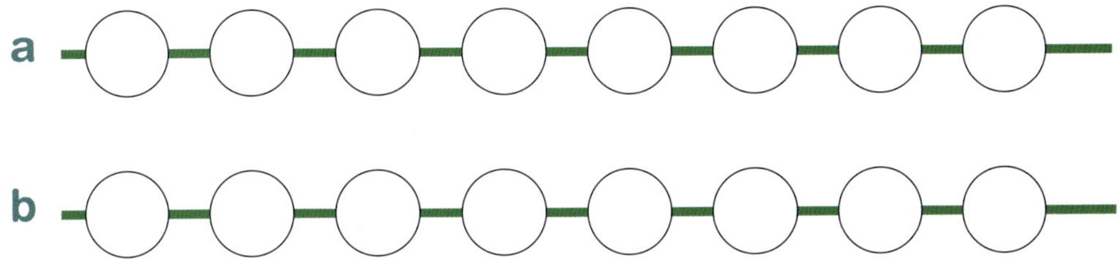

a

b

25C Comparing quantities

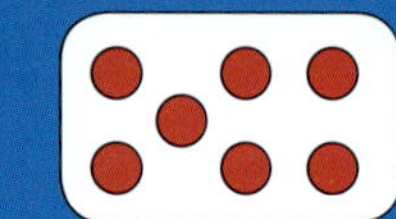
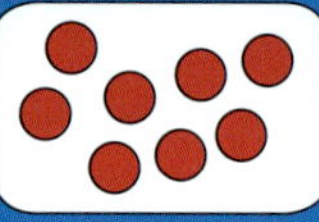

1 **Circle** the picture if we have enough to give our group one each.

☐ children

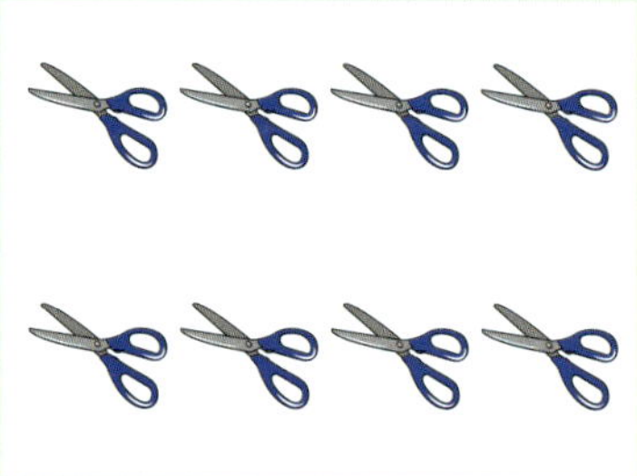

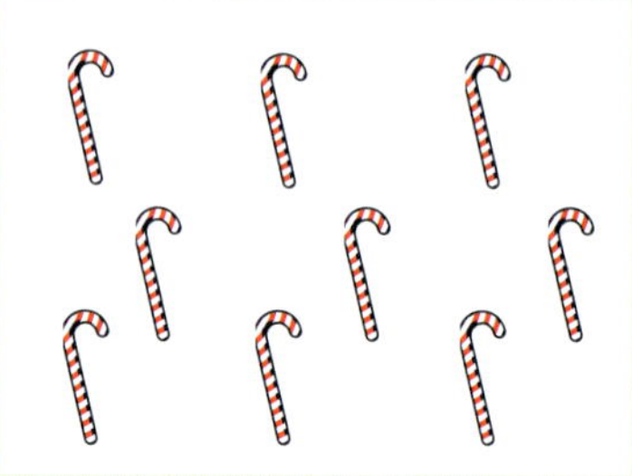

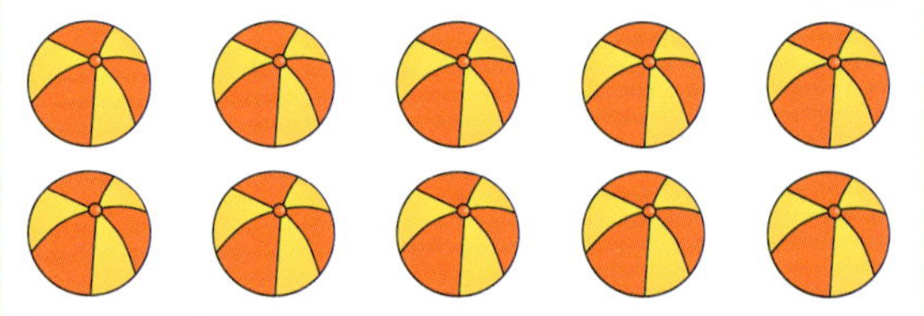

2 **Circle** the item if we have enough money to buy it.

☐ dollars

© PEARSON AUSTRALIA 2024 • *AUSTRALIAN SIGNPOST MATHS F* • ISBN 9780655708742

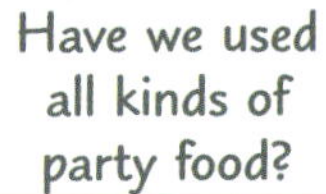

1 Party favourites

a How many liked ? ☐

b How many liked ? ☐

c How many liked ? ☐

d How many liked ? ☐

e Colour the food liked most.

f Circle the food liked least.

g How many more students liked fruit than cakes? ☐

INVESTIGATION

Ask students to put up their hand if they think more than half the class likes Vegemite. Ten students will be chosen and asked if they like Vegemite. Put a tick next to "yes" or "no" for each student.

Do you like Vegemite? Yes or no?									
yes									
no									

26A Groups of equal size

1 Colour the group with the most objects. Talk about which has more / less.

a

b

c

2 Make the groups the same. Talk about equal groups.

a

b

Handful of blocks

Each student takes a handful of blocks. They place their blocks in rows, side by side. Change the number of blocks to make the two groups equal. Explain what you did.

© PEARSON AUSTRALIA 2024 • *AUSTRALIAN SIGNPOST MATHS F* • ISBN 9780655708742

26B Matching equal groups

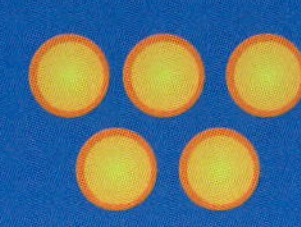

1 Match these groups so that the number on one side is the same as the number on the other side.

Making equal groups

Place 8 counters in a row. Under this row make another row of 8 counters. Make other equal rows of counters to show equal groups.

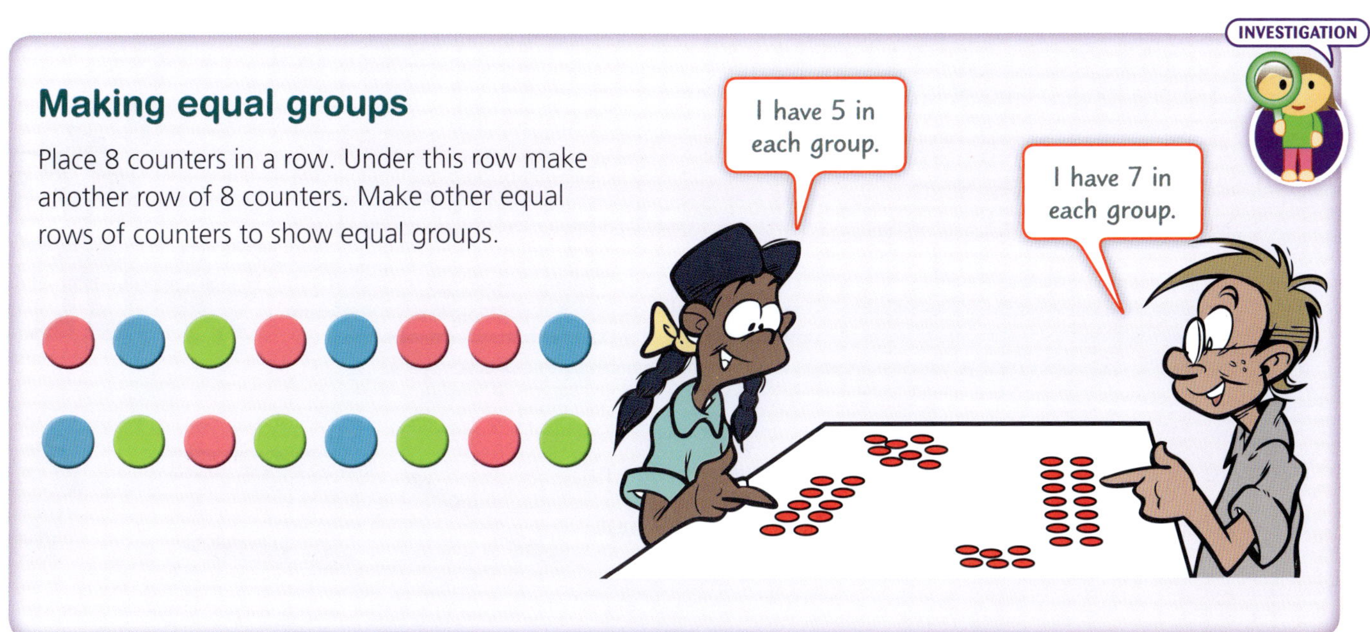

© PEARSON AUSTRALIA 2024 • *AUSTRALIAN SIGNPOST MATHS F* • ISBN 9780655708742

26C Comparing lengths

Direct comparison

CONCEPT

1 Compare the lengths in each part.

a A B

☐ is longer. ☐ is shorter.

Talk about how you knew which was longer.

b C D

☐ is longer. ☐ is shorter.

c E F

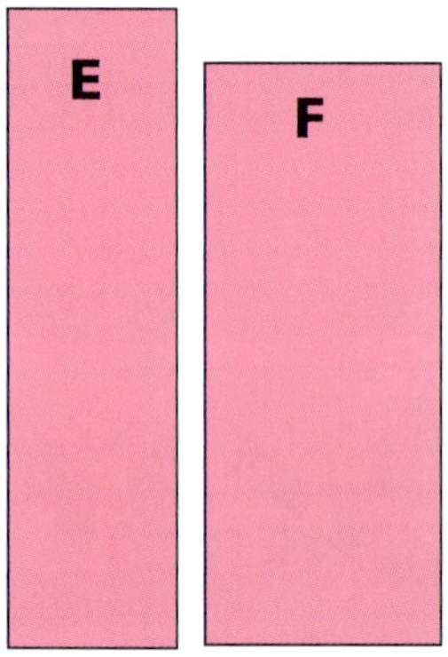

☐ is taller.

☐ is shorter.

2 ✔ Tick the longest line. ✘ Cross the shortest line.

a

b

ACTIVITY

Compare the lengths of three objects of about the same length.

Say which is the longest and tell someone how you found out.

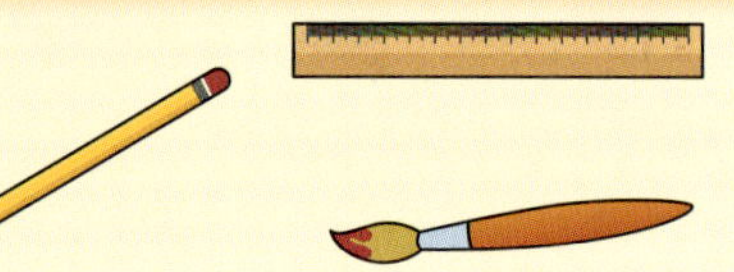

© PEARSON AUSTRALIA 2024 • *AUSTRALIAN SIGNPOST MATHS F* • ISBN 9780655708742

Data displays

1 Use the pictures to complete the graph. Discuss possible responses.

Class pets

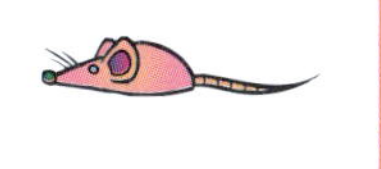

fish	mice	birds

a How many fish? ☐

b How many mice? ☐

c How many birds? ☐

d How many pets altogether? ☐

INVESTIGATION

Collecting information

10 students will be chosen to say if they have a brother. Put a tick next to "yes" or "no" for each student. Discuss the possible results.

Do you have a brother? Yes or no?										
yes										
no										

© PEARSON AUSTRALIA 2024 • *AUSTRALIAN SIGNPOST MATHS F* • ISBN 9780655708742

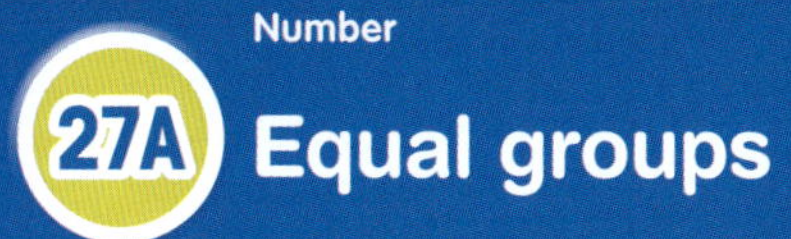

27A Equal groups

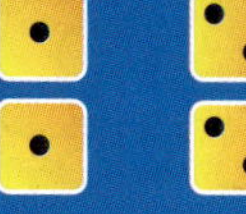

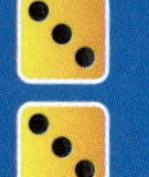

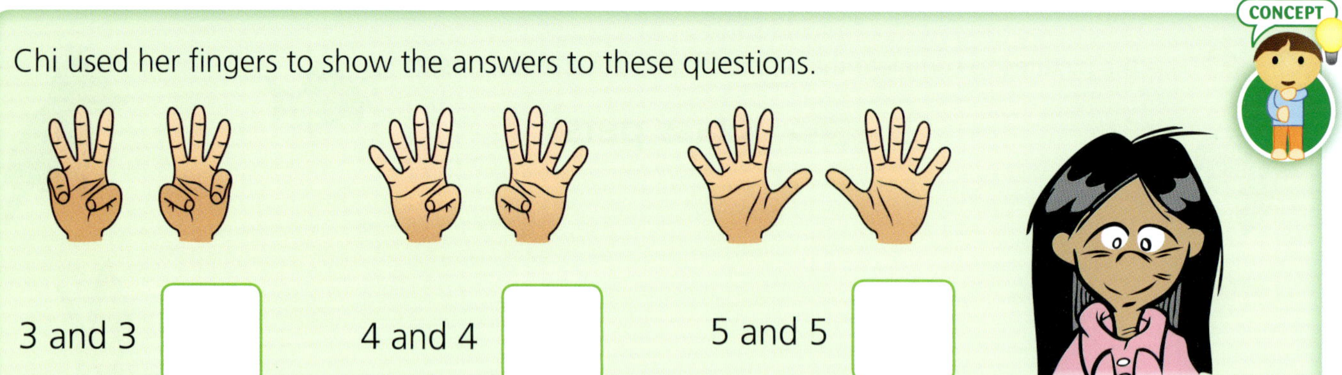

Chi used her fingers to show the answers to these questions.

3 and 3 ☐ 4 and 4 ☐ 5 and 5 ☐

1 Count to find the number of blocks in:

a 2 groups of 4

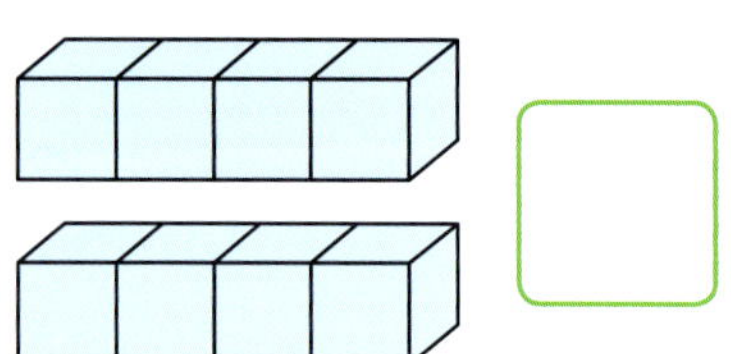

b 2 groups of 2

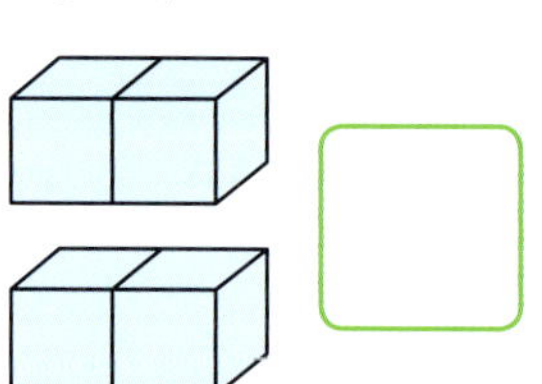

c 2 groups of 3

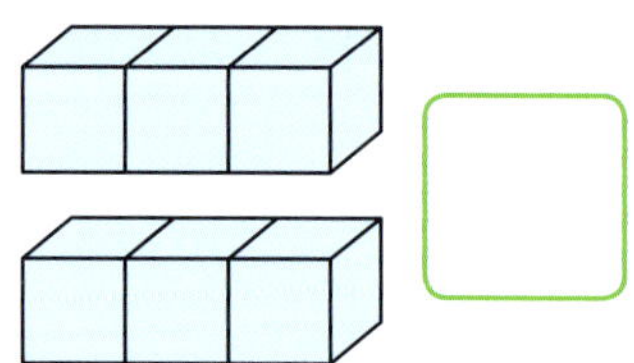

d 2 groups of 6

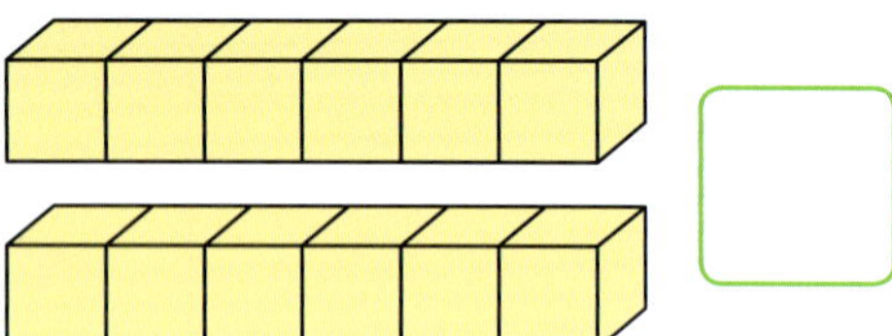

e 2 groups of 5

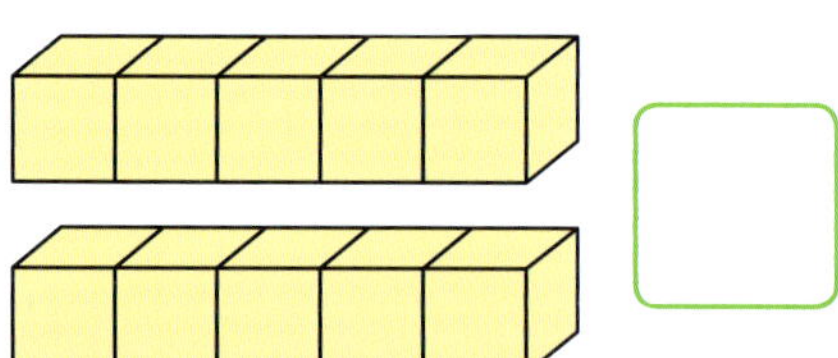

2 Count to find the number of blocks in:

a 3 groups of 4

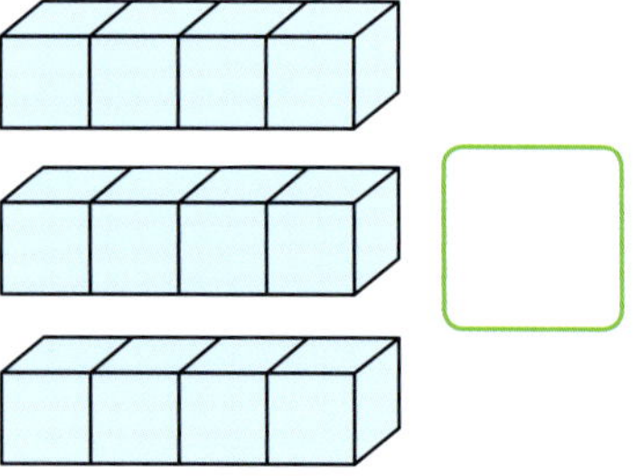

b 3 groups of 2

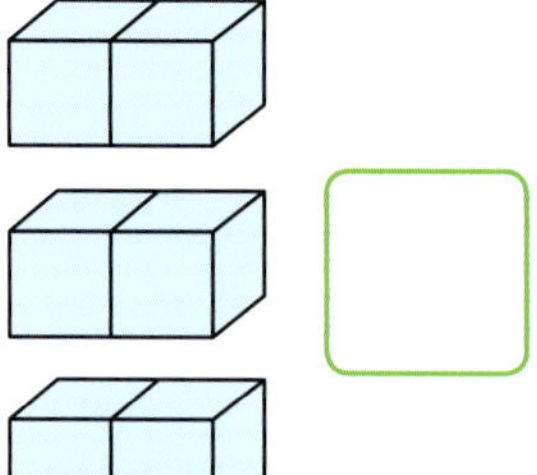

c 3 groups of 3

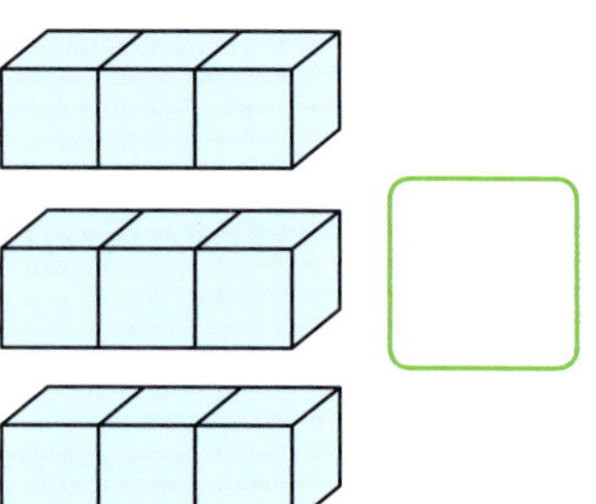

Challenge: Learn the answers to 3 and 3, 4 and 4, 5 and 5, 6 and 6, 7 and 7, 8 and 8.

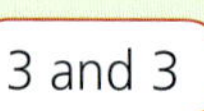

© PEARSON AUSTRALIA 2024 • *AUSTRALIAN SIGNPOST MATHS F* • ISBN 9780655708742

27B Using grouping to share

CONCEPT

How many children can be given 3 counters?

15 counters

I have circled groups of 3.

There are 5 groups of 3 in 15 counters.

5 children can be given 3 counters each.

Use counters to model each question.

1 How many groups are there? **Circle** the groups.

a 12 marbles, 4 in each group. ☐ groups

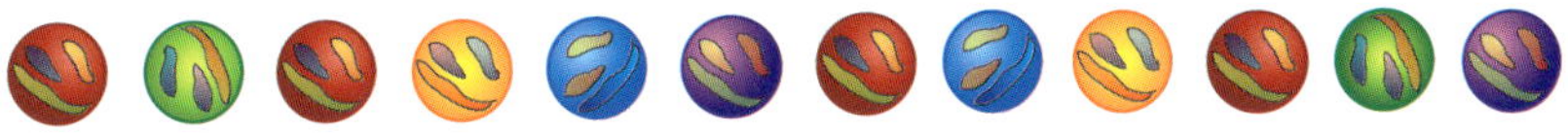

b 8 bottles, 2 in each group. ☐ groups

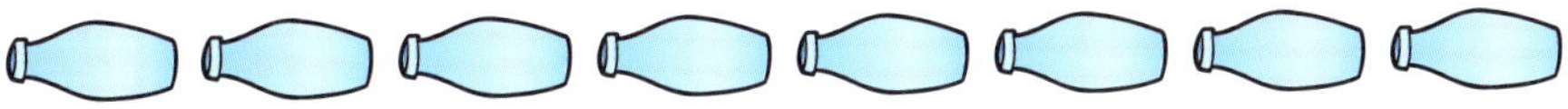

c 15 counters, 5 in each group. ☐ groups

2 Here we have groups of 3 toys.

a How many groups of 3 are there altogether? ☐ groups

b How many toys are in 4 groups of 3 toys? ☐

c How many toys are in 3 groups of 3 toys? ☐

3 Use these groups to find how many counters are in:

a 5 groups of 2 ☐

b 8 groups of 2 ☐

© PEARSON AUSTRALIA 2024 • *AUSTRALIAN SIGNPOST MATHS F* • ISBN 9780655708742

27C Telling the time

Clockwise: hands turn to the right.

CONCEPT

This is 4 o'clock.

This also shows 4 o'clock.

1 Write the time.

☐ o'clock

☐ o'clock

☐ o'clock

☐ o'clock

☐ o'clock

☐ o'clock

2 Draw something you might do at each time.

© PEARSON AUSTRALIA 2024 • *AUSTRALIAN SIGNPOST MATHS F* • ISBN 9780655708742

27D Using o'clock

1 Trace the missing words.

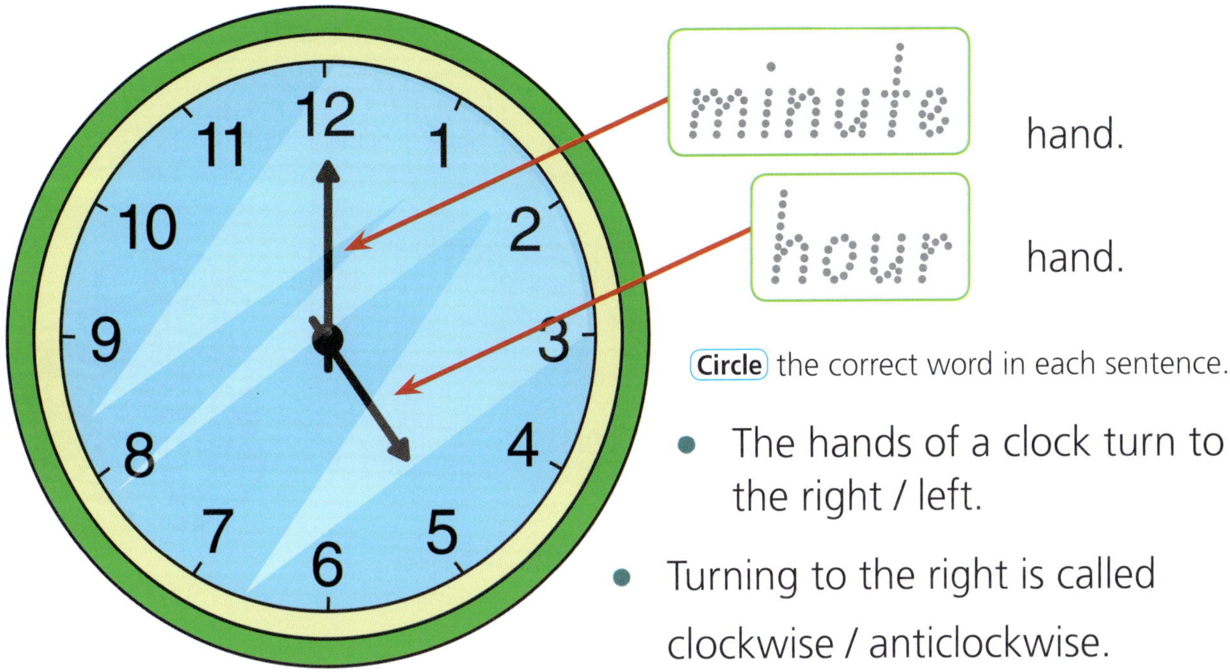

Circle the correct word in each sentence.

- The hands of a clock turn to the right / left.
- Turning to the right is called clockwise / anticlockwise.

2 Write the time.

The little hand shows the hour.

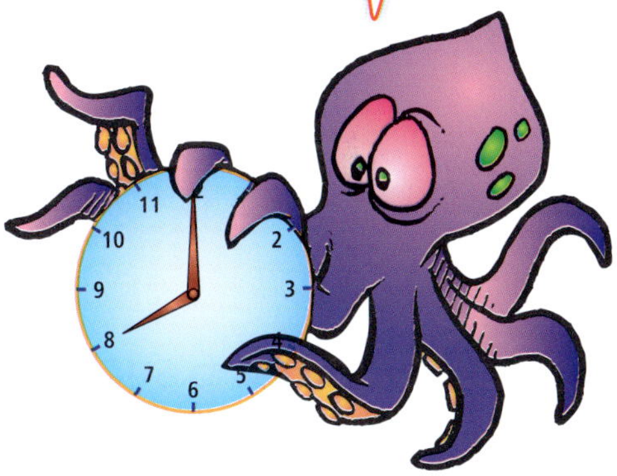

a 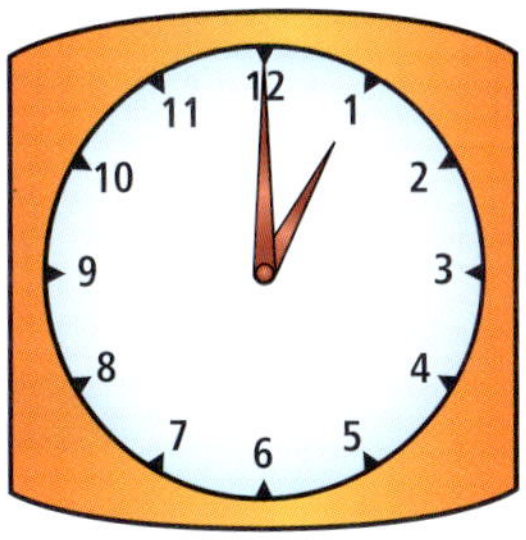 ☐ o'clock

b ☐ o'clock

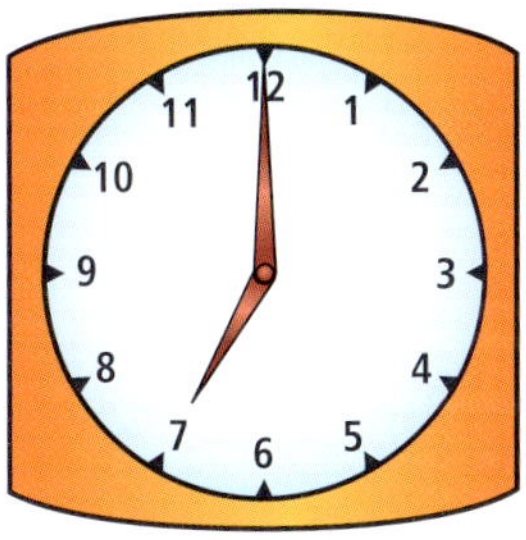

c ☐ o'clock

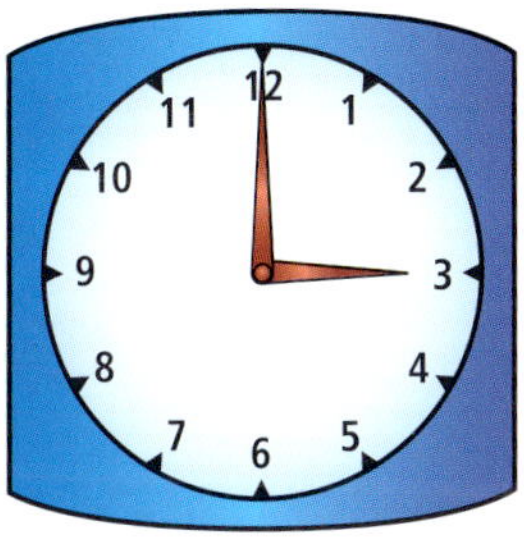

d ☐ o'clock

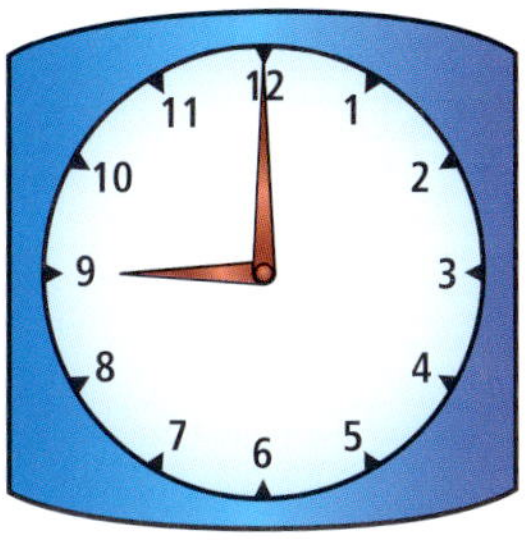

e ☐ o'clock

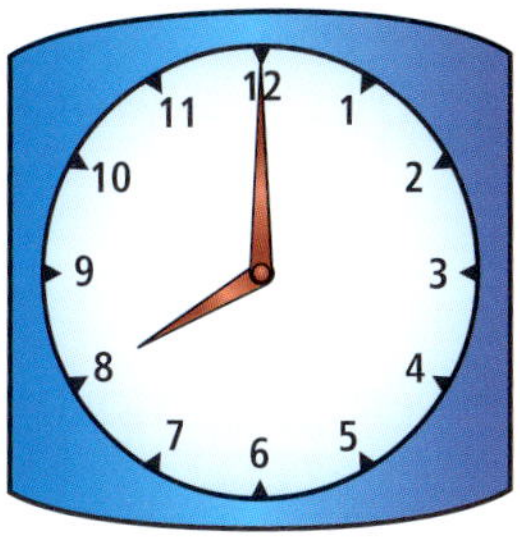

28A How many more?

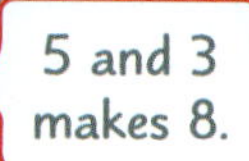

CONCEPT

I have 3 stickers.

I need 5 to fill my chart.

I need 2 more stickers.

5 is 3 and 2 more.

1 **a** Jo has 2 stickers.
She needs 4 altogether.

She needs ☐ more stickers.

4 is 2 and ☐ more.

b Ali has 4 stickers.
He needs 5 altogether.

He needs ☐ more sticker.

5 is 4 and ☐ more.

c Sam has 6 stickers.
She needs 8 altogether.

She needs ☐ more stickers.

8 is 6 and ☐ more.

ACTIVITY

- Make a class sticker chart.
- Talk about how many more stickers are needed to fill the chart if we had one sticker? … two stickers? and so on.

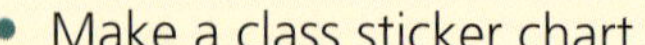

© PEARSON AUSTRALIA 2024 • *AUSTRALIAN SIGNPOST MATHS F* • ISBN 9780655708742

CONCEPT

Peter used a pile of counters to make 3 equal groups.

Count the counters. How many altogether?

1 a

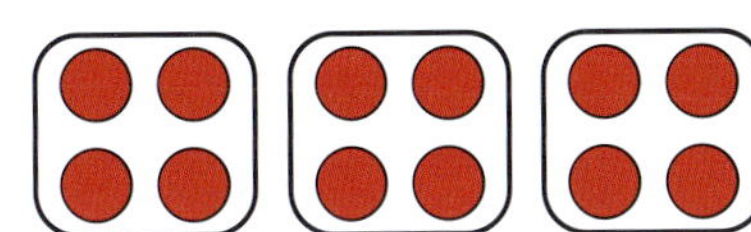

How many counters are in 3 groups of 4?

b

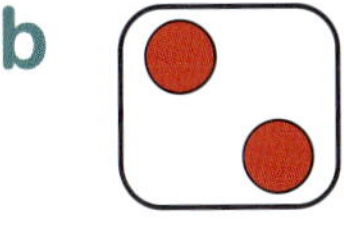

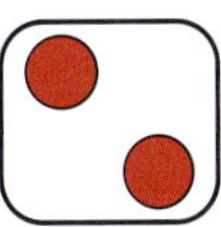

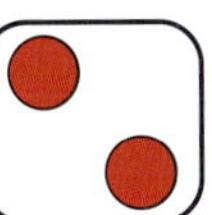

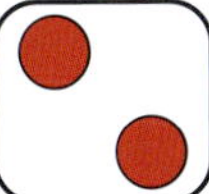

How many counters are in 4 groups of 2?

2 Count how many blocks are in:

a

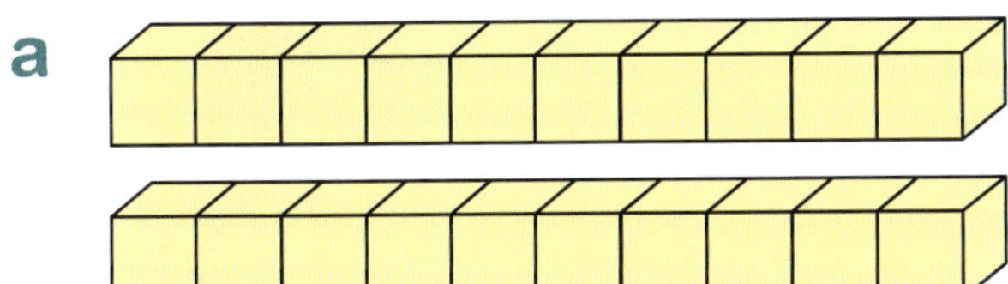

2 groups of 10

b

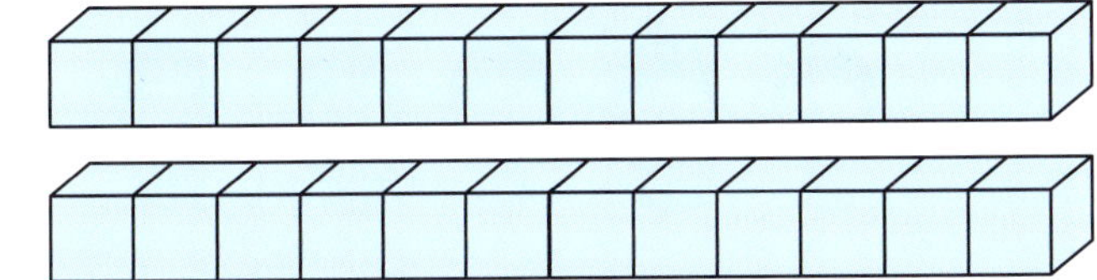

2 groups of 12

c

3 groups of 3

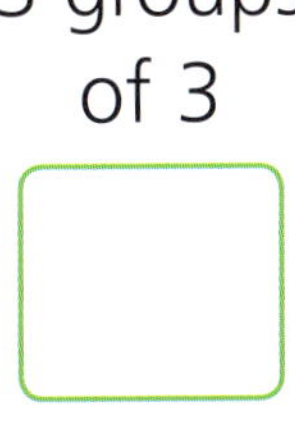

d

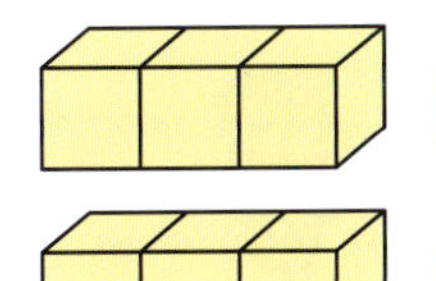

4 groups of 3

ACTIVITY

- Make equal groups of counters, count them, then write what you found.

3 groups of 6

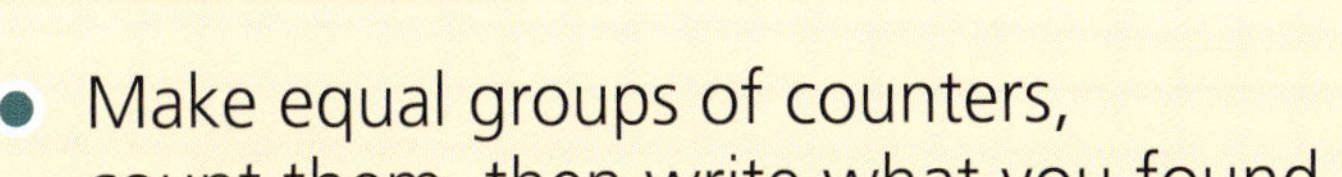

© PEARSON AUSTRALIA 2024 • *AUSTRALIAN SIGNPOST MATHS F* • ISBN 9780655708742

28C Patterns using sounds and actions

1 Talk about these sound patterns.

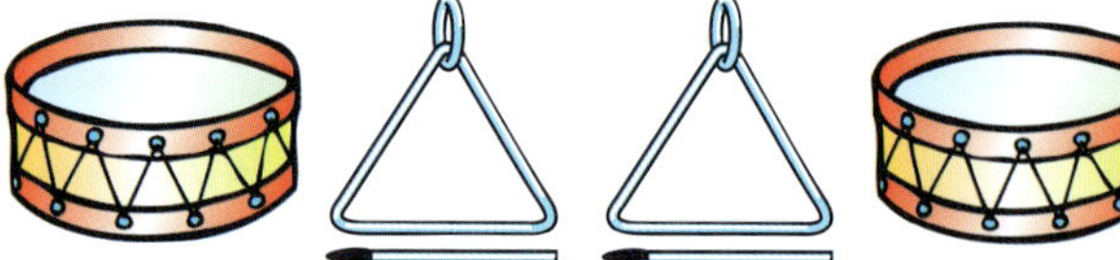 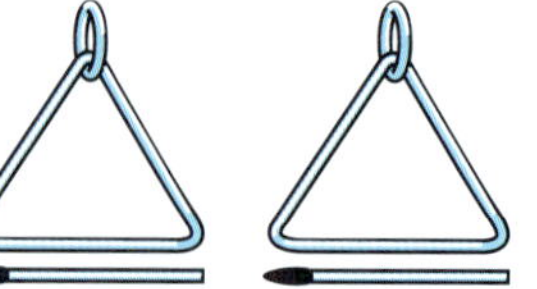

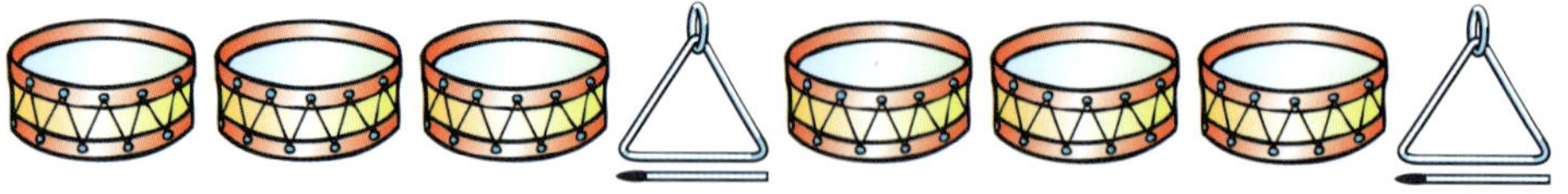

Talk about patterns made by the sound of waves, clocks, telephones, taps and police sirens.

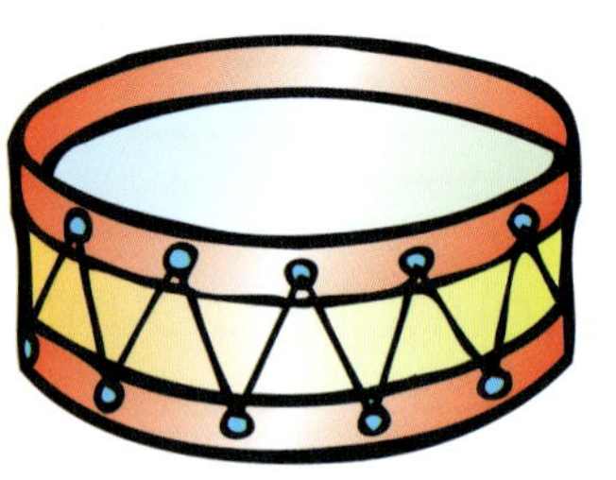

2 Say the numbers and letters to make sound patterns.

1	2	1	2	1	2	1	2	1
soft	loud	soft	loud	soft	loud	soft	loud	soft
a	b	a	b	a	b	a	b	a

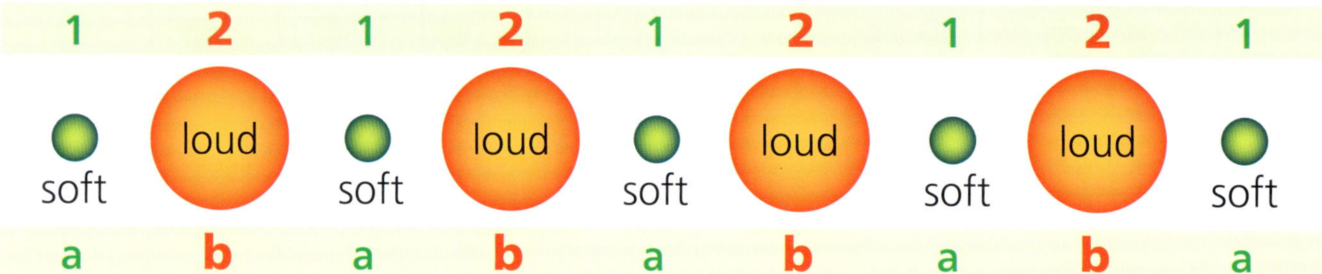

Make sound patterns of your own.

whoosh ... splat ... whoosh ... splat

ding ... ding ... bang ... ding ... ding ... bang

3 Talk about these action patterns. Act them out with friends.

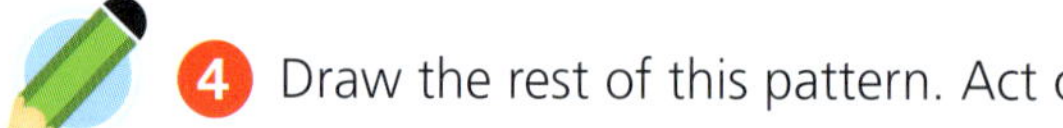

4 Draw the rest of this pattern. Act out the pattern.

Make action patterns.

clap ... clap ... stomp ... clap ... clap ... stomp

stand ... lift your hands ... sit ... stand ... lift your hands ... sit

© PEARSON AUSTRALIA 2024 • *AUSTRALIAN SIGNPOST MATHS F* • ISBN 9780655708742

28D Using data displays

1 Make a display to show the number of boys and girls in your class. Colour a square for each student.

girls

There are ☐ girls.

boys

There are ☐ boys.

a How many students are there altogether? ☐

b There are more ☐ than ☐.

ACTIVITY

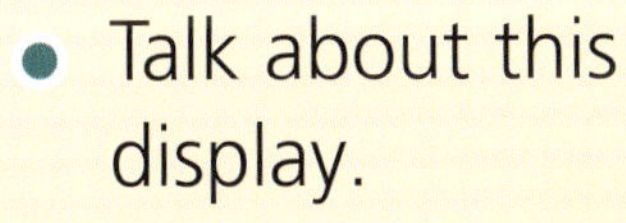

- Talk about this display.
- Write a name for this data display.

- Ask a friend a question about the display.

© PEARSON AUSTRALIA 2024 • *AUSTRALIAN SIGNPOST MATHS F* • ISBN 9780655708742

29A Sharing

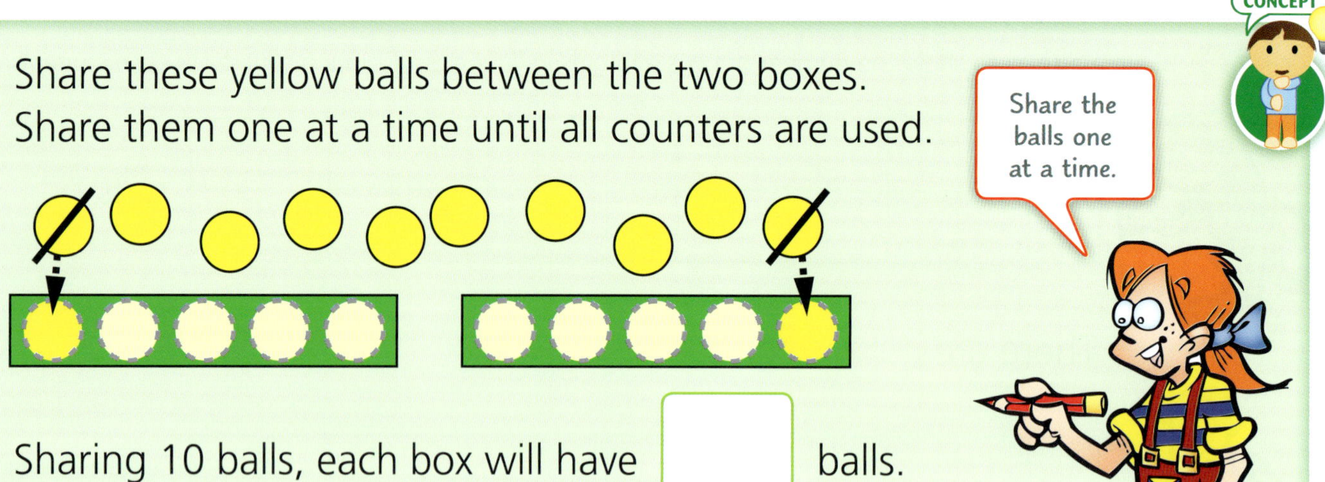

Sharing 10 balls, each box will have ☐ balls.

1 Share these balls into 2 groups. Draw each ball as it is shared.

How many are in each share?

a 6 balls are shared. ☐

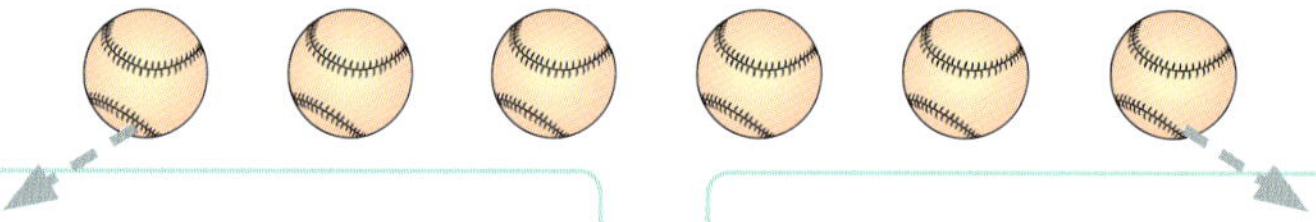

b 4 balls are shared. ☐

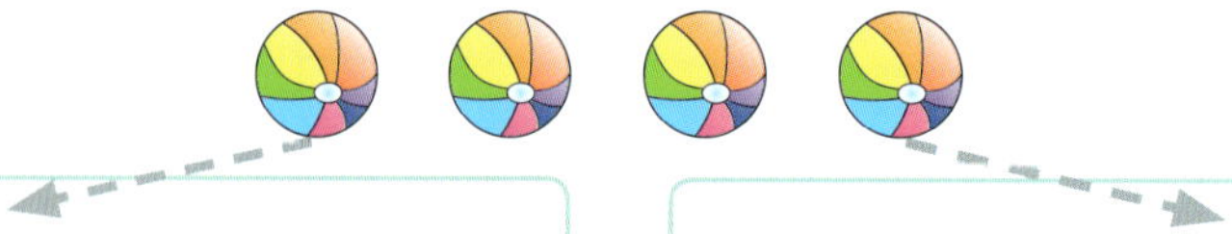

c 8 balls are shared. ☐

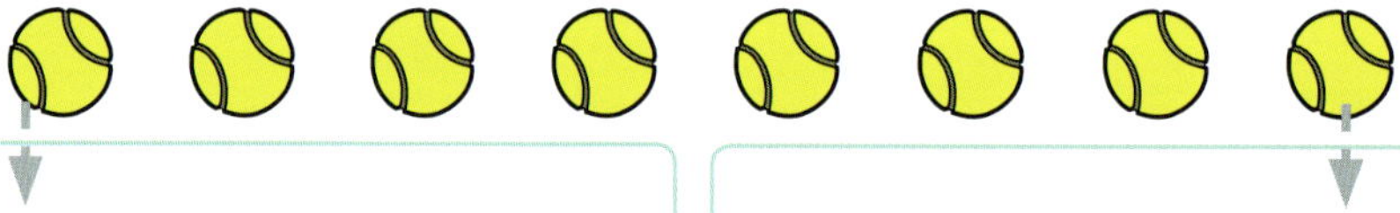

d 10 balls are shared. ☐

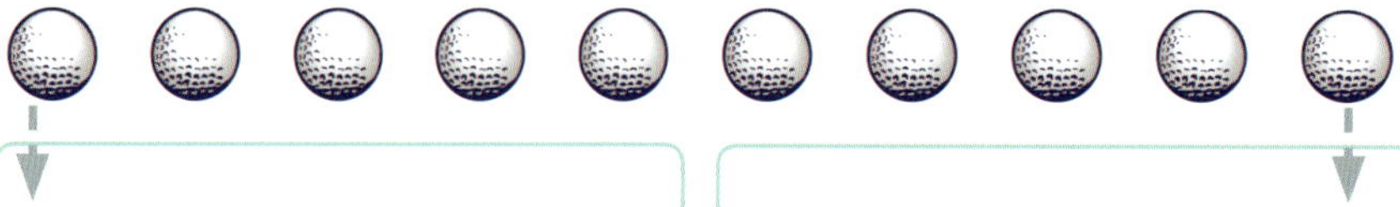

Take turns to share counters with a friend.

Take a pile of counters and share them one at a time.

If there is a counter left over, put it aside.

© PEARSON AUSTRALIA 2024 • *AUSTRALIAN SIGNPOST MATHS F* • ISBN 9780655708742

Sharing

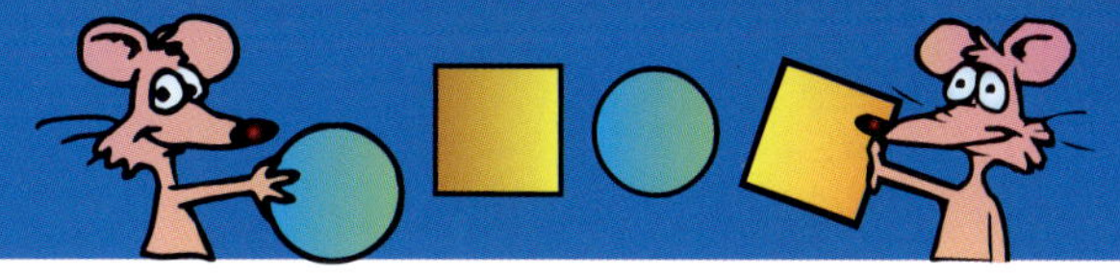

ACTIVITY

1 Use these boxes to share counters between 2 people.

a Start with 8 counters. Share these between 2 people.

How many is each given?

In a fair share, each person gets the same number of objects.

b Start with 12 counters. Share these between 2 people.

How many is each given?

How many have been shared?

2 Use these boxes to share counters among 3 people.

a Start with 15 counters. Share these among 3 people.

How many is each given?

b Start with 12 counters. Share these among 3 people.

How many is each given?

How many have been shared?

© PEARSON AUSTRALIA 2024 • *AUSTRALIAN SIGNPOST MATHS F* • ISBN 9780655708742

29C Comparing capacities

1 Circle the correct containers. Explain why you chose those containers.

2 Colour a container that holds more than the glass. ✔ Tick a container that holds less than the glass. Circle the container that holds about the same as the glass.

3 Each container was filled and then tipped into the same empty jar. Discuss.

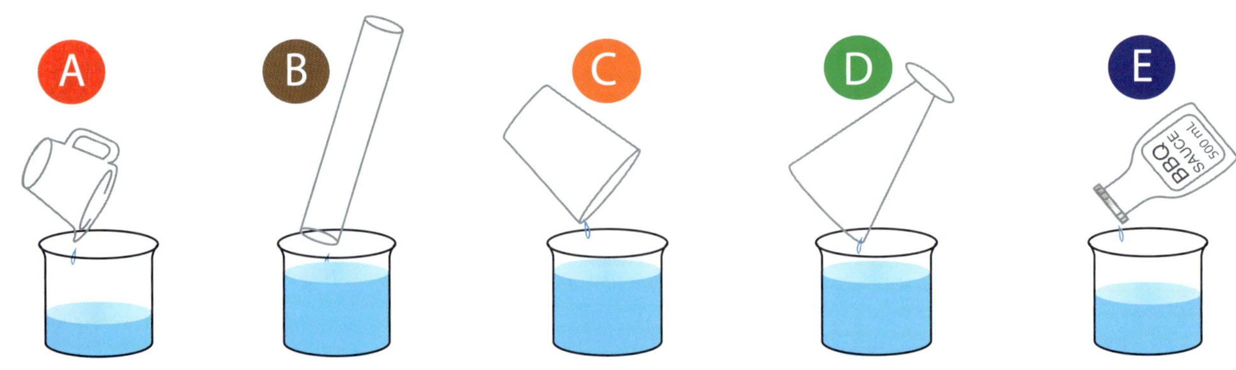

Can containers of different shapes hold the same amount?

Which jar is about half full?

© PEARSON AUSTRALIA 2024 • *AUSTRALIAN SIGNPOST MATHS F* • ISBN 9780655708742

29D Comparing objects

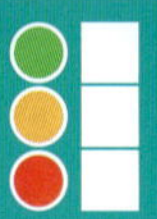

1

Which student is the:

a tallest?  b shortest?  c lightest? 

2

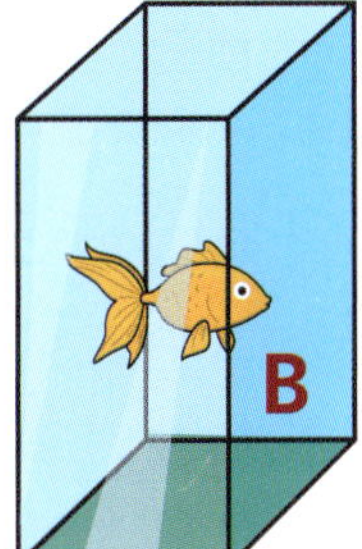

Which fish tank:

a is tallest?  b is shortest?  c holds most? 

ACTIVITY

Order your school bag (**A**), lunch box (**B**), pencil case (**C**) and drink bottle (**D**):

a tallest to shortest

b heaviest to lightest

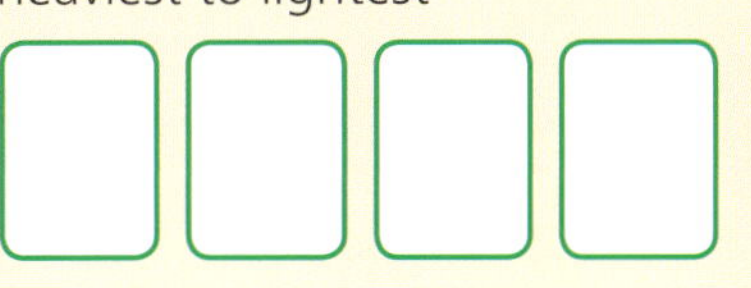

c holds most to holds least

d easiest to use to hardest to use

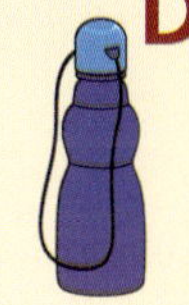

30A Sharing in other ways

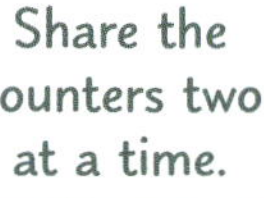

Share these yellow counters between the two boxes.
Share them two at a time until all counters are used.

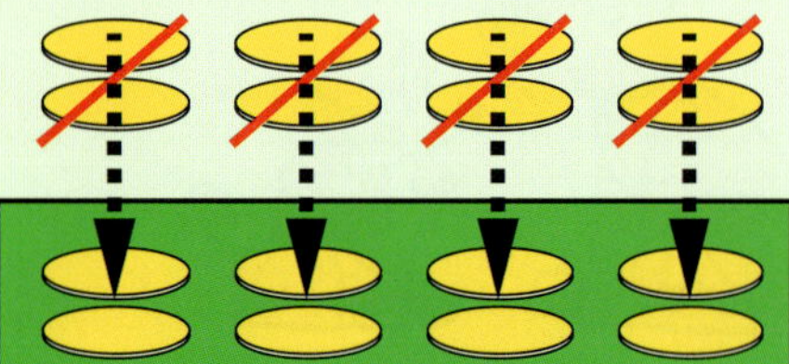
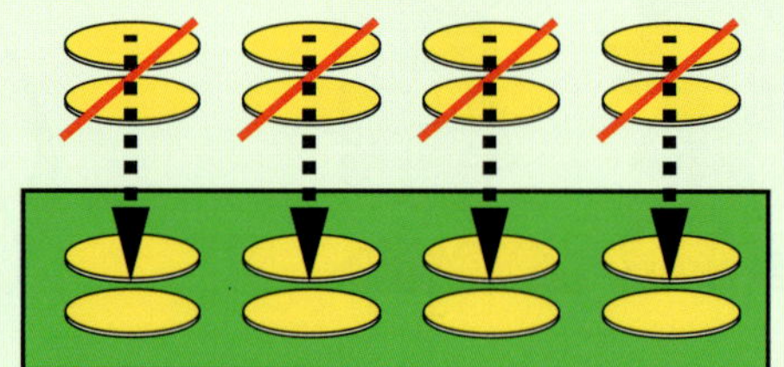

Sharing 16 counters, each box will have  counters.

1 Share two at a time into 2 groups. Draw them as they are shared.

How many are in each share?

a

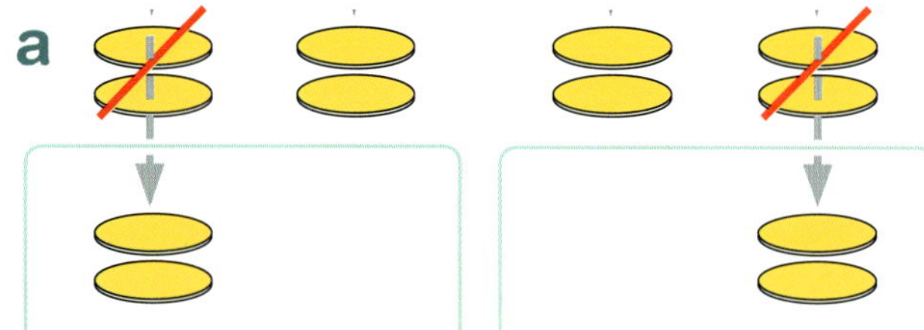

8 counters are shared. ☐

b

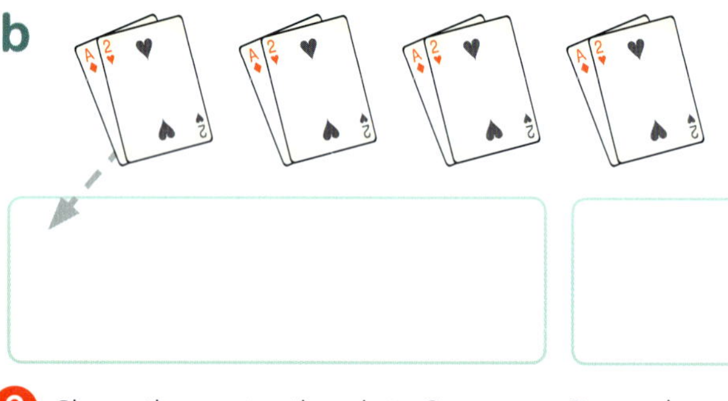

12 cards are shared. ☐

2 Share three at a time into 2 groups. Draw them as they are shared.

a

18 cards are shared. 

Make two groups of counters. Line them up in two rows, one row above the other.
Move counters from one group to the other to make two fair shares. Discuss.

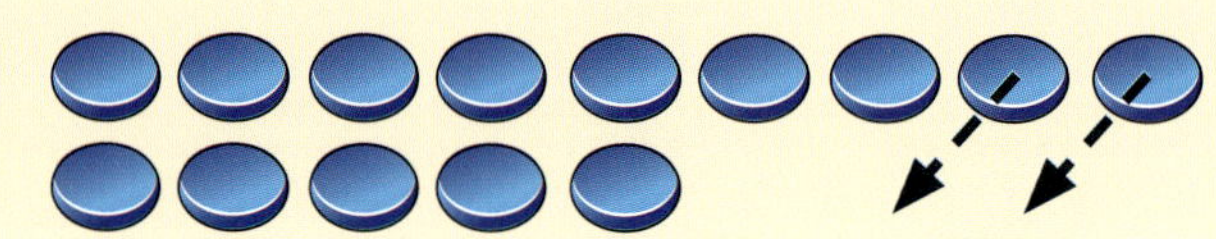

© PEARSON AUSTRALIA 2024 • *AUSTRALIAN SIGNPOST MATHS F* • ISBN 9780655708742

Sharing among 3 or more

Share these red balls among the three boxes.

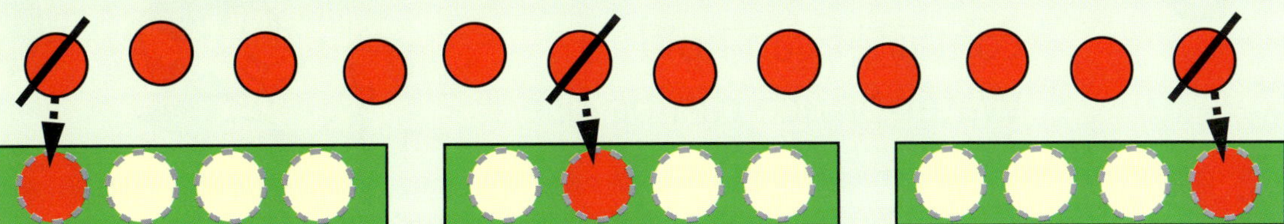

Sharing 12 balls among 3 boxes, each box will have ☐ balls.

1 Share these balls into 3 groups. Draw each ball as it is shared.

a

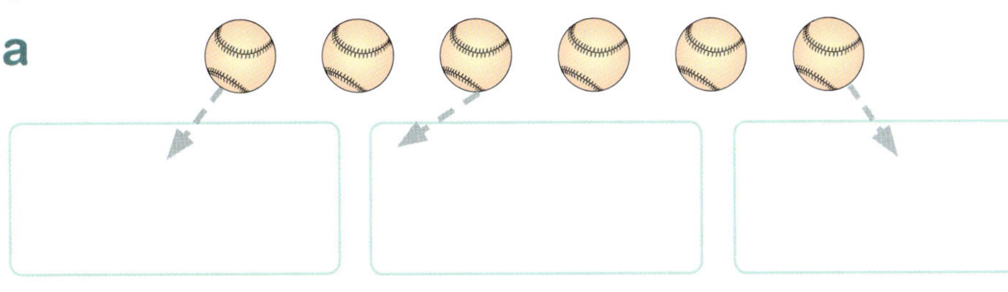

How many are in each share?

6 balls are shared. ☐

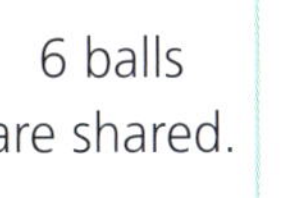

b

9 balls are shared. ☐

2 Share these balls into 4 groups. Draw each ball as it is shared.

a

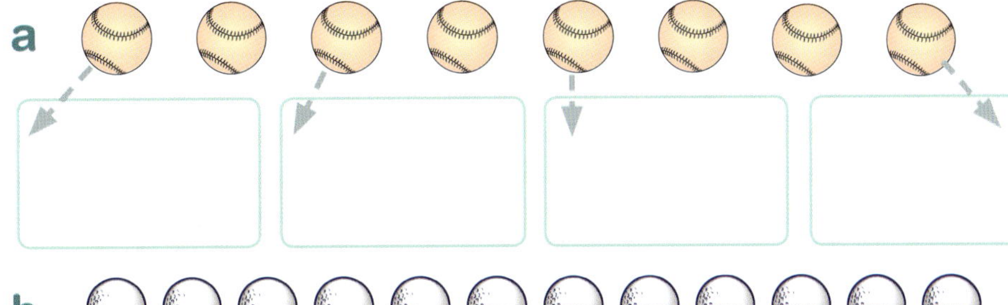

8 balls are shared. ☐

b

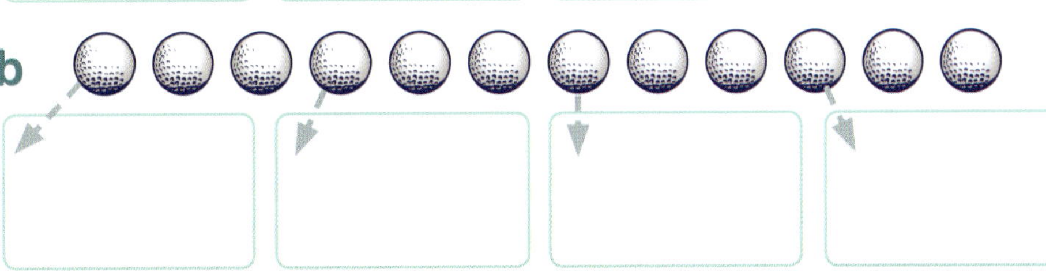

12 balls are shared. ☐

Take turns to share a number of playing cards among 3 or 4 people.

Share them one at a time, starting with the person on the left.

The person with the most picture cards wins.

30C Comparing capacity

CONCEPT

- Capacity is the amount a container can hold.
- Water or rice can be used to fill a container.

These two containers were filled then poured into the jars.

Do A and B hold the same amount?

1. The containers were filled then poured out. **Circle** the container in each question that holds more. **Circle** both containers in the question if they hold about the same amount.

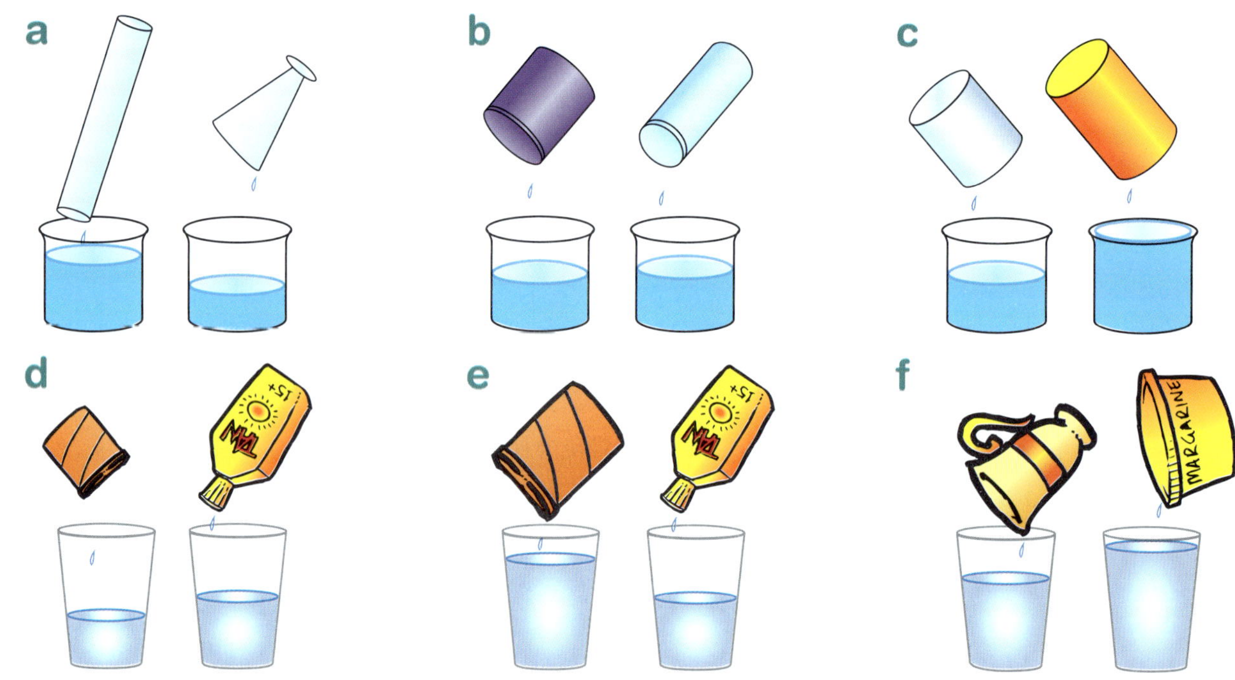

2. Harry has two piles of rice. He wants to find out which is the larger pile. He puts each pile into a glass. **Circle** the pile that is larger.

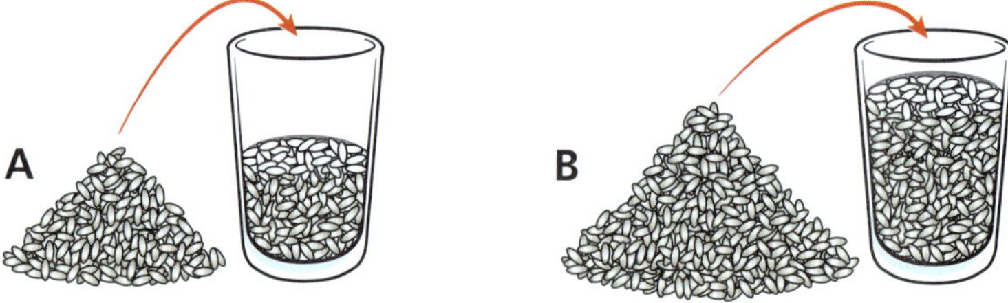

ACTIVITY

Make your own piles. Find out which is the larger pile. Talk about what you did.

© PEARSON AUSTRALIA 2024 • *AUSTRALIAN SIGNPOST MATHS F* • ISBN 9780655708742

Comparing capacity

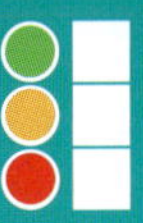

CONCEPT

To find which holds more:

- Fill a container with water or sand.
- Pour it into the other container.
- If it overflows, the first container holds more.

1 In each case, **circle** the container that holds more. Discuss.

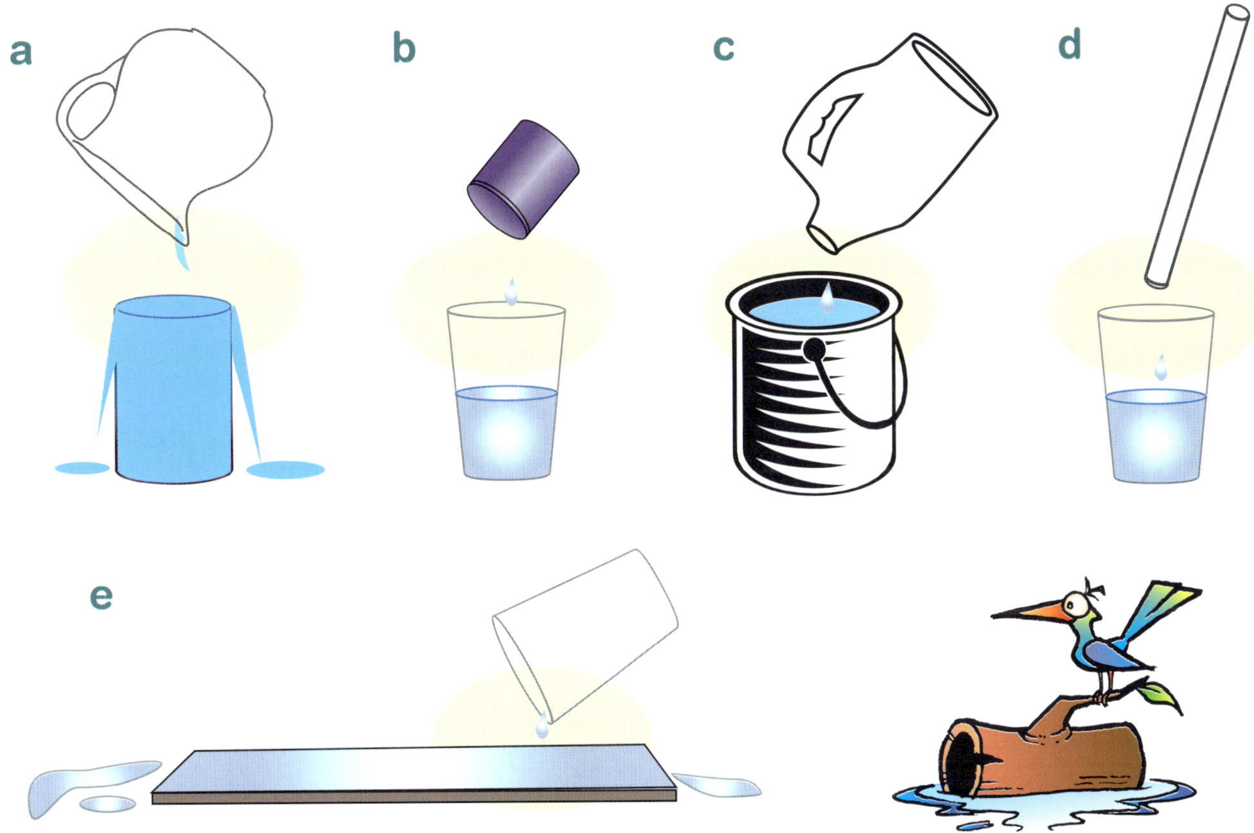

2 Pour water from one container into another to find out which one holds more. Colour the container that holds more.

© PEARSON AUSTRALIA 2024 • *AUSTRALIAN SIGNPOST MATHS F* • ISBN 9780655708742

Left   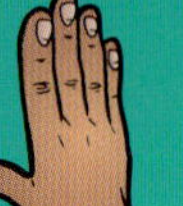 Right 

ACTIVITY

Draw:

- a cow inside the paddock
- a duck near the pond
- birds flying under the clouds
- a house on the hill
- a flower next to the tree
- yourself to the right of the tree.
- a car to the left of the fence.

Are you left-handed (L) or right-handed (R)? ☐

© PEARSON AUSTRALIA 2024 • *AUSTRALIAN SIGNPOST MATHS F* • ISBN 9780655708742

31B Recording the weather

1 A class made this daily weather chart.

Week 1	rainy Sun	rainy Mon	cloudy Tues	sunny Wed	sunny Thurs	sunny Fri	sunny Sat
Week 2	windy Sun	cloudy Mon	cloudy Tues	windy Wed	sunny Thurs	sunny Fri	rainy Sat

Discuss the results above and use them to complete this chart.

Weather								Total
sunny								
rainy								
windy								
cloudy								

a How many days were  ? ☐

b How many days were  ? ☐

INVESTIGATION

12 children will be asked what their favourite activity is out of these choices.
Each student first guesses which activity will be chosen most often. Draw a face for each child.

Which of these do children like the most?

swimming										
bike riding										
playing soccer										

© PEARSON AUSTRALIA 2024 • *AUSTRALIAN SIGNPOST MATHS F* • ISBN 9780655708742

31C Comparing distances

INVESTIGATION

- Colour the label to show who is closer: the captain or the pirate. **Circle** the label to show who is further away.

captain

pirate

1 2 3 4 5 6 7 8 9 10

captain	captain	captain	captain
or	or	or	or
pirate	pirate	pirate	pirate

- Join the numbers to reach the treasure. Start at 1.

© PEARSON AUSTRALIA 2024 • *AUSTRALIAN SIGNPOST MATHS F* • ISBN 9780655708742

Pattern blocks

INVESTIGATION

- Use pattern blocks to cover each picture.
- Colour each picture so the shapes that join have different colours.

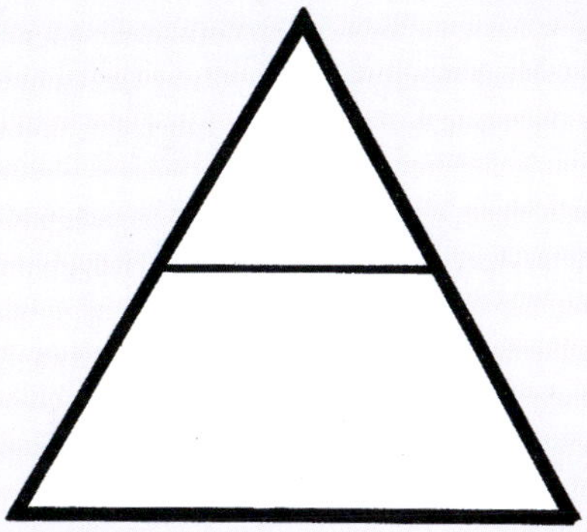

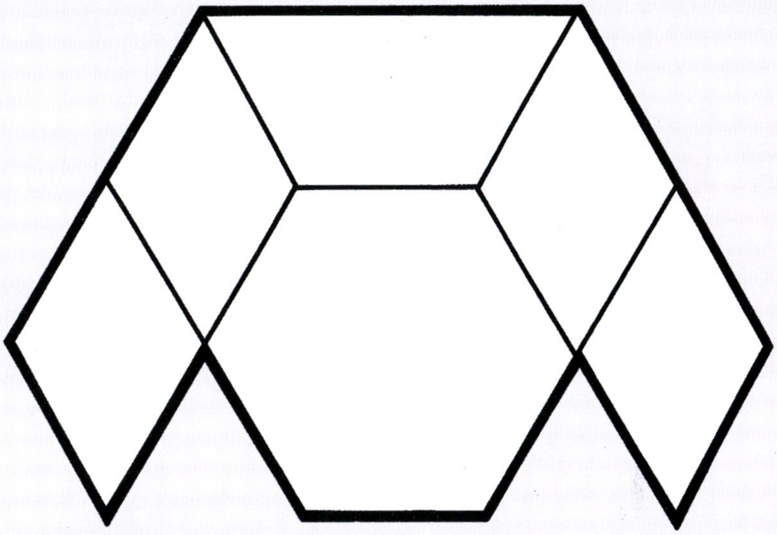

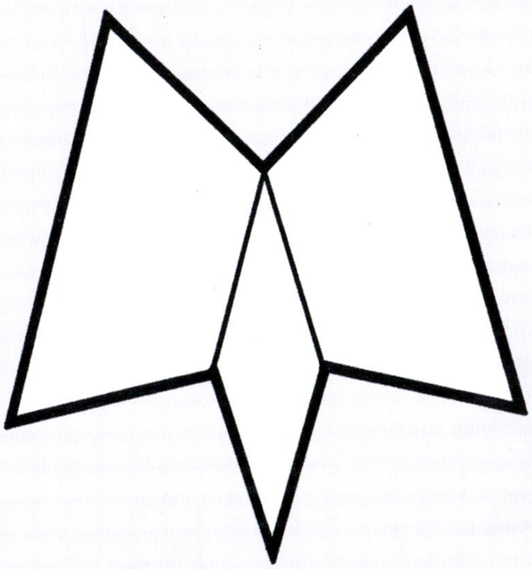

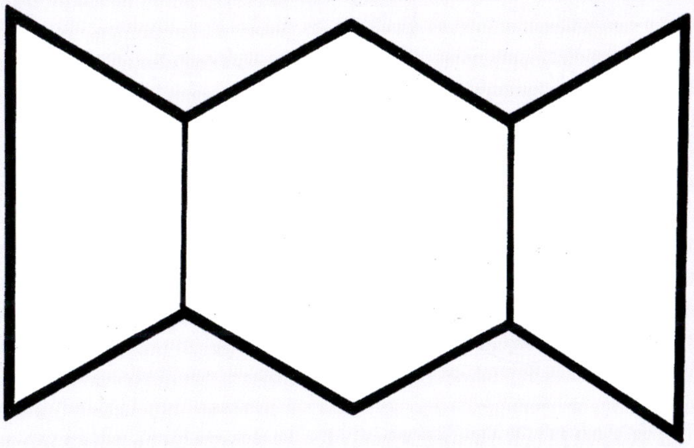

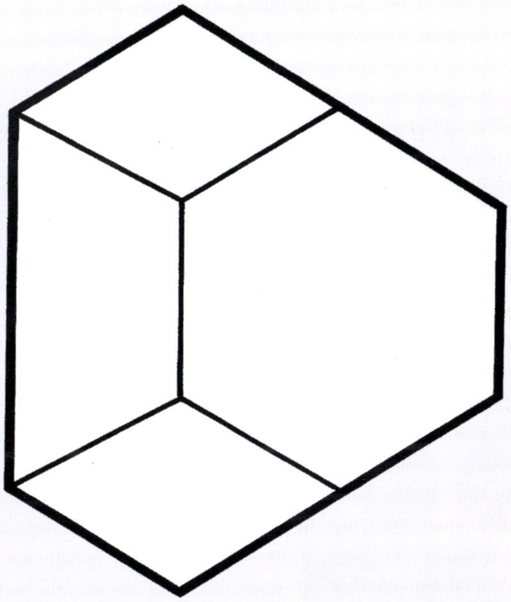

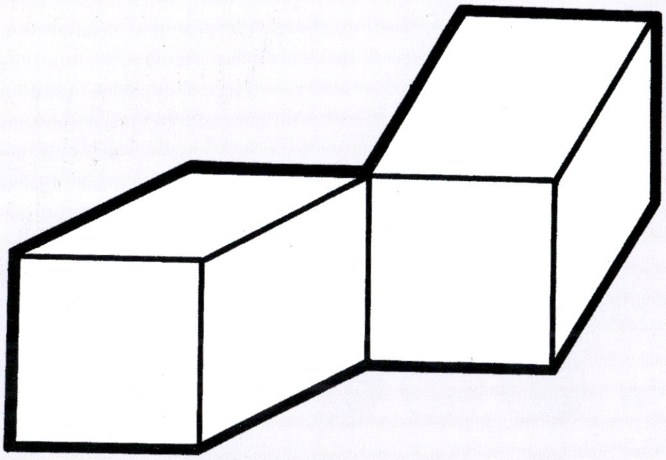

32A Sorting and classifying coins

1 Discuss these coins. Colour the gold coins yellow and the silver coins green.

How many of each coin are there?

5c		10c		20c	
50c		$1		$2	

2 How many coins in each row?

a

b

© PEARSON AUSTRALIA 2024 • *AUSTRALIAN SIGNPOST MATHS F* • ISBN 9780655708742

32B Australian money

❶ Write the value of each coin.

❷ Match each banknote to the correct label.

$5
five dollars

❸ Write the value of the banknotes in order from smallest to largest.

© PEARSON AUSTRALIA 2024 • *AUSTRALIAN SIGNPOST MATHS F* • ISBN 9780655708742

Identifying and addressing areas of need

An essential part of a teacher's role is identifying and addressing areas of student need.

This includes recognising areas where memory is fading and discovering any concepts that have been missed or misunderstood.

Testing is a great way to identify areas of need, but is only really useful when the results are used to help the student.

It is important to build a strong foundation when teaching new concepts and skills.

It is also important to revise / re-teach areas of weakness you discover so that these areas will not be barriers to the future learning of related concepts.

Progress tests and retests (see adjacent page)

Progress tests 1 to 5 are found in the online Teacher Resource.

After each test, notes and answers are supplied.

Progress test questions are cross-referenced to appropriate Student Book pages.

Progress retests 1 to 5 are found in the Teacher Resource.

The remediation records pages are used to provide a record of each student's progress.

These are found in the online Teacher Resource.

For each error recorded, the question should be discussed and using the Student Book cross-reference provided, practice should occur. Retesting should follow using the progress retests.

Summary

1 Test recent work.

2 Enter any mistakes in the Remediation records.

3 Use this record to direct your revision / re-teaching.

4 Retest using the matching retest questions to ensure understanding.

Teaching and learning

Successfully teaching content and skills is a complex process.

A **good textbook** is an important tool alongside **effective teaching and planning**.

Knowledge, understanding and skills must be embedded in the student's mind so that recall continues with time. This will be done using:

(1) instruction, (2) practice, (3) drill, (4) review.

Instruction involves explicit explanation, investigation and the use of good educational resources.

Practice forms neural pathways within the brain.

Drill strengthens neural pathways. The stronger the pathways become, the longer the understanding or knowledge is retained. 'Overlearning' prolongs recall.

Review revitalises weakened neural pathways.

© PEARSON AUSTRALIA 2024 • *AUSTRALIAN SIGNPOST MATHS F* • ISBN 9780655708742

Progress test 2

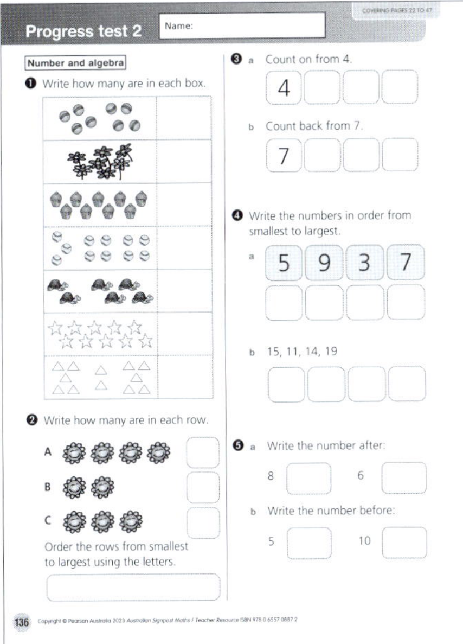

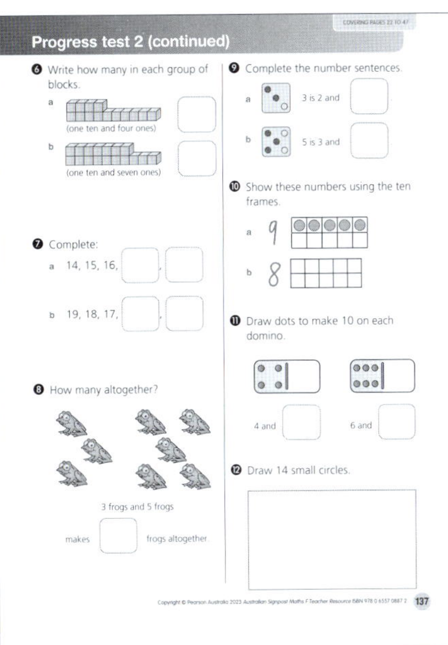

Progress retest 2

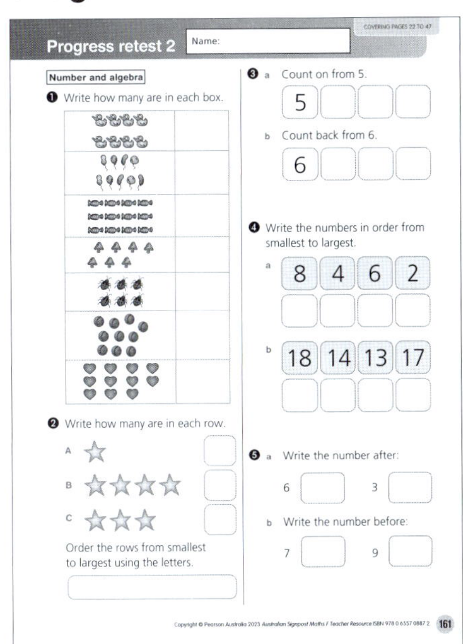

Notes and answers for Progress test 2

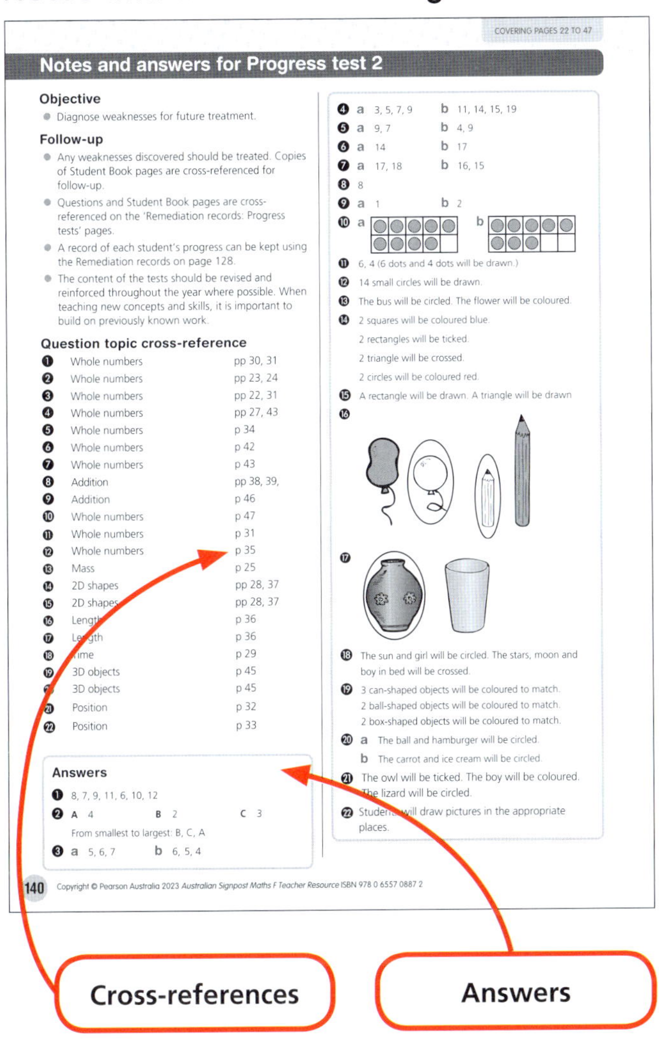
COVERING PAGES 22 TO 47

Notes and answers for Progress test 2

Objective

- Diagnose weaknesses for future treatment.

Follow-up

- Any weaknesses discovered should be treated. Copies of Student Book pages are cross-referenced for follow-up.
- Questions and Student Book pages are cross-referenced on the 'Remediation records: Progress tests' pages.
- A record of each student's progress can be kept using the Remediation records on page 128.
- The content of the tests should be revised and reinforced throughout the year where possible. When teaching new concepts and skills, it is important to build on previously known work.

Question topic cross-reference

1	Whole numbers	pp 30, 31
2	Whole numbers	pp 23, 24
3	Whole numbers	pp 22, 31
4	Whole numbers	pp 27, 43
5	Whole numbers	p 34
6	Whole numbers	p 42
7	Whole numbers	p 43
8	Addition	pp 38, 39,
9	Addition	p 46
10	Whole numbers	p 47
11	Whole numbers	p 31
12	Whole numbers	p 35
13	Mass	p 25
14	2D shapes	pp 28, 37
15	2D shapes	pp 28, 37
16	Length	p 36
17	Length	p 36
18	Time	p 29
19	3D objects	p 45
20	3D objects	p 45
21	Position	p 32
22	Position	p 33

Answers

1 8, 7, 9, 11, 6, 10, 12
2 A 4 B 2 C 3
From smallest to largest: B, C, A
3 a 5, 6, 7 b 6, 5, 4
4 a 3, 5, 7, 9 b 11, 14, 15, 19
5 a 9, 7 b 4, 9
6 a 14 b 17
7 a 17, 18 b 16, 15
8 8
9 a 1 b 2
10 a b
11 6, 4 (6 dots and 4 dots will be drawn.)
12 14 small circles will be drawn.
13 The bus will be circled. The flower will be coloured.
14 2 squares will be coloured blue.
2 rectangles will be ticked.
2 triangle will be crossed.
2 circles will be coloured red.
15 A rectangle will be drawn. A triangle will be drawn
16
17
18 The sun and girl will be circled. The stars, moon and boy in bed will be crossed.
19 3 can-shaped objects will be coloured to match.
2 ball-shaped objects will be coloured to match.
2 box-shaped objects will be coloured to match.
20 a The ball and hamburger will be circled.
b The carrot and ice cream will be circled.
21 The owl will be ticked. The boy will be coloured. The lizard will be circled.
22 Students will draw pictures in the appropriate places.

140 Copyright © Pearson Australia 2023 Australian Signpost Maths F Teacher Resource ISBN 978 0 6557 0887 2

Remediation records: Progress tests

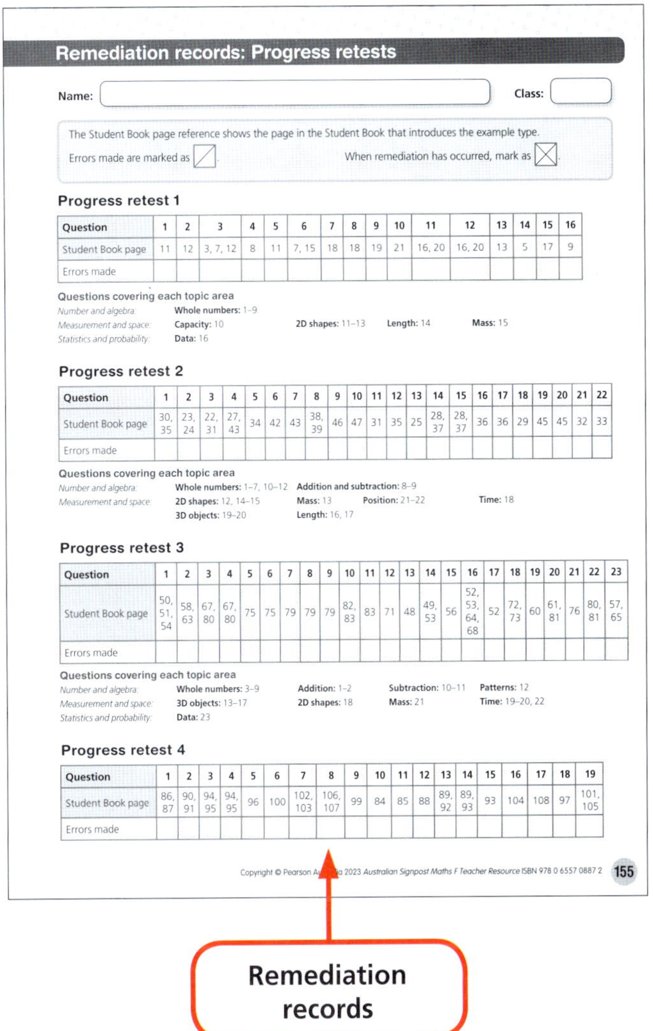

Remediation records: Progress retests

Name: Class:

The Student Book page reference shows the page in the Student Book that introduces the example type.
Errors made are marked as ⧄. When remediation has occurred, mark as ⊠.

Progress retest 1

Question	1	2	3	4	5	6	7	8	9	10	11	12	13	14	15	16
Student Book page	11	12	3, 7, 12	8	11	7, 15	18	18	19	21	16, 20	16, 20	13	5	17	9
Errors made																

Questions covering each topic area
Number and algebra: **Whole numbers:** 1–9
Measurement and space: **Capacity:** 10 **2D shapes:** 11–13 **Length:** 14 **Mass:** 15
Statistics and probability: **Data:** 16

Progress retest 2

Question	1	2	3	4	5	6	7	8	9	10	11	12	13	14	15	16	17	18	19	20	21	22
Student Book page	30, 35	23, 24	22, 31	27, 43	34	42	43	38, 39	46	47	31	35	25	28, 37	28, 37	36	36	29	45	45	32	33
Errors made																						

Questions covering each topic area
Number and algebra: **Whole numbers:** 1–7, 10–12 **Addition and subtraction:** 8–9
Measurement and space: **2D shapes:** 12, 14–15 **Mass:** 13 **Position:** 21–22 **Time:** 18
3D objects: 19–20 **Length:** 16, 17

Progress retest 3

Question	1	2	3	4	5	6	7	8	9	10	11	12	13	14	15	16	17	18	19	20	21	22	23
Student Book page	50, 51, 54	58, 63	67, 80	67, 80	75	75	79	79	79	82, 83	83	71	48	49, 53	56	52, 53, 64, 68	52	72, 73	60	61, 81	76	80, 81	57, 65
Errors made																							

Questions covering each topic area
Number and algebra: **Whole numbers:** 3–9 **Addition:** 1–2 **Subtraction:** 10–11 **Patterns:** 12
Measurement and space: **3D objects:** 13–17 **2D shapes:** 18 **Mass:** 21 **Time:** 19–20, 22
Statistics and probability: **Data:** 23

Progress retest 4

Question	1	2	3	4	5	6	7	8	9	10	11	12	13	14	15	16	17	18	19
Student Book page	86, 87	90, 91	94, 95	94, 95	96	100	102, 103	106, 107	99	84	85	88	89, 92	89, 93	93	104	108	97	101, 105
Errors made																			

Copyright © Pearson Australia 2023 Australian Signpost Maths F Teacher Resource ISBN 978 0 6557 0887 2 155

Cross-references

Answers

Remediation records

Number charts

1	2	3	4	5	6	7	8	9	10
11	12	13	14	15	16	17	18	19	20
21	22	23	24	25	26	27	28	29	30

1	2	3	4	5	6	7	8	9	10
11	12	13	14	15	16	17	18	19	20
21	22	23	24	25	26	27	28	29	30
31	32	33	34	35	36	37	38	39	40
41	42	43	44	45	46	47	48	49	50
51	52	53	54	55	56	57	58	59	60
61	62	63	64	65	66	67	68	69	70
71	72	73	74	75	76	77	78	79	80
81	82	83	84	85	86	87	88	89	90
91	92	93	94	95	96	97	98	99	100

© PEARSON AUSTRALIA 2024 • *AUSTRALIAN SIGNPOST MATHS F* • ISBN 9780655708742

Ten frames

© PEARSON AUSTRALIA 2024 • *AUSTRALIAN SIGNPOST MATHS F* • ISBN 9780655708742

Adding two groups

and

makes

altogether

Counting on
How many fingers are hidden?

Play this game with a friend.
The other hand can be used to hide fingers.

© PEARSON AUSTRALIA 2024 • *AUSTRALIAN SIGNPOST MATHS F* • ISBN 9780655708742

Before and after to 10

1	2	3	4	5	6	7	8	9	10

After:

2	3
4	
3	
1	
7	
6	
5	
8	
9	

Before:

3	4
	2
	3
	6
	9
	8
	5
	10
	7

Missing numbers:

4	5	6
	2	
2		4
6		8
	7	
	4	
7		9
3		5
5		7

Extra support page 5 Adding 1 or 2

We can count on to add 1.
4 and 1 (4 ... **5**)

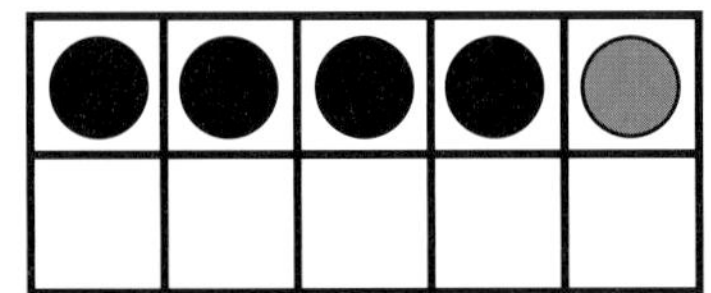

4 and 1
makes 5

1 and 4 is the same as ***4 and 1***.
We start at 4 and count on 1.

We can count on to add 2.
6 and 2 (6 ... **7**, **8**)

6 and 2
makes 8

2 and 6 is the same as ***6 and 2***.
We start at 6 and count on 2.

1 **a** 1 and 1 ☐ **b** 4 and 1 ☐ **c** 3 and 1 ☐

d 6 and 1 ☐ **e** 8 and 1 ☐ **f** 2 and 1 ☐

g 9 and 1 ☐ **h** 7 and 1 ☐ **i** 5 and 1 ☐

2 **a** 2 and 2 ☐ **b** 1 and 2 ☐ **c** 5 and 2 ☐

d 6 and 2 ☐ **e** 4 and 2 ☐ **f** 8 and 2 ☐

g 0 and 2 ☐ **h** 7 and 2 ☐ **i** 3 and 2 ☐

3 **a** 1 and 7 ☐ **b** 2 and 4 ☐ **c** 2 and 6 ☐

d 2 and 5 ☐ **e** 1 and 5 ☐ **f** 1 and 9 ☐

g 2 and 7 ☐ **h** 1 and 8 ☐ **i** 2 and 8 ☐

© PEARSON AUSTRALIA 2024 • *AUSTRALIAN SIGNPOST MATHS F* • ISBN 9780655708742

Subtracting 1 or 2

We can count back to subtract 1.
5 take away 1 (5 … **4**)

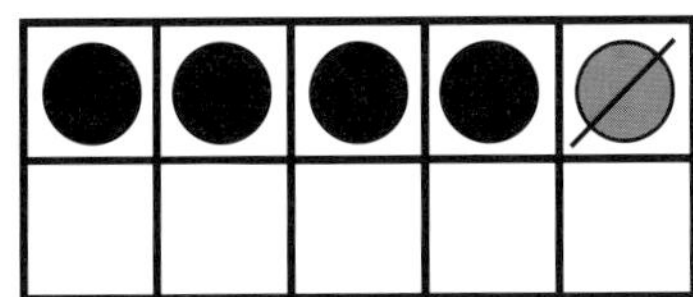

5 take away 1
leaves 4

We can count back to subtract 2.
8 take away 2 (8 … **7**, **6**)

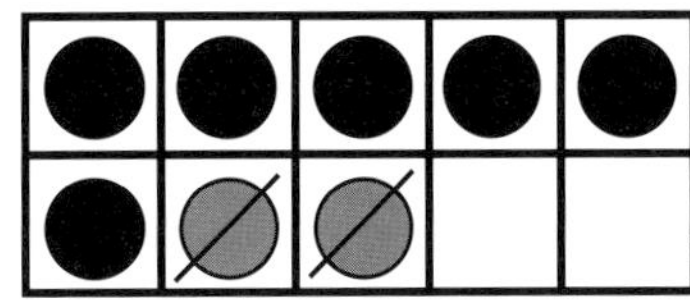

8 take away 2
leaves 6

1 a 6 take away 1 ☐ **b** 4 take away 1 ☐

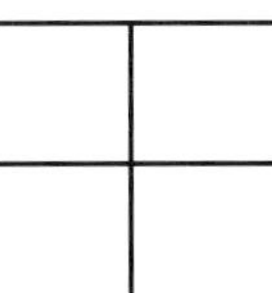

c 8 take away 1 ☐ **d** 7 take away 1 ☐

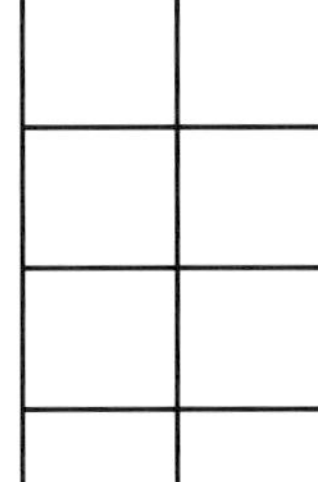

e 5 take away 1 ☐ **f** 9 take away 1 ☐

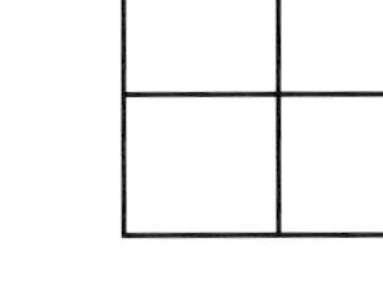

2 a 4 take away 2 ☐ **b** 7 take away 2 ☐

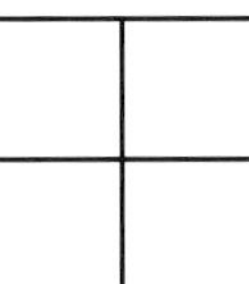

c 9 take away 2 ☐ **d** 5 take away 2 ☐

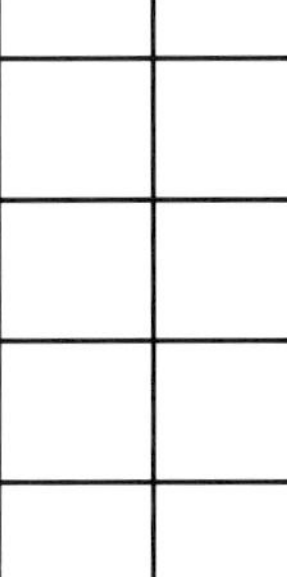

e 8 take away 2 ☐ **f** 6 take away 2 ☐

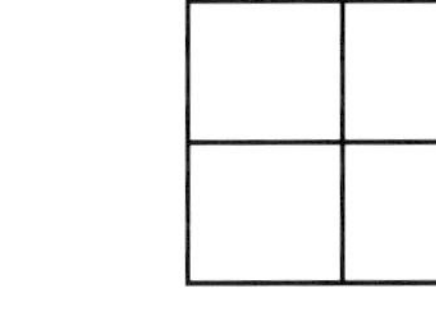

3 a 8 take away 1 ☐ **b** 7 take away 1 ☐

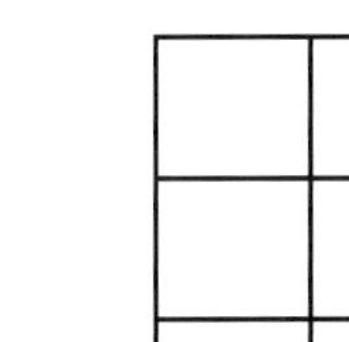

c 7 take away 2 ☐ **d** 6 take away 1 ☐

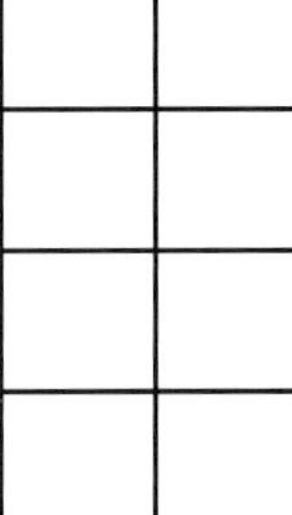

e 9 take away 1 ☐ **f** 8 take away 2 ☐

g 9 take away 2 ☐ **h** 6 take away 2 ☐

Addition number facts to 10

4 and 3 makes 7

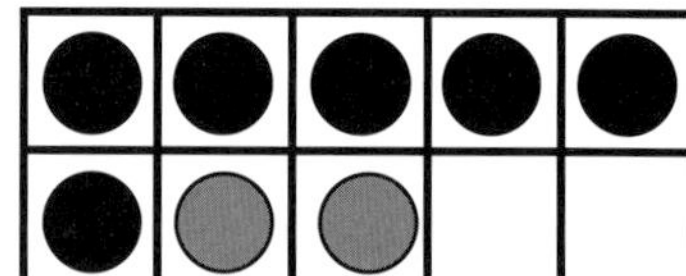

6 and 2 makes 8

1 **a** 1 and 1 ☐ **b** 2 and 2 ☐ **c** 3 and 3 ☐

d 4 and 4 ☐ **e** 5 and 5 ☐ **f** 4 and 1 ☐

g 3 and 2 ☐ **h** 1 and 2 ☐ **i** 3 and 0 ☐

2 **a** 7 and 2 ☐ **b** 3 and 5 ☐ **c** 7 and 1 ☐

d 6 and 3 ☐ **e** 4 and 6 ☐ **f** 4 and 3 ☐

g 2 and 6 ☐ **h** 4 and 5 ☐ **i** 5 and 2 ☐

3 **a** 7 and 3 ☐ **b** 3 and 4 ☐ **c** 3 and 7 ☐

d 2 and 7 ☐ **e** 1 and 8 ☐ **f** 3 and 6 ☐

g 8 and 2 ☐ **h** 5 and 3 ☐ **i** 6 and 4 ☐

© PEARSON AUSTRALIA 2024 • *AUSTRALIAN SIGNPOST MATHS F* • ISBN 9780655708742

Number bond houses

10	
1	9
2	8
3	7
4	6
5	5
6	4
7	3
8	2
9	1

9	
1	8
2	7
3	6
4	5
5	4
6	3
7	2
8	1

8	
1	7
2	6
3	5
4	4
5	3
6	2
7	1

7	
1	6
2	5
3	4
4	3
5	2
6	1

6	
1	5
2	4
3	3
4	2
5	1

5	
1	4
2	3
3	2
4	1

4	
1	3
2	2
3	1

3	
1	2
2	1

7	
	1
5	
	3
3	
	5
1	

8	
7	
	2
5	
	4
	5
2	
	7

10	
1	
	8
3	
	6
	5
6	
7	
	2
9	

Say the number bonds in a line, giving the answers as you go.
Line A would be 7 = 1 + ■, 6 = 3 + ■, 9 = 3 + ■, 8 = ■ + 5.

A

7
1

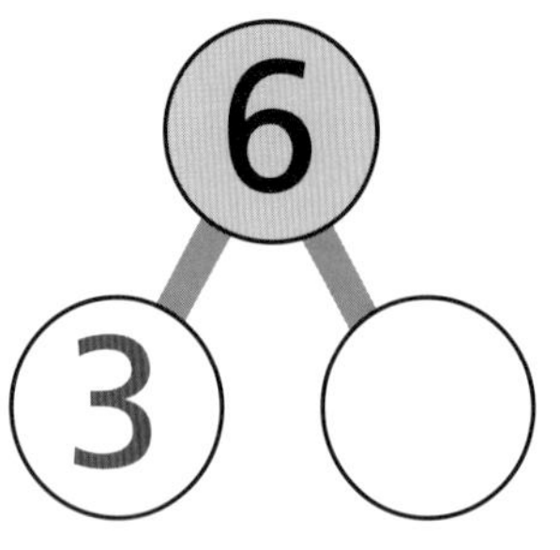

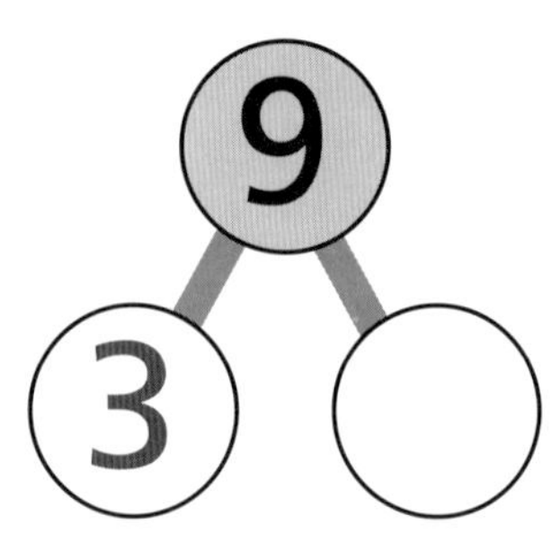

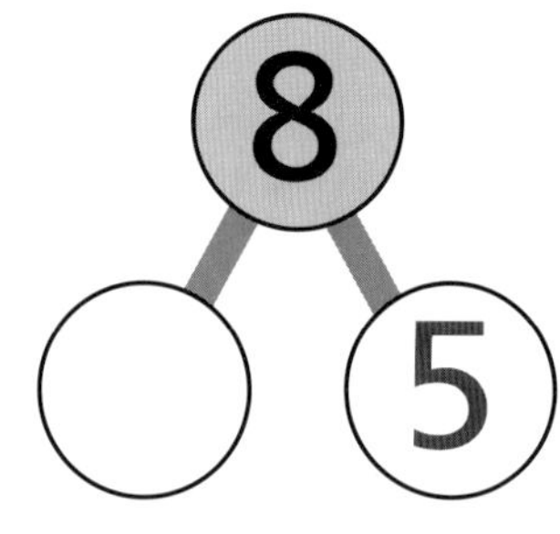

B

4
1

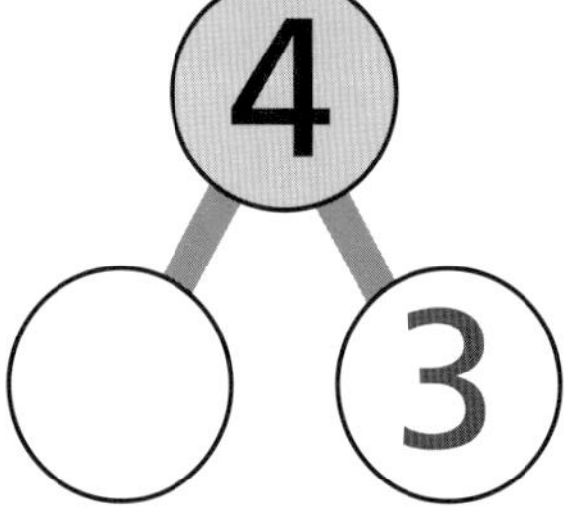

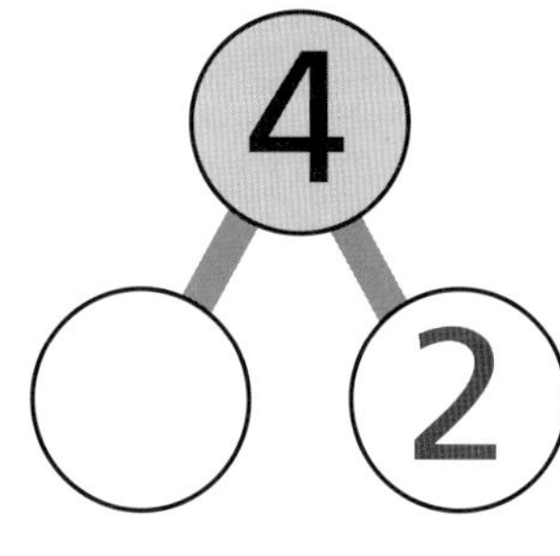

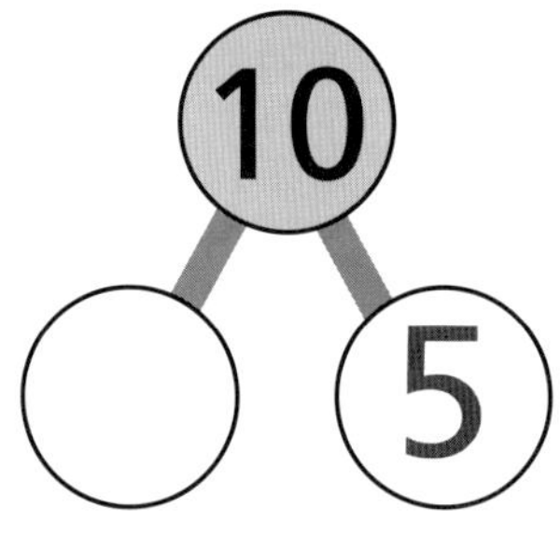

C

10
1

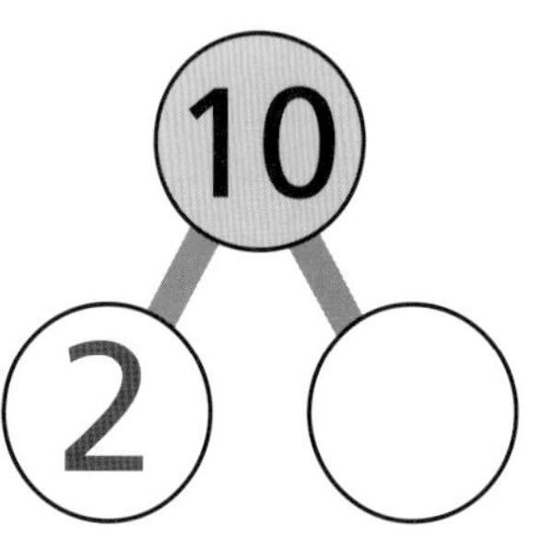

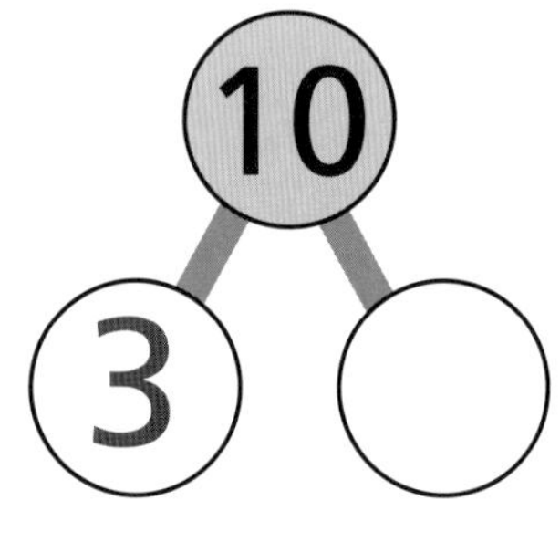

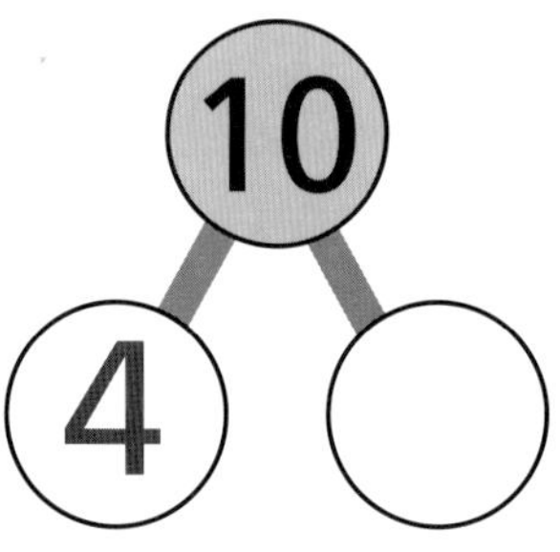

D

10
5

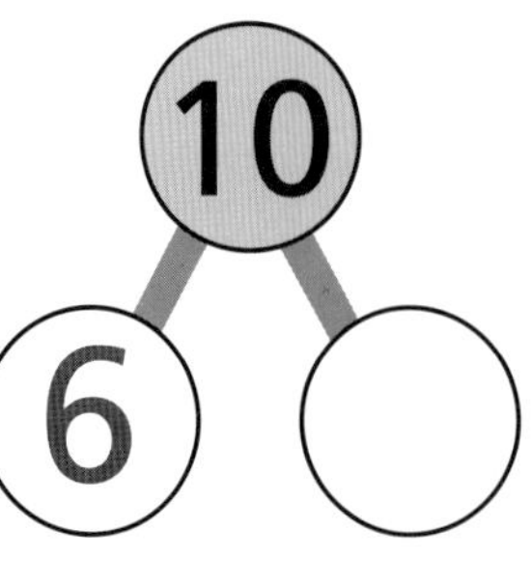

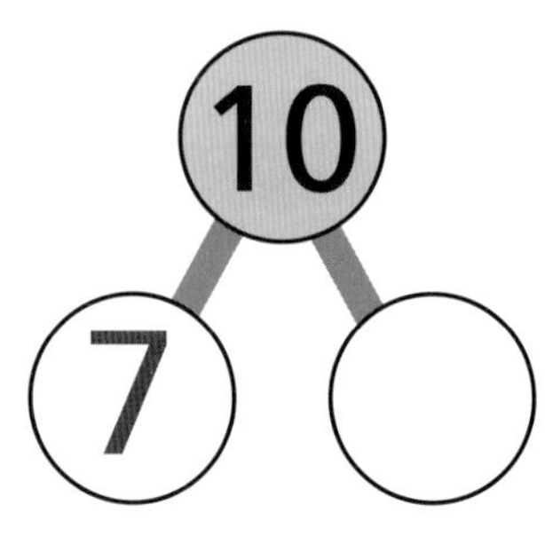

10
8

© PEARSON AUSTRALIA 2024 • *AUSTRALIAN SIGNPOST MATHS F* • ISBN 9780655708742